Angie Debo

THE OKLAHOMA WESTERN BIOGRAPHIES
RICHARD W. ETULAIN, GENERAL EDITOR

Angie Debo

Pioneering Historian

Shirley A. Leckie

UNIVERSITY OF OKLAHOMA PRESS : NORMAN

Also by Shirley A. Leckie

(with William H. Leckie) *Unlikely Warriors: General Benjamin H. Grierson and His Family* (Norman, 1984)
(ed.) *Colonel's Lady on the Western Frontier: The Correspondence of Alice Kirk Grierson* (Lincoln, 1989)
Elizabeth Bacon Custer and the Making of a Myth (Norman, 1993)

Library of Congress Cataloging-in-Publication Data

Leckie, Shirley A., 1937–
    Angie Debo : pioneering historian / Shirley A. Leckie.
        p.   cm. — (The Oklahoma western biographies; v. 18)
    Includes bibliographical references and index.
    ISBN 0-8061-3256-6 (cloth)
    ISBN 0-8061-3438-0 (paper)
    1. Debo, Angie, 1890–   2. Historians—Oklahoma—Biography.
    3. Oklahoma—Historiography.   4. Southwest, New—Historiography.
    5. Indians of North America—Oklahoma—Historiography.   6. Indians of
    North America—Southwest, New—Historiography.   I. Title.   II. Series.

E175.5.D43 L43 2000
976.6'05'092—dc21

                                                          00-026210

Angie Debo: Pioneering Historian is Volume 18 in The Oklahoma Western
Biographies.

The paper in this book meets the guidelines for permanence and durability of
the Committee on Production Guidelines for Book Longevity of the Council
on Library Resources.∞

2   3   4   5   6   7   8   9   10

To Nicole, Claire, Robin, Cecilia, Emily, Aaron, and Trevor

Contents

Illustrations

Series Editor's Preface

STORIES of heroes and heroines have intrigued many generations of listeners and readers. Americans, like people everywhere, have been captivated by the lives of military, political, and religious figures and of intrepid explorers, pioneers, and rebels. The Oklahoma Western Biographies endeavor to build on this fascination with biography and to link it with two other abiding interests of Americans: the frontier and the American West. Although volumes in the series carry no notes, they are prepared by leading scholars, are soundly researched, and include a list of sources used. Each volume is a lively synthesis based on thorough examination of pertinent primary and secondary sources.

Above all, the Oklahoma Western Biographies aim at two goals: to provide readable life stories of significant westerners and to show how their lives illuminate a notable topic, an influential movement, or a series of important events in the history and culture of the American West.

Shirley A. Leckie's biography of Angie Debo is an important addition to the Oklahoma series. The first book-length study of this notable western woman and historian, Leckie's volume makes noteworthy contributions in the fields of western, gender, and Native American history. In Leckie's provocative and clearly written life story, she delineates the pathbreaking contributions Debo made in western historical writing, particularly in her new, ethnographic approach to the history of American Indians in the West and Southwest.

Leckie's book is thoroughly researched. Drawing extensively on Angie Debo's published work, Leckie also carefully examines her subject's manuscript correspondence and other unpublished material. Leckie's discussions of recent scholarship on Native Americans, as well as Debo's role in this burgeoning historiography, are particularly valuable.

The heroine of Leckie's sparkling story will captivate readers of all backgrounds. Angie Debo, a sympathetic figure of great ambition and courage, should inspire scholars, students, and general readers alike.

In short, Shirley Leckie clearly achieves the major goals of the Oklahoma Western Biographies. She deals with a notable westerner whose life illuminates larger happenings in western history.

RICHARD W. ETULAIN

University of New Mexico

Acknowledgments

THIS work would never have been completed without the interest and assistance of many individuals and associations. I thank Richard Etulain for his encouragement throughout the course of my research and writing and his careful reading and criticism of a preliminary draft. As soon as I began my research, Glenna Matthews generously shared her often-moving insights into the life and character of Angie Debo, her close friend. Later, she suggested ways of improving an early draft. Albert Hurtado's comments also helped me strengthen this work.

Hugh and Ramona O'Neill, Debo's close friends and neighbors, gave me invaluable information and have become my treasured friends. Carter Blue Clark contributed unstintingly from his store of memories and knowledge, and so did Connie Cronley and Richard Lowitt. Peter Petersen showed me around Canyon, Texas, and put me in contact with individuals who had known Debo in Canyon. I also gained invaluable insights from Raymond Bryson, Gerry Schaefer, Gloria Valencia-Weber, Betty Mubiru, Anne Morgan, Rennard Strickland, Barbara Abrash, Martha Sandlin, Kenny Brown, Danney Goble, David Baird, Frederick J. Rathjen, Suzanne Schrems, the late B. B. Chapman, LeRoy Fischer, Michael Harrison, and Pattie Loughlin.

Historians depend on librarians and archivists, and Heather Lloyd, head of Special Collections and University Archives at Oklahoma State University, has my immense gratitude. I also thank John Lovett and Brad Koplowitz, librarian and assistant curator, respectively, of the Western History Collection at the University of Oklahoma; Joe E. Todd, archivist at the Oklahoma Historical Society; and Betty Bustos, archivist at the Research

Center of the Panhandle-Plains Historical Museum at Canyon, Texas. Finally, I thank the Text and Academic Authors Association, which awarded me a research grant, and the University of Central Florida for a sabbatical in 1994, which permitted me to begin my research.

Teresa Decio, graduate student in the Department of History, served as a research assistant. Heather Ruland, graduate secretary in the Department of History, helped with proofreading. My dear friend, Peggy Brown, of Norman, Oklahoma, shared her home with me when I journeyed to Oklahoma for research trips. Maria Gabrielle Swora, my daughter and anthropologist, read over portions of the manuscript that dealt with her field and directed me to important works. I am also grateful to Ursula Smith for her excellent care in copyediting this manuscript. As always, my husband, William H. Leckie, was a true comrade, providing me with his scholarly insights and his memories of Edward Everett Dale and helping me untangle my prose. The flaws and mistakes in this work are entirely mine.

Finally, an endnoted copy of the original manuscript is located in the Angie Debo Collection of the Manuscript Division of the Edmon Low Library at Oklahoma State University, Stillwater. Other copies can be found in the Western History Collections at the University of Oklahoma in Norman and at the University of Central Florida library in Orlando, Florida.

SHIRLEY A. LECKIE

Winter Springs, Florida

Angie Debo

Introduction

IN the fall of 1988 a haunting film appeared as part of the premier season of the PBS series *The American Experience.* "Indians, Outlaws and Angie Debo," produced by Barbara Abrash and Martha Sandlin, presented a riveting interpretation of the life of the Oklahoma historian who wrote on Native Americans and pioneers in her state. Born in 1890, the year the frontier closed according to the interpretation of scholar Frederick Jackson Turner, Angie Elbertha Debo died at ninety-eight, several months before the documentary was shown nationwide.

The film depicts the aged historian reminiscing in her home and participating in the Prairie City Days celebration in Marshall, Oklahoma. It also describes her family's arrival in Oklahoma Territory in 1899, a decade after the first and most famous land run of April 22, 1889.

Since her town had no four-year high school before 1910, Debo was twenty-three when she graduated in 1913. Five years later, she earned a bachelor's in history from the University of Oklahoma and in 1924 a master's from the University of Chicago. She received a Ph.D. in history from Oklahoma in 1933.

In the film, she states, "the history field was . . . barred against women. There wasn't anything at all that a woman could do to enter it." The background narrator adds, "Even with a Ph.D., Angie Debo would never hold a position in a history department of a university."

Asking only for "a fair field and no favors," Debo turned to writing American Indian history. She investigated the end of the Cherokee, Choctaw, Creek, Chickasaw, and Seminole republics in Indian Territory and their incorporation into the new state of

3

Oklahoma. During that inquiry she discovered that "all of eastern Oklahoma was dominated by a criminal conspiracy to cheat the Indians out of their property" and that this conspiracy reached into the state legislature. "I didn't know those things were so," she continued, in recalling the beginnings of her research. "Nobody had ever written about that history of Oklahoma, and when I got into it, I couldn't honestly back out." Although Debo documented her account thoroughly, the potentially explosive nature of her findings led to the cancellation of her contract with the University of Oklahoma Press. Four years passed before Princeton University Press published her manuscript as *And Still the Waters Run*.

Despite all setbacks, Debo wrote, edited, or coauthored thirteen books in her lifetime. In the PBS film, the late scholar of American Indians, Arrell Gibson, characterized Debo as a "lone wolf," capable of sustaining her scholarship in relative isolation and without collegial support. He also described her as a courageous and articulate activist who worked untiringly to attain greater justice for Native Americans.

In 1985, in recognition of the various contributions she had made to American Indians, to her state, and to her profession, Oklahoma placed Debo's portrait in the capitol rotunda. The first woman so honored, her portrait hangs there alongside those of the Cherokee scholar, Sequoyah; the American Indian athlete, Jim Thorpe; humorist Will Rogers; Robert Kerr, former governor of Oklahoma and U.S. senator; and Carl Albert, former speaker of the U.S. House of Representatives.

Although "Indians, Outlaws and Angie Debo" was a glowing tribute, the issues raised by the historian's life and career deserve greater analysis than any one-hour film can present. Certainly the obstacles she encountered in publishing *And Still the Waters Run* provided dramatic unity to the production, but she was more than a scholar who tackled a controversial subject with courage and tenacity. She was a pioneer whose work paved the way for a more realistic and inclusive view of the history of the trans-Mississippi West.

Debo also contributed to changes in the field of American Indian history. Richard White, in reviewing the PBS film for the 1989 *Journal of American History,* credited her with having "invented the 'new' Indian history long before there was a name for it." Four years later, in the American Historical Association pamphlet, *Teaching American Indian History,* Terry Wilson (Potawatomi) published the results of a survey he had conducted among scholars in the field. "Only a single book published before 1945 was mentioned more than once and it was the sixth most frequently listed," Wilson reported. The work was *And Still the Waters Run.*

On the surface, Debo seems at first an unlikely candidate for the role of revisionist historian. In her undergraduate and graduate studies at the University of Oklahoma, she came under the influence of Edward Everett Dale. As Frederick Jackson Turner's student, Dale celebrated the movement of pioneers into western areas as the experience that set the United States apart from other nations. Given Debo's indebtedness to Dale and thus to Turner as well, the eventual direction of her career seems surprising—until other factors are considered.

From childhood on, Angie Debo was a maverick. Her innate qualities included an independent spirit, a dogged determination, a hunger for learning, and an agile mind. In addition, her family background and environmental influences shaped her personality in distinctive ways.

Her parents, Lina and Edward Debo, were farmers who escaped tenancy by acquiring their own acreage and then found that the land could not support their aspirations. Edward Debo's entry into the hardware business turned disastrous, and he found himself reduced in his fifties to wage-earning status. Thus an intimate knowledge of disappointment and economic hardship predisposed Debo to affiliate with the less fortunate. In addition, because she grew up during the Progressive Era, her adolescent role model was the charismatic Oklahoma reformer, Catherine Ann Barnard, an impassioned and eloquent crusader for exploited workers and children.

Family and community relationships, moreover, strengthened Debo's inherent optimism and her belief in her abilities. Inspired by a strong mother, who was her husband's full-fledged partner, she came of age in a developing region, which meant that there was always more work than there were laborers. The need for competent people was so great that skilled and talented women found ready employment in this region of Oklahoma Territory. In the early twentieth century Marshall had a female dentist, a primary schoolteacher who was divorced, and several women among the town's business and community leaders. In that context, although Debo understood that women faced prejudice, she believed that higher education and a willingness to work hard would bring her professional opportunities. These, in turn, would permit her to employ her creative powers and enjoy at least a modicum of financial security.

Instead, in her mid-forties, even with a prize-winning book to her credit, Debo found herself unemployed. Though the Great Depression certainly played a role in her dismissal from West Texas State Teachers College, other women with less seniority and less impressive credentials retained their teaching positions. There is no doubt that Debo's ambition and assertiveness—traits that would have served her well as a man—contributed to her firing.

Resilient and willing to take chances, Debo became an independent scholar, subsisting on fellowships and grants and drifting in and out of paid employment. By the time she was fifty, years of disappointing setbacks and unremitting poverty had left this strong woman emotionally battered as she struggled to salvage her professional career.

Raised on the same Protestant work ethic as men and having sacrificed marriage and family life in the interest of a career, Debo never gained the material rewards men of lesser abilities enjoyed. For one who came from a developing area in the trans-Mississippi West, where the ethos of expanded opportunities was embedded in the historiography of the region and where her mentor considered himself a living embodiment of the validity of the American dream, Debo might have been devastated by such disappointments.

Instead, these personal hardships seemed to deepen her sensitivity to the plight of minorities, especially American Indians. Her experiences confirmed what her scholarly research revealed: The idea that the West was the land of opportunity and personal progress needed qualifying. It depended on who you were.

Steeled by the school of hard knocks, she became what historian Peggy Pascoe calls an "intercultural broker." It was a role women often assumed when firsthand experience with sexual discrimination illustrated the "contradictions" inherent in a society that purported to be a "frontier" offering opportunity to all. Rather, as Pascoe notes, the trans-Mississippi West is more accurately described as a "cultural crossroads," a place where men and women of different races, classes, and ethnicities interact from widely disparate positions of power, privilege, and autonomy.

As an intercultural broker, Debo moved beyond her scholarly origins. Well into the twentieth century, historians, following in Turner's footsteps, celebrated a white male saga of westward expansion. Popular textbooks, such as those written by Frederic Paxson, Ray Allen Billington, and Thomas D. Clark, depicted Euro-American men mastering the West and its indigenous people in the nineteenth century and subsequently consigning them to reservations or attempting to assimilate them into the larger society.

By plunging into the archives and following the evidence wherever it led her, Debo embarked on a journey that led to a different understanding of her state, her nation, and herself as well. Given her preparation in the Turnerian school and her willingness to move beyond her mentor and ask how the westward movement appeared from the perspective of those who lived in the region known as "free land," Debo became a plank in the bridge connecting the "Old Western History" to the "New Western History" that emerged in the 1980s. The latter, more encompassing in its subjects and concerns, views national expansion into the trans-Mississippi West as "conquest" rather than as the extension of Thomas Jefferson's "Empire of Liberty."

Since the majority of Debo's writings deal with the history of American Indians, she is remembered today for her accomplishments in that field. Her works have staying power; focusing mainly on Indian-white relations, they are narrated as fully as possible from the Indian point of view. And, in incorporating the works of ethnologists and Debo's own fieldwork, they pioneered in an early form of ethnohistory.

Finally, by moving Native Americans to the center of her historical analysis and by exploring their history beyond the end of the Indian wars and well into the twentieth century, Debo anticipated a key element of the "New Indian History." She presented Native peoples as both changing and yet continuing ethnic groups in today's world rather than mere props destined for assimilation into the white man's saga of conquest.

Although Debo, in part through her own choices, never enjoyed the security of a tenured position, her scholarly productivity eventually brought her professional acclaim. Her activism and spirited defense of civil liberties won her additional recognition beyond her chosen field.

It was actually the rise of the modern, post–World War II feminist movement that engendered a national appreciation for Debo's work and a heightened interest in her life. When Debo was in her seventies, scholars began searching for the social, economic, and cultural roots of ideologies that held that men, simply by being men, were entitled to authority, autonomy, and the lion's share of material rewards and honors. In this context, although some scattered works narrating female accomplishments had appeared earlier, the foundation for an enduring body of knowledge that incorporated women into the historical narrative was laid for the first time. That sense of honoring women's past paved the way in turn for "the creation of feminist consciousness." The latter, historian Gerda Lerner tells us, is essential for "the formulation of the kind of abstract thought needed to conceptualize a society in which differences do not connote dominance."

Recently, scholars looking beyond the socially constructed roles that constrict women and men and place barriers in the path of nonconformists have moved into a new area of understanding. They have examined the ways that unconsciously gendered language, analysis, and attitudes have often categorically deprecated women and their work and contributions, scholarly and other-wise. For it is in these areas that women have faced the most formidable hurdles to equality.

In that context and acknowledging the long odds Angie Debo had overcome to maintain her career in an era when women were barred from full participation in the more prestigious occupations, feminist scholars in Oklahoma in the 1980s obtained funding to conduct oral history interviews with her. Their efforts, combined with a growing desire among many other Oklahomans to honor her as a "state treasure," paved the way for placing her portrait in Oklahoma's capitol rotunda. In a closely allied effort, these same feminist scholars and a variety of groups and institutions raised money for the production of "Indians, Outlaws and Angie Debo," a work that captured the historian's personality indelibly on film.

After her death, Debo's papers and the transcripts of the oral history interviews were deposited in the manuscript division of the Edmon Low Library at Oklahoma State University. Scholars will mine this treasure trove for years to come. In this way, the historian, by agreeing to interviews late in life, despite declining health and energy, has left behind important information about growing up as a female on the prairies of Kansas and Oklahoma. The record now delineates the impact of regional factors on her life, work, and personal identity.

Through this manuscript collection, Debo also bequeathed modern scholars information regarding the odyssey she made as a historian. By examining her early training and her scholarly influences, one gains a rare glimpse into the process by which a lifelong student, though indebted to others, learned to trust her own insights and her own distinctive perspective. As World War II was concluding, Debo's reading and analysis convinced her that the history of Indian-white relations in the United States was the story of her country's "real imperialism." From her rural base, she realized that, unless her compatriots acknowledged the injustice perpetrated against Native peoples and other minorities—and altered that historic pattern—their leadership in the postwar era would remain morally compromised.

Debo's travels abroad after her mother's death in 1954 broadened her perspective and clarified her understanding of the impact of failed racial policies on American society as a whole. Furthermore, her activism from the mid-1950s on deepened her convictions and, hence, the moral authority she brought to her writings. Her long-standing involvement in the Indian Rights Association and the Association on American Indian Affairs convinced her that Native peoples needed self-determination and all the benefits promised in the earlier treaties by which they had given up their lands. She fought tenaciously for these rights during the last thirty-five years of her life.

By the time Debo was in her eighties and nineties, she had traveled far from the mental landscapes of her childhood. As she noted in June 1985, "There's no spot on the globe that is as far away from my knowledge and understanding as the Indian Territory was when I was growing up in the Territory of Oklahoma." Placing herself on the other side of Turner's frontier and viewing the story of westward expansion from the perspective of Native Americans, she saw a different reality behind the idealized version of the history she had inherited from her extended family and her beloved mentor, Edward Everett Dale.

By moving beyond her own origin myth, Angie Debo, the daughter of sodbusters, paved the way for change in herself and her profession. In her writings, she challenged the widespread myth of national innocence and insisted that her compatriots honor their commitments, not only for the sake of Native peoples but because they owed it to their better selves.

Armed with such knowledge, Angie Debo's readers can embark on their own odysseys. Their journeys can carry them a long way toward home, the place that promises reconciliation with their collective past.

CHAPTER I

The New Land

ON November 8, 1899, Edward and Lina Debo with their two children—nine-year-old Angie and Edwin, a year younger—arrived in Marshall, Oklahoma Territory. As Edward conferred with a real estate agent about the farmland he had purchased, the young girl, seated beside her mother, peered out of a covered wagon at the houses, a story and a half tall; their red barns; and the "green wheat stretching to the low horizon." Where, she wondered, were the Indians? She knew they lived in Oklahoma, but all she had seen so far during her family's travels from Welcome, Kansas, to this small town were homesteaders in frame or sod houses and an occasional rancher or cowboy.

Returning to his separate wagon, sagging with farm equipment, Edward signaled his wife to follow in hers, which was crammed with furniture, dishes, utensils, canned fruit, clothing, and a few precious books. After driving about five miles southward, the family arrived at their new home. It was, Angie discovered, a one-room shack, probably twenty by twenty feet. The farmer who had patented the land in 1889 had sold out when property values increased beyond expectations. Like many others, he was seeking new profits farther west.

Spotting a tree near a creek, the two children climbed its branches, looking for a place where their father could build a playhouse. Meanwhile the parents unpacked the family's belongings and prepared the evening meal. In their mid-thirties, Edward and Lina Debo were starting over, but each brought to this venture a resiliency forged from previous encounters with hardship.

Following their marriage in 1889, Angie's birth on January 30, 1890, on a rented farm in Beattie, Kansas—and Edwin's birth some twenty-two months later—Edward and Lina had managed through hard, unremitting labor and painstaking frugality to escape tenancy. Despite declining prices of farm commodities and a widespread depression, by 1893 they had acquired railroad land in Welcome, a hamlet about twenty miles south of Manhattan, Kansas. With the nine hundred dollars they cleared after selling out four years later, they were making, they hoped, a final move. They were settling in "Old Oklahoma," the region opened in the famous land run of April 22, 1889.

When the couple signed a mortgage for the five hundred dollars still owed, they were confident that rising real estate prices would amortize their indebtedness. All the publicity and recent talk of the "great commercial awakening" in Oklahoma strengthened their faith in their decision. Two monthly train excursions from the East were bringing thousands of settlers into the territory. Given such widespread interest, land values would surely increase. More important, Oklahoma soil produced abundant harvests of tall wheat. Although prices had declined after soaring above a dollar a bushel two years earlier, they were still high by historic standards.

Like many other families, the Debos were accompanied by relatives. In their case it was Lina's parents and her unmarried siblings who moved with them to this last frontier and established their own home nearby. Twenty-eight-year-old Bertella Rosina, better known as Bird, was Angie's favorite aunt. Following her fiancé's murder seven years earlier, Bird had been photographed, at Grandmother Angeline Cooper's insistence, in a black dress and widow's veil. Ever since then, Bird had seen herself as the "heroine of a romantic novel." Lina, impatient with her mother's and her sister's theatrics, informed Angie that their actions were foolish and arose from Angeline Cooper's attachment to "sentimental stories" that exaggerated the "romantic strain in her nature"—to everyone's misfortune.

In this and other situations, Lina taught her daughter that, although she was her grandmother's namesake, emulating her traits would not be wise. Instead, she was to meet life's inevitable hardships with equanimity and as much courage as she could muster. One must extend compassion to those who suffered, but one should never extract drama or sympathy from tragedies or willingly play the victim's role.

When winter came, Edward began transforming the shack into a three-room house. In the evening, while Angie helped her mother prepare meals and Edwin assisted his father with carpentry, Edward recalled his family's adventures and hardships. His ancestors, originally from France, had settled along the Rhine after Napoleon Bonaparte had expanded his authority into the region following the Peace of Amiens in 1802. When Napoleon was defeated thirteen years later, the Debos found themselves chafing under Prussian rule. In 1854, Peter Debo, Edward's father, emigrated to the United States. Later he met and married Elizabeth Hoppmeier, a German immigrant of Peru, Illinois.

Edward, as the couple's second son, helped his father pull ice barges down the Mississippi. Eager to prosper, he tried railroading before acquiring a homestead near Rock Island, Nebraska. After his farm proved disappointing, he moved to Cheyenne, Wyoming, which struck him as "too lawless." Later he joined his sister Lisetta, the wife of William Tilden of Beattie, Kansas. She, in turn, introduced him as the "cyclone shucker" to her close friend, Lina Cooper. Twenty-six-year-old Edward Debo was the only man in the county capable of husking and cribbing a hundred bushels of corn daily throughout the harvest season.

During these family evenings, Edward's accounts encouraged Lina to reminisce in turn about her childhood. She had grown up listening to father Alfred Cooper's tales of his overland journey to California in 1859, a trek made mostly by men rather than by families. Cooper arrived a decade too late for the small prospector, and not surprisingly, he returned home thinner from illness and richer only in his memories. Still searching for a better life, Alfred then moved his growing family to northeastern Iowa and in 1879 to Rooks County in northwestern Kansas. There fourteen-year-old Lina helped her family build a sod house, a dwelling whose roof leaked when it rained and that attracted the usual centipedes, spiders, and snakes. Although the family missed the great grasshopper plague of 1874, Lina recalled later infestations. Swarms of insects, which seemed to "drop out of the western Kansas sky," destroyed crops and, at times, invaded homes, ravaging clothing, curtains, and upholstery.

As the second of seven children and the oldest daughter, Lina was responsible for caring for five younger children. Her duties left little time for schooling, and, she was soon "working out." Her family welcomed the fifty cents she earned daily by helping new mothers with housekeeping. Meanwhile, the Coopers were experiencing serious reverses as they contended with droughts, declining commodity prices, the high costs of shipping crops, and the rising costs of equipment. In 1883, faced with a "starving time," Alfred Cooper moved his family to Beattie, Kansas, in the northeastern part of the state, close to the Nebraska line. Whatever her memories of hardships, Lina, like her husband, was proud of her family's perseverance. For both husband and wife, tales of pioneering endurance represented their primary bequest to the new generation growing up in Oklahoma.

The couple, however, differed from their families of origin in one important way. Lina and Edward limited their progeny to two offspring. Although physical incapacities on the part of one or the other may have accounted for this fact, very likely the two were determined, despite a farming background that rendered children an economic asset, to limit their family size. In that way, they were able to give Angie and Edwin more time, energy, and care, thereby increasing their chances for advancement in later life.

Angie had kept a diary sporadically in the past, but the move to Oklahoma, which all pioneers saw as historically significant, heightened the importance of recording her experiences. In the pages of her journal, she noted that her mother showed her how to plant onions and other vegetables. Later Lina taught her to set a hen and care for baby chicks. Angie was also responsible for a cow and her calf and assisted her mother with the pigs.

With food requirements met, mother and daughter then planted roses, peonies, dahlias, and chrysanthemums, many from seedlings and small plants that Lina had brought from Kansas. Despite the unending demands of farm life, flowers were essential.

They brought beauty and gentility to everyday life, qualities easily lost amid the monotony and drudgery of constant work. Someone, perhaps Lina or Grandfather Cooper, also taught Angie to identify the region's birds. The best loved and most welcomed was the mockingbird whose April song signaled the arrival of spring.

Edwin, for his part, herded cattle, and when his father plowed, the boy harrowed the soil before Grandfather Cooper sowed the sorghum seed. Following the rainy season in May and June, male members of the extended family helped Edward and Edwin prepare for the fall planting of winter wheat as the hot, oppressive winds of July and August bore down on them. It was grueling, backbreaking labor.

Several months after the planting, Angie and her mother drove to the fields to see the ripening wheat. One day, when "the sky was blue the way Oklahoma skies can be," Lina showed rare emotion. "When I look out on the country like this, the tears come to my eyes," she told her daughter. "I don't know why." Angie understood, for the surrounding beauty and fertility moved her in the same way. She too loved the new land.

More than anything, however, the young girl loved school. During the five to six months that classes were in session, she and Edwin trudged along the two-mile path to Rosenberg School, a frame building south of their home. Often they took a shortcut through a neighbor's pasture that crossed Horse Creek with its plum thicket and redbud trees. At the one-room schoolhouse, they joined other children and youths of widely varying ages and skills to study grammar, arithmetic, geography, history, and according to the records, physiology. The latter course, offered in many schools throughout the country, dealt with health issues—most especially, the dangers of drinking alcoholic beverages.

In their study of history, the students probably learned about Oklahoma's first people, the Wichita-Caddos, Kiowa Apaches, Cheyennes, Arapahos, Comanches, Osages, and Quapaws. Then, very likely, they turned to the movement of European explorers into the region, beginning with the Spanish expedition led

by Francisco Vásquez de Coronado in 1541 and early in the
next century, the French exploration under Bernard de la
Harpe. Official United States exploration, they learned, began
in 1806.

The students also examined the movement of the Cherokees,
Creeks, Choctaws, Chickasaws, and Seminoles into Indian Territory. These tribes were always referred to as the Five Civilized
Tribes to distinguish them from the Plains Indians farther west.
Their arrival in Indian Territory was presented as the beginning
of "civilization." Much class time, however, was spent discussing
the recent "runs" and the subsequent movement of non-Indian
families into Oklahoma Territory, in search of a better life on this
last frontier.

Angie's first teacher in Oklahoma was twenty-nine-year-old
Stella Noble, a divorced mother of three. Though the census
records list Noble as a divorcée, Debo remembered her as a
"widow," which was undoubtedly what adults told children in
an era when divorce was considered disreputable. Despite the
stigma, Marshall's residents employed Noble as a schoolmistress
largely because the rapidly growing region desperately needed
teachers. Aside from Noble, most of Angie's instructors were still
in their teens, with no education beyond eighth grade. Passing
the territorial examination qualified them to become schoolmis-
tresses, although they seemingly had to meet other requirements
as well. One former instructor recalled being told to "put my
hair up and my skirts down."

Whatever their age or background, teachers were extraordinary creatures to Angie. When she grew up, she informed her
family, she wanted to be "an old maid and teach school." Despite
her youth, she already knew that married women, except for
widows or those with incapacitated husbands, seldom became
wage earners.

In Oklahoma, unlike Kansas, Lina no longer helped in the
fields. Barnyard and household chores consumed her days. Since
farm equipment always needed replacing and upgrading, labor-
saving household appliances received low priority among less
prosperous families. That fact added to Lina's burdens as she

faced a heavy workload. In one fortnight, according to a letter Lina sent her daughter once when Angie was away from home, in addition to preparing three large meals a day, she tended to the horses, cleaned the house, washed and ironed the clothes, relined old shirt collars for Edward, and made over Angie's blouse. She also planted the vegetable and flower gardens and weeded the lawn and her family's portion of the road along their property. Then, after caring for the hens and their eggs and chicks, she picked cherries at a nearby farm. When she returned home, she canned the cherries, along with eighteen quarts of string beans and beet greens.

Lina also raised and sold turkeys, which provided the funds for Angie's reed organ, available locally after the Denver, Enid and Gulf Railroad arrived in Marshall in 1902. A young woman from a local farm family now traveled the region giving lessons to about thirty youngsters, mostly girls. When Angie joined that group, Lina rejoiced that her daughter enjoyed advantages she had never known.

Years later, Debo characterized her mother as "a practical feminist." Nothing in family records indicates that Lina was a "reluctant pioneer" or saw herself simply as her husband's helpmate. Instead, she informed her daughter that a wife, by working in her home, "was entitled to an equal use of a joint account."

Lina also served outside the home as a Sunday school teacher for the Methodist Church. Since the circuit-riding minister filled the pulpit every other Sunday in the early 1900s, Lina remained her congregation's most reliable source of religious instruction. Once when her mother was late for class, Angie wrote in her diary, "it was like the fellow that was going to be hung. There wasn't going to be anything done till he got there."

Edward, a man described as "not contemplative," usually avoided religious services, but he always assisted his wife at church. Each week he fetched the large boxes of Sunday school material from the post office. Before worship, his daughter recalled years later, he "lighted the fires throughout the winter and attended to the summer ventilation." After a snowstorm, he shoveled the walkways.

Although Marshall boasted the broadest Main Street in Oklahoma, in 1903 it still lacked a high school. After finishing eighth grade and passing her territorial examination, Angie waited impatiently for completion of the brick building that would offer her more schooling.

At thirteen Angie contracted measles, which progressed to pneumonia. She might have suffocated had Lina not drawn on her vast store of folk medicine and pharmacology. (Debo recalled years later that her mother, highly skilled in home nursing, had saved the lives of at least four persons "by swift, decisive action in crises, while other neighbors stood helplessly by.") Rather than calling a doctor, a last resort in rural areas of the plains and prairies, Lina gave her daughter an emetic. Before long, Angie vomited a jellolike substance. With her lungs cleared, she breathed more easily. Afterwards she lost her golden brown hair and for several months was almost bald. At last it grew back, but darker and never again as abundant as during her childhood.

As she entered adolescence, Angie became increasingly interested in the larger world. When the *Kingfisher (Okla.) Free Press,* published in a nearby settlement, carried the story that Czarist troops had fired on petitioning workers at the Winter Palace in St. Petersburg on January 9, 1905, known in history as "Bloody Sunday," Angie became engrossed in the Russian Revolution. As she devoured news of the subsequent strikes, riots, naval mutinies, and assassinations, she felt conflicting emotions—torn by a repulsion to violence yet hoping Russia would be freed from the forces of autocracy. Unfortunately, 1905 ended as it had begun, with a workers' insurrection in Moscow, followed by government retaliation.

Marshall's new schoolhouse had, by now, opened its doors to an increasingly diverse group of students. Like other areas of the plains and prairies, the territory was attracting large numbers of immigrant families from Europe, most commonly from Germany and Bohemia. Daily, Angie rode Queen, her pony, to the brick building three and a half miles from home. There she studied English, Latin, algebra, and geography.

On February 2, 1906, Angie's ninth-grade class debated the question, "Resolved: That a nation or nations should interfere with and slow the barbarities that are now being perpetrated in Russia." Angie argued for the negative, since she attributed much of the disorder to Czar Nicholas's vacillation and weakness. As she saw it, the recent atrocities committed by the masses were responses to atrocities the nobility had inflicted earlier on peasants and workers. Whatever the bloodshed, Angie hoped that the common people would never again submit to their chains and that "out of this confusion [would] yet come one of the leading nations of the world." Debo's lifelong fascination with the struggles of the Russian people had begun. More important, she was already intensely interested in issues of social justice.

Unfortunately, when Angie finished ninth grade in June of 1906, no other classes were available. Facing a dead end, she waited for a teaching vacancy in a rural school. In the meantime she kept abreast of current news by devouring the local weekly and listening to men talk of politics at the general store.

Edward Debo was a Democrat. That meant that he saw the high tariff, which inflated the price of farm equipment, as the chief source of injustice for small farmers like himself. Nonetheless, the entire family supported the current president, Republican Theodore Roosevelt. Teddy, as they fondly called him, demonstrated his willingness to curb the power of that engine of progress and exploitation—the railroad. Western agrarians had long complained that the carriers charged as much as four times the eastern rate for transporting their commodities and freight. When Roosevelt won passage of the Hepburn Act in 1906, which allowed the Interstate Commerce Commission to set maximum rates for transmitting goods, Oklahoma farmers looked forward to greater prosperity.

According to Mabel Clark, a correspondent of Debo's during her teen years, Angie briefly "set her cap" on a young Bohemian. But neither that relationship, whatever its extent, nor any other friendship with a male deepened into genuine courtship. Angie, wanting a career, withdrew as soon as any young man showed more than passing interest. And her admirers, discouraged, eventually gave up pursuit.

One day during that frustrating period when further schooling was unavailable, Angie accompanied Edwin to town to purchase

kerosene for their lamps. On the way home, they tossed a sack
of flour they had also bought at the general store into the wagon.
When they arrived home, Lina discovered that the kerosene had
penetrated the flour's burlap covering. Though she threw out
the dampened portion of the flour, she discovered that, unfortunately, the pungent odor had permeated the entire bag. Even
so, having no additional money to replace the flour, Lina used it
to bake the family's biscuits, cakes, and pies.

Instead of rebuking their offspring, Lina and Edward joked
about the matter. In later reminiscences, the couple characterized their good-natured response to misfortune as evidence they
had mastered the "spirit of Oklahoma." Like other families who
had undergone a "starving time," the Debos endured privation
with good humor. In this way, Lina and Edward instilled in their
offspring a cheerful stoicism. Moreover, by tying this quality to
regional values, they deepened their children's sense of identity
as Oklahomans.

Although the Debos were increasingly attached to the territory, the lack of educational opportunities wore on Angie's spirits. She found one source of stimulation in the lecture circuit that
brought famous figures to town. A speech by the temperance
advocate Carry Nation, recently of Kansas but now living in
Guthrie, thirty miles from Marshall, provided a welcome break
in the routine of farm life. Angie later described Nation as "the
dumpy little woman with the brisk manner and the keen wit," a
rather inept depiction since Nation was almost six feet tall. More
accurately, Debo remembered her as having swayed the crowd.
"Those who had come to scoff remained to join up—this time
a 'Prohibition Federation' of Republicans and Democrats who
were expected to renounce their parties," Debo observed as the
territory prepared for statehood.

When vacancies finally opened in the neighboring schools,
Angie began teaching in Logan and Garfield Counties. Even
though she enjoyed earning a salary of one hundred dollars every
three months, she missed her family, for she moved constantly,
boarding in one farmhouse and then another, and never really
feeling at home.

Teaching, moreover, was not an easy job. Instructors had to make a fire each morning in the winter and keep it going. Year-round, they had to sweep out the schoolhouse. Classroom discipline also presented problems, for the dearth of recreational facilities left many students without outlets for their exuberant spirits. A favorite game among the older boys was to see if class disruptions could drive a novice instructor to quit in discouragement even more quickly than they had driven off the teacher she had replaced. Angie, although small and slender and new in her profession, ruined any such plans by establishing firm control in her classroom from the beginning.

At the same time, she was kind. With a shy child, she would never ask direct or discomforting questions. Instead, she elicited any response she could to a statement and then sought a kernel of truth in the student's answer.

In November 1907 Angie missed the ceremonies in Guthrie that marked Oklahoma's transition to statehood. The earlier spring panic on Wall Street had left the local bank short of currency, and train fare was difficult to come by. Moreover, Angie and her parents worried about the red patches the green bug infestation had left on the wheat fields following a summer drought. In that context it seemed best to save on expenditures. Nonetheless, Debo followed news accounts of events with mounting interest.

Her attention was especially focused on her idol, Catherine Ann Barnard. At thirty-two, "our good angel, Kate," as she was known, was the new state's commissioner of charities and corrections.

Earlier, in August 1906, when delegates from the Indianhoma Farmers' Union and the Twin Territorial Federation of Labor had assembled at Shawnee, Barnard had exhorted them to support planks outlawing child labor and mandating compulsory schooling. In addition, she had called for greater safety standards for workers and for the eight-hour workday. When these issues became a part of the state constitution, which also created the office of Charities and Corrections, everyone knew that, although Oklahoma women lacked suffrage, Kate Barnard would be elected to lead that department.

Angie, fascinated by the five-foot, ninety-pound dynamo with profuse dark curls and alert eyes, had absorbed all the relevant facts about her heroine. Like herself, Barnard had lived in Kansas before moving to Oklahoma. In her twenties she had become director of the Provident Association of Oklahoma City, and in that capacity she had forged a strong alliance with female organizations interested in social reform, especially the Oklahoma Federation of Women's Clubs. Acquainted with both rural and urban poverty through personal experiences and through her travels to eastern cities and interviews with Jane Addams and Jacob Riis, among others, Barnard wanted the new state to give workers, especially children, greater protections.

After Congress accepted Oklahoma's constitution, President Roosevelt signed the enabling legislation on November 16, 1907. On that day Indian Territory and Oklahoma Territory were united in a ceremony on the steps of Guthrie's Carnegie Library. A mock marriage between a woman of Cherokee descent and an Oklahoma City businessman, dressed as a cowboy, symbolized the creation of the new state.

Afterwards Kate Barnard rode in a carriage in the inaugural parade. Although Charles N. Haskell, a Democrat with progressive leanings from Muskogee, was sworn in as Oklahoma's first governor, many saw the celebration as Barnard's day of triumph. After all, she had received more votes than any other officeholder in the newly created state. In truth, she played no role in the actual ceremonies and later described her carriage as a "broken down, battered, and frayed buggy." She soon discovered that her quarters in the state office building consisted of a small cubicle on the third floor next to the men's room. Her power was minimal and her salary was the lowest, next to the lieutenant governor's, of all state officials.

Seventeen-year-old Angie Debo knew nothing of this reality as she avidly devoured every detail of Barnard's career in the local newspapers. Consciously and unconsciously, Debo was influenced by her heroine's personal magnetism and her work on behalf of Oklahoma's less powerful citizens.

In 1910, after Marshall added the last three years to its high school curriculum, Angie resumed her education. A civic-minded clubwoman who extended her homemaking into the larger community was behind this development. A recent arrival from Pierson, Iowa, and a mother herself, Lola Clark Pearson had been campaigning for a full secondary school curriculum since her election as president of the Marshall Woman's Club, an organization she had founded in 1905. Her ally was U. F. Clemons, the manager of a local grain elevator. Together, they urged fellow citizens to make Marshall, which was never destined to become a leading city of the interior, at least a place that educated its youth.

In 1912, another drought wiped out the crops in the region, and the green bug infestation reappeared. Edward and Lina, increasingly disappointed in their farm, sold it and bought a hardware store in town. Again they were starting over.

In the meantime, Angie was excelling at school. At one point an English teacher, impressed by her agile mind and superb writing skills, took her aside. She had to attend college, the teacher told her, "because when you get older you're going to write books and things that the rest of us will be reading." That afternoon, Angie walked home "on clouds."

During her high school years Debo participated in a debate about giving women the right to vote. Arguing for the affirmative, she invoked the principles of the Declaration of Independence and the Constitution. She reminded her audience that, under the current system of government, power was derived from the consent of the governed—in other words, the people. Surely women were people. But females, one half the population, were subject to taxation without representation since they could neither vote nor make laws. In short, according to democratic principles, women needed suffrage. Otherwise the state government should declare its statutes "enacted by the ruling class or the oligarchy of the state of Oklahoma." After arguing that women were entitled to vote on the basis of justice, Angie noted that, given their special role within the family, they needed suffrage to protect their homes and children. Rather than threatening their "womanly nature," voting would enable them to "train their children to higher ideals of citizenship."

Although Angie never participated in the suffrage movement, she obviously gave the question of woman's role in society careful thought. Throughout her speech she wove insights into the accomplishments of suffrage leaders Elizabeth Cady Stanton and Susan B. Anthony and Women's Christian Temperance Union leader Frances Willard. It was clear that she had consulted history books. But, in the end, it was probably Lina's practical feminism that played the greatest role in shaping her daughter's attitudes toward the necessity of enfranchising women.

In June 1913, the townspeople assembled in the high school auditorium to honor Marshall High School's first graduating class. As the nine students marched down the aisle, wearing the finest clothes their parents could make or buy, the crowd erupted in cheers. It was a proud moment for the town, the first in the area to offer its youth a high school diploma.

After her graduation, Angie returned to teaching in the rural schools. Then, in 1915 she fell gravely ill with typhoid fever. Again Lina saved her life, expertly nursing her back to health. After she recovered, Angie enrolled at the University of Oklahoma, a small school dating back to 1892 and located in Norman. Eager to learn the craft of writing, she selected English as her major. But, when she discovered that her education was preparing her to correct student papers and little else, she switched to geology, since she loved nature and the outdoors.

On Mother's Day, 1916, as she finished her freshman year, Angie wrote Lina, expressing appreciation for her love and support. Earlier, she acknowledged, her mother had "been chained down on that old farm and nothing could be done to make that nightmare tolerable." But armed with a degree, Angie vowed she would give her mother a life that included luxuries, such as "a diamond ring [for] every finger and thumb," frequent trips to the movies, and weekly visits to Europe. "[E]very one of your dishrags shall be of silk," she told her. And these dreams were not just castles in the air. She was determined to improve her mother's life. "Just watch and see," she told Lina.

Angie was grateful to her mother, for despite hardships and setbacks, Lina had given her children "an uncommonly happy childhood." Neither of her children could claim to be "self-made," she noted. With soaring optimism, Angie now looked forward to a future of material success, and she wanted to share her abundance with her parents—most especially with her mother. More than anyone else, Lina had given her the confidence to pursue her ambitions and dreams.

CHAPTER 2

Student and Teacher

WHEN Angie Debo learned that geology offered few opportunities for women, she became disillusioned with the field. Since she had enjoyed an earlier course on American history and government taught by Edward Everett Dale, she enrolled in one of his other classes in January 1917.

The tall, slim, "unprofessorial figure" was different from Angie's other teachers. Gentle and unassuming in manner, Dale strode into the classroom with his "cowboy walk, his soft voice, and his alert far-seeing eyes." His thesis adviser at Harvard, Frederick Jackson Turner, had introduced him to "a new heaven and earth in the field of American History," and he sought to inspire the same enthusiasm in the sons and daughters of pioneers seated before him.

Oklahoma, Dale taught them, had provided the setting for the last act of an amazing drama. The Five Tribes, the state's original pioneers, had entered the eastern portion, then known as Indian Territory, early in the nineteenth century, armed with finely honed diplomatic skills gained from their earlier dealings with European powers and their tenacious, although ultimately unsuccessful, efforts to protect themselves from removal from their southeastern homelands. Their struggles to ensure the best interests of their people against an encircling population further enhanced their political acumen. Thus, when Oklahoma became a state, although Indians numbered only 6 percent of the population, they supplied, Dale estimated, 20 to 25 percent of its most notable leaders.

The western portion of the state had been populated by traders, military men, cattlemen, and pioneering families, who had swept westward in successive waves across newly opened territories, seeking opportunities unavailable in older settled regions. Dale claimed that, as each of these waves "revert[ed] to primitive conditions," society rebuilt itself anew. Owing less each time to European influences, it became in the process more indigenously American. In so theorizing, Dale was building on Frederick Jackson Turner's ideas as expressed in "The Significance of the Frontier in American History," Turner's address to the American Historical Association at the 1893 Columbian Exposition in Chicago.

Since Oklahoma Territory had been the last area thrown open, its people were the most American of all. According to Dale, when they joined themselves with the Native peoples to the east in Indian Territory, they created a state that encapsulated the entire history of the United States. Moreover, in his own lifetime, Dale had experienced the process by which these elements had come together. Having "grown up on the prairies" of Oklahoma Territory, he had "observed its change from the frontier of the hunter to that of the cowboy, the pioneer settler, and the prosperous farmer, and had witnessed the coming of towns and cities and all the complex organizations of commercial and industrial life." Within a few years, he had seen "that body of unwritten law known as 'Cow Custom,'" transformed into "statutory law by action of the territorial or state legislatures." Thus, history was not some abstract body of knowledge involving only the elite and the renowned. History was what he, his students, and their families had lived through.

Angie was enthralled by Dale's lectures and excited by one of his assignments—to write a history of her hometown. She wrote it using the methods of researching and writing that Dale taught. Years later, she claimed that she relied on his training throughout her career. "[I]t is my belief," she said, "that much of the bad historical writing we read comes from faulty note-taking and note-organizing techniques."

As Dale provided a narrative that explained United States history and shared the techniques for producing it, he also wove stories of his life into his lectures with wry, self-deprecating humor.

Angie soon learned that, as the son of a small farmer from Greer County, the area bordering the Kiowa-Comanche Reservation around the North Fork of the Red River, he had grown up viewing himself as a Texan. But in 1896, when he was seventeen, he became an Oklahoman when the U.S. Supreme Court ruled that the South Fork, rather than the North Fork, was the source of the Red River, the boundary of Texas. Thus Greer County, located between the two forks, belonged to Oklahoma.

Orphaned two years later, young Edward Dale tried ranching, but with homesteaders flooding into the area, the days of the open range were over. In his twenties he served as a schoolmaster at various locations in western Oklahoma, while he attended summer sessions to further his education. At Cloud Chief, the lack of housing forced him to live one summer in a wagon. Later, he boarded at a dugout with so little privacy that he "managed his dressing under an improvised tent of bedclothes while his hostess was preparing breakfast in the opposite corner." That experience, among others, taught him to see the pioneer wife as a noble, overburdened woman who had moved westward only to please her husband. Living in crude housing, she treasured her few remaining pieces of china, silver, or glass and dreamed, he wrote in *Frontier Ways: Sketches of Life in the Old West* (1959), of the day "when she would have a home into which these things would properly fit."

By 1906 Dale, now a principal, was attending summer sessions at the territorial teacher's college, or normal school, at Edmond. Angie and the other students always laughed when he explained that, without a high school diploma, he was placed in the "the sub-normal department." Six years later, at age thirty-three, he received his bachelor's degree from the University of Oklahoma. And two years after that, in 1914, equipped with a master's from Harvard, he accepted an instructorship at his alma mater.

For Debo, Dale was a kindred soul who had overcome many of the same barriers she faced. This former cowboy, regal in his simplicity and speaking in country cadences similar to hers, gave her inchoate dreams shape and direction. Determined to follow in his footsteps, she changed her major to history.

During these years, the Debo hardware business failed. In his fifties and no longer an independent farmer or businessman, Edward became a lineman for the Santa Fe Railroad. He rose quickly to foreman, and, before long, by practicing their usual frugality, he and Lina had settled their accounts.

While the Debos were suffering setbacks, Marshall and nearby towns were prospering. With the Great War well into its third year in 1917, the continuing demand for wheat sent prices soaring to two dollars a bushel. Pioneering farmers who had held on through luck and perseverance looked back in self-congratulation. Land, once free except for a small filing fee, was now worth thousands of dollars a section, making many in Logan County people of means as the United States entered the war in April on the side of England and France.

Debo, aware that her brother, who had contributed to her college expenses, was facing conscription and her parents were still struggling financially, hurried to finish a four-year program in three. Discovering a "fair field and no favors," she won accolades from her professors as she excelled academically. Still, she sometimes envied the young women from more prosperous families who arrived on campus wearing the latest modified sheaths. Many were members of sororities, which gave them a sense of belonging and left her feeling excluded. For the first time, Angie felt the pain of belonging to a social class others saw as inferior.

She was living in an era of change. During these years, the youth of America were already revolting against their parents' customs and conventions. Pictures of young women wearing bobbed hair had adorned the covers of the popular *Ladies' Home Journal* as early as 1915. Inside its pages young women sported shortened hemlines, although the flapper would not appear until the 1920s. Moreover, young men and women now related to one another with less formality and a greater sense of camaraderie. In an issue of the *University of Oklahoma Magazine*, dated March 1918 and one of the few Angie saved, was an article titled "My Ideal Woman." According to the writer, identified only as "a man," this woman would be first and foremost "an ideal wife," and, in that role, not a helpmate but instead a good comrade. Although Angie had renounced matrimony because she saw a wife's responsibilities as incompatible with a career, she undoubtedly endorsed the standards the article prescribed. The ideal woman would "be of the fiber that will stand adversity without becoming embittered and share prosperity without exalting herself."

Within weeks after Debo's graduation in May 1918, Pvt. Edwin Debo drilled at Camp Stanley near San Antonio, Texas, in preparation for Central Officer Training School at Camp Taylor in western Kentucky. Several months later, on November 11, an incessant whistle announcing the armistice awoke Debo as she slept at a friend's house. "We lay there too moved for speech except a sentence of deep thankfulness," she recalled years later. She then dozed off again, imagining "a peace that I thought would last forever."

The war was over and her brother had escaped overseas service. Although demobilization proceeded so rapidly that laid-off armament workers swelled the ranks of the unemployed, Edwin, who had graduated from Marshall High School in 1915, eventually found a teaching position in a rural school. Soon after, undoubtedly with Angie's assistance as repayment for his earlier help with her education, he enrolled in the Agricultural and Mechanical College in nearby Stillwater.

The opening of the new decade brought changes for Oklahoma women. In addition to experiencing less formality in their relations with men, the state's females, enfranchised in a 1918 referendum, voted for the first time in November 1920. Ten weeks earlier, Tennessee, the thirty-sixth state to ratify the Nineteenth Amendment to the Constitution, had given the ballot to all American women. Debo, following in her father's footsteps, cast her first vote for the Democratic presidential ticket, which included James Cox, former governor of Ohio, and Franklin Delano Roosevelt, assistant secretary of the navy since 1913. The victory of Republican candidate, Warren G. Harding, demonstrated, however, that the earlier era of reform was irretrievably gone. Moreover, the U.S. Senate had rejected involvement in collective security by voting against America's participation in the League of Nations, a measure proposed by Woodrow Wilson in the last year and a half of his presidency.

These trends weighed on Debo's mind when she left her teaching position at Enid High School in 1923. With her brother's education assured, she was determined to pursue a master's degree outside of Oklahoma. Her timing was good. Faced with a dearth of male students since the late war, graduate schools were more readily welcoming women, and females now constituted about 40 percent of those working toward advanced degrees.

Angie, like many western women from rural areas, felt a pull toward the urban environment. Determined to pursue her studies at a large city university, she narrowed her alternatives to Columbia University in New York City and the University of Chicago. In the end, she chose the latter because of its superiority in international studies, her major area of interest.

Another factor may also have influenced her choice. Debo, who always scrutinized her options, probably knew that Chicago had become more accommodating to females largely because of its dean of women, Marion Talbot. A graduate of the Massachusetts Institute of Technology, Talbot had come to Chicago in 1892 as an administrator and as professor of sanitary science. Committed to seeing women get the same chance at education as men enjoyed, she often reminded her superiors that females won proportionately more of the highest academic honors than did their male counterparts. Moreover, although women received fewer fellowships than men, their attrition rates were lower.

By fall 1923 Angie felt increasingly at home in the university's Gothic buildings. Talbot's efforts had won off-campus women a reading room and a pleasant lounge at the Woman's Union. In addition, they had their own gymnasium and swimming pool in Ida Noyes Hall.

At Chicago Debo majored in history and minored in political science. Because her Christian faith had been of vital importance to her since childhood, she chose a course in the psychology of religion as an elective. Her lecture notes from this course show the ways in which her studies were forming her: "Our culture is disintegrating—no traditions no standards no loyalty in the sense other ages have had them & in the sense human nature craves them. There must be some way by which we can express our natural championship of causes and ideals and yet do it in a scientific way." One way, she noted, was to view religion as "consciousness of social values and then try to promote [those values]," while still respecting ". . . the values of traditional and dogmatic systems."

These ideas, echoing the social gospel of the earlier Progressive Era, may have been Angie's summation of the instructor's statements—or they may have represented an attempt to reconcile classroom information with her own commitment to Christianity. At any rate, her religious faith, still intact, expressed itself later in a desire to champion social values through "causes and ideals." History, with its emphasis on critically and objectively examining sources and evidence, would provide the "scientific way."

One of the professors who had attracted Angie to Chicago was James Fred Rippy. His course, The Americas in World Affairs, offered her the opportunity to study the origins of her country's historic isolationism. Shortly before Christmas 1923, as Debo examined foreign policy during the Revolutionary period, she made a surprising discovery.

Many historians saw isolationism in the United States as originating from President George Washington's Proclamation of Neutrality in 1793, following the outbreak of war between France and England. Angie uncovered an earlier statement that suggested otherwise. John Adams, during the 1775 Continental Congress debates over obtaining aid from France against the mother country, had admonished his compatriots "not to enter into any alliance with her, which would entangle us in any future wars in Europe." Furthermore, Adams noted, the colonies should "lay it down, as a first principle and a maxim never to be forgotten, to maintain an entire neutrality in all future European wars." These caveats, he noted later, met with "[a]ttention and approbation" from friends and foes alike.

Surprised by Debo's finding, Rippy encouraged her to investigate further. If her evidence revealed a larger pattern overlooked by earlier scholars, she had made an important discovery. Even if not, her research would reinforce traditional ideas concerning the origins of isolationism in American foreign policy.

Angie had found her thesis topic when she learned that others shared Adams's sentiments. Later in life, she characterized her good fortune as "simply a stroke of luck," although admittedly, "it took a little discernment on my part to see the importance of it." Isolationism, she discovered, had originated in the early settlements when individuals like William Penn had seen the New World as a refuge from the conflicts and wars of the Old World and a place for "starting anew in a virgin continent." Carrying the story forward, Debo learned that, whether they were patriots supporting the Revolution or Tories remaining loyal to England, American colonists feared European entanglements. Thus, even before the thirteen colonies had declared their independence, isolationism was a principle of their foreign policy, a fact that European powers understood.

William E. Dodd, Debo's professor in a course on the Old South, found her discoveries so intriguing that he waived the requirements for a term paper and accepted her thesis in its stead. Enamored of Woodrow Wilson (as his biography of that figure indicated), Dodd believed with other progressive historians that a study of the past could prove useful to understanding present problems.

But not all Chicago professors agreed with Dodd about history's potential for solving modern dilemmas. Andrew C. McLaughlin, chair of the history department, had lost a son to combat in the recent war. In all likelihood, it was after President Wilson had failed to win greater self-determination for colonized peoples and some minorities at Versailles and faltered in bringing the United States into the League of Nations that McLaughlin and others at Chicago turned against him. Increasingly disillusioned with the aftermath of the war fought to make "the world safe for democracy," their faith in history as a means of shedding light on international problems gave way to pessimism.

Still, in this era of the "New History" championed by James Harvey Robinson, formerly of Columbia University but now founder and first director of New York City's New School for Social Research, some scholars continued to maintain that their discipline could illuminate the context out of which contemporary dilemmas had arisen. In 1920 Frederick Jackson Turner had expressed it this way: "A just public opinion and a statesmanlike treatment of present problems demand that they be seen in their historical relations in order that history may hold the lamp for conservative reform."

Whatever Debo's view of "conservative reform," she never wavered in her belief that historical understanding could lead to more intelligent policy making in the present and future. If that struck some Chicago professors as naive, Rippy and Dodd were not among them. Rippy, who emphasized the necessity of remaining objective and impartial in writing history, was already exploring the economic and political roots of American hegemony in Latin America. Although he would soften his criticism of his country's policies in *The United States and Mexico* (1926), his later work, *The Capitalists and Colombia* (1931), would involve a study of United States imperialism. Since Debo would later view American Indian history as America's "real imperialism," Rippy was influencing her in subtle and almost subliminal ways that would reverberate throughout her life.

At Chicago, Debo made other discoveries about history and historians. Reading through the secondary literature on her topic, she encountered scholars who, largely because they had never read the original documents, falsely accused the United States of violating its 1778 treaty with France. Although the new nation had not assisted her ally in the 1793 war between France and England, two treaties had, in fact, been concluded—one of commerce and another of alliance. The United States and France interpreted the first differently. When it came to the second, both sides concurred that Americans bore no responsibility for assisting the French in Europe. Nor did the French ask Americans for help in defending their West Indies. However, the Washington administration, fearing that they might, argued that the treaty of alliance no longer bound the United States, since the government involved had been overthrown by the French Revolution.

During her year at Chicago, Debo's scholarship won the respect of her instructors. Moreover, she encountered no discrimination in the classroom because of her sex. Although "hard hearted" and demanding in their requirements, her professors "fanned the flame" of student interest and assisted students in every way. One young man they strongly encouraged was Henry Steele Commager, who later became one of the nation's foremost historians. Angie remembered him as a tall, quiet youth whose gangly legs were always wrapped around his chairs as he pored over his books.

In addition to enjoying her classes, Debo found the city of Chicago an exhilarating environment. With guidebook in hand, she toured the vast metropolis systematically, relying on the elevated trains to travel anywhere day or night, despite the gang wars of organized crime in that era. Undoubtedly she wandered through the galleried rotunda of Marshall Field's department store, gazing in awe at its magnificent Tiffany dome. Certainly she toured the Field Museum of Science in its new location on Lake Shore Drive and took in the Transportation Building, designed by Dankmar Adler and Louis Sullivan. Close by was Jackson Park where, at the World Columbian Exposition, Frederick Jackson Turner had given his famous 1893 address to the American Historical Association. Debo also visited Jane Addams's Hull House on the west side, where 80 percent of the population came from abroad or were the children of immigrants. Although other students teased her about her methodical approach to sightseeing, they were soon asking her to escort them around the city.

Debo always enjoyed walking, and in Chicago her favorite strolling place was along the Lake Michigan shoreline. The wide expanse of water, so reminiscent of the prairies, made her feel at home. When time permitted, she sat on her favorite perch, a pier that extended into the lake. There, where she studied her texts, she undoubtedly paused at times to watch the play of light on the lake's surface or study the changing sky. At other times Angie strode along the area between the lake and Michigan Avenue, which was often awash in mud in the 1920s. One day, young workers from the nearby skyscrapers were outside playing baseball in the street during lunchtime. Angie watched with pleasure. The city that attracted people of many nationalities speaking different languages seemed almost like a foreign land to her. But as she watched youth engaged in this common pastime, all of them, whatever their nationality, seemed truly American.

Among fellow graduate students at Chicago, one Richard Loeb impressed Angie—despite his background of wealth and privilege. He seemed charming and amiable, and she learned at a departmental dinner that he had earned his bachelor's degree at sixteen. Returning to her room at 6024 Woodlawn, Debo stood in front of her mirror, arranging her hair and reflecting that, until now, she might have been prejudiced against people from different, more affluent backgrounds. Her roommate, a young woman majoring in Latin and Greek, was not so sure about Loeb. She knew his good friend, the precocious nineteen-year-old law student Nathan Leopold, and she detested him. Nonetheless, both women were shocked several months later when Loeb and Leopold confessed to the abduction and murder of fourteen-year-old Bobby Franks, admitting that their only motive was to commit the perfect crime.

In that era, a master's degree opened the door to teaching in higher education; the Ph.D. remained the credential for researchers. As June 1924 approached, Debo searched for a faculty appointment at a college or university. Unfortunately, all but one of the thirty institutions that contacted Chicago ruled out employing a woman. The sole exception would take a female only if a man was unavailable.

Although Angie knew that women faced prejudice, she had grown up when opportunities in college teaching had still been relatively plentiful for her sex. At the turn of the century, openings for females in higher education had outpaced those in medicine and law, largely because of the earlier expansion of women's colleges and teacher training schools. Moreover, even within her hometown, Debo recalled that women of ability had found opportunities in business and in the professions. Frances Stiffen, for example, had served as Marshall's dentist during Angie's adolescence. Nothing had prepared her for the blatant discrimination she now encountered.

Beneath the surface, long-term trends were working against women teachers in higher education. Although the growth of female institutions of higher education had given women 36 percent of the positions at colleges and universities in the 1880s, that ratio had declined to 20 percent between 1890 to 1910 as many female institutions began to employ male teachers. Male or coeducational institutions, however, did not turn to women; indeed, the reverse was occurring. The rise of the modern university, which stressed graduate training through seminars and the scholarly productivity of faculty, had led to a decline in the opportunities available to women aspiring to join their faculties. Females were considered less capable of conducting the sustained research that would bring honor and renown to a university or college department.

In this changing context, the University of Chicago, which still welcomed women as students at both the undergraduate and graduate level, offered them more hope than fulfillment. As historian Ellen Fitzpatrick notes, among the nine alumnae who had earned their doctorates from Chicago between 1892 and 1907, "not a single one secured a regular faculty appointment at a coeducational institution upon her graduation." By contrast, "[t]wo-thirds of their male classmates were so employed." Nor had the situation improved in 1916, when the federal government's *Biennial Survey of Education* revealed that close to 79 percent of college and university faculty were men. Among professional schools, the percentage stood at almost 98 percent. Five years later, the American Association of University Professors noted that almost half, or 47 percent, of the schools it surveyed reported "no woman holding a professorship of the first rank in the academic faculty." Instead, the few females who taught at colleges and universities remained, for the most part, on the lowest rungs of faculty positions. These trends were reflected in Chicago's faculty as a whole. By 1924, a year before women faculty would lodge a formal protest before the University of Chicago's president and the board of trustees, only Marion Talbot and two other females held the rank of full professor.

Debo had some intimation of these trends, but, like others in similar situations, she hoped her situation would prove the exception to the rule. She sought advice from the one woman who held a formal academic position on Chicago's history faculty. Frances Ada Knox, an extension assistant professor, responded that during wartime or other periods of emergency when men were unavailable, schools "had to take a woman—temporarily." Knox had performed so well that Chicago had kept her on after the war. Angie read between the lines. Even if a woman found employment, she had to work harder than her male colleagues to hold her position.

Although such realizations generated resentment and sadness, Rippy's enthusiasm for her thesis lifted her spirits. She was delighted when the *Smith College Studies in History* published it in the April-July 1924 volume, with Rippy listed as first coauthor. Although he read the galleys and page proofs, it was Angie's work entirely. Seeing it in print gave her a faith in her abilities that future setbacks never destroyed.

When Debo returned to Marshall, she contacted colleges far and wide. Eventually her persistence led her to teacher training institutions. Of the two with openings, she selected West Texas State Teachers College in Canyon, Texas, where enrollment totalled about two thousand students. (The other school was never identified.) Founded in 1910 as a training school for teachers, West Texas students, the offspring of pioneering ranchers, were similar to those attending the University of Oklahoma. Debo hoped to inspire in them the same appreciation for their families' historic role in the West that Dale had inspired in his students.

There was another reason Angie went to Canyon. The chair of the department, Lester Fields Sheffy, had served as a graduate assistant in the University of Chicago's history department the year she had earned her master's. Furthermore, he and her thesis adviser had become friends, and the two would correspond off and on for many years. Very likely, James Rippy, who was proud of Debo, prevailed upon Sheffy to consider her for an opening, and the latter, knowing the quality of her work, was willing to help. But Sheffy assigned Debo to the demonstration school attached to the college; she would hold no faculty rank in the West Texas history department itself.

The demonstration school provided youth in the region the opportunity to finish high school as a way of entering college. It also functioned as a training center for college students studying to become teachers. As Debo signed her first contract, she promised herself that in her spare time she would continue studying international relations, keeping alive her dream to return to Chicago for further study in that field.

Before classes started in Canyon, Angie visited Edward Dale in Norman. As she shared with him her experiences in graduate school, she noted the pessimism that permeated much of Chicago's history department. Some professors, she added, believed that "nothing could be learned from the past; the only reason for studying history was the intellectual pleasure of knowing it. There was no human progress." At this, Dale broke into a huge grin. "What nonsense," he replied. If Edward Everett Dale believed in anything, it was the inevitability of progress.

At the same time, Dale probably harbored little concern over the growing conservatism of the 1920s. When he had returned to Harvard to complete his doctorate under Turner in September 1919, the Boston police were on strike. Buckling on his six-gun, Dale had volunteered as a peacekeeper until the National Guard arrived, summoned by the governor of Massachusetts, Calvin Coolidge. Later, Coolidge would refuse to rehire the striking policemen, declaring, "There is no right to strike against the public safety by anybody anywhere any time." Dale's autobiography, *The West Wind Blows,* published posthumously in 1984, showed that his concern, above all, was that order must prevail; he stood squarely on the side of management.

In Canyon Angie rented a room at Fred Scott's boardinghouse adjacent to the campus. After the sixty-year-old retired cowboy and his wife, Montie Jane, served the evening meal, he often reminisced about the years he had worked for Charles Goodnight and his JA Ranch. Scott recalled proudly that he and other cowboys had driven twenty-three hundred head of cattle to Dodge City in 1884 with Old Blue, the legendary steer, leading the herd for the last time.

Mostly, however, the tall, lanky cowhand had worked as a line rider, patrolling the outer reaches of Goodnight's far-flung ranch in search of stray cattle. At times he had encountered danger. Once a hostile Indian had appeared unexpectedly in the door of his cabin while he was warming himself by the fire and his gun was on the other side of the room. Obviously, he survived this encounter and others, but his stories of such adventures brought the Canyon region to life for Debo. They also revived her interest in southwestern history. Unfortunately, her fascination with the area placed her on a collision course with Lester Sheffy, who considered the West, especially the study of ranching, his specialty.

Angie remembered her colleagues at West Texas as "old-time teachers," who often held only bachelor's degrees. Nonetheless, respectful of their attempts to improve educational opportunities in the Panhandle, she threw herself wholeheartedly into her courses. She also contributed as fully as possible to college life.

The administration pressured teachers and students to conform to strict community mores. In the mid-1920s, school officials, noting that West Texas was "a College of Christian ideals," still held religious assemblies five days a week. Andrew Jackson Hill, the president of the college, moreover, proudly informed the *Randall County News* in November 1925 that "Every church in Canyon has a member of the faculty as its Sunday School superintendent." Other instructors taught individual classes. Angie conducted Sunday school classes in the local Methodist Church and during the week served as faculty adviser for the Young Women's Christian Association. These activities, combined with a heavy teaching load, left little time for research and writing.

Debo, as a female instructor, knew that she had to conduct herself with strict propriety since seemingly harmless actions often brought swift reprisal. When A. K. Knott interviewed retired college professors in the late 1970s for an oral history project, he learned from Olin Hinkle, former teacher of social sciences at West Texas, that a local Baptist minister had excommunicated young men and women in the mid-1920s for swimming together in the same pool. Georgia O'Keeffe, who had been, in effect, the art department at the school in 1916 and

1917, recalled chafing under the restrictions of a straitlaced environment.

Nonetheless, however strict the surroundings at West Texas, there was always an irrepressible quality in Angie Debo, and it frequently surfaced during these years. Energetic and tireless, she thought nothing of donning jodhpurs and boots and taking students and church groups on overnight outings into Palo Duro Canyon, one of her favorite sites. Without any trail to guide them—roads were carved out only later by the Civilian Conservation Corps and other depression-era work crews—Debo and the youth she chaperoned made their way to Prairie Dog Town Fork, the small creek at the bottom of the canyon that fed into the Red River. There they camped, buffered by magnificent sandstone bluffs as high as eight hundred feet. In a location that had once sheltered the nomads of the High Plains, the Kiowa, Comanche, and Cheyenne, Debo and her charges roasted chicken and potatoes over an open fire as the sky turned dark following sunset.

During the late 1920s, Angie acquired her own automobile. Although unreliable, her vehicle gave her expanded opportunities to explore. Early one morning, as she was driving south of Canyon, near Plainview, Texas, she saw the rays of the rising sun hit the surface of the setting moon. "It was just as plain as it is when you strike a match," she said. For her, it was "a new experience with the sky," and "the thrill of that experience" never left her.

More than any other facet of nature, Angie loved the wide expanse of the west Texas sky. Its ever-changing panorama in the High Plains country deepened her attachment to the West. As she recalled to her friend, Tulsa freelance writer Connie Cronley, whenever she returned to Canyon after a visit home, "My spirits just soared as soon as I felt myself come up on those high plains—so level you could plow a furrow from Amarillo to the New Mexico line."

But however much she loved west Texas, Debo was becoming restless. Year after year, she remained in the demonstration high school while others, with backgrounds similar to hers, moved to the history department and were listed among the college faculty.

Most notable among them was Hattie Anderson, who had a master's from the University of Missouri, though earlier she had spent a year at Chicago. Three years older than Debo, Anderson, like many others of that era, had alternated schoolteaching with attendance at universities to become a college teacher. Another woman, Mary McLean, with only a bachelor's degree, taught with Debo in the demonstration school the first year she arrived at West Texas. As soon as she received a master's from Columbia University, however, Sheffy moved McLean to the college's history department, where she was promoted to associate professor. J. Evetts Haley, with a master's from the University of Texas, never taught in the demonstration school but instead started as an associate professor in the history department when he joined the college in 1927. Geraldine Green followed in his footsteps the following year. For some reason, Debo was barred from the college faculty even though she was known as an excellent teacher.

No record explains why Lester Sheffy discriminated against Angie in this manner. Possibly her assertiveness struck him as improper for a female. Businesslike and professional in all aspects of her life, she spoke out fearlessly on issues. Her forthright demeanor undoubtedly antagonized those who expected females to be compliant and outwardly subservient when dealing with men in positions of authority.

Moreover, although Angie loved teaching, she still longed to write, especially when the haunting beauty and the immense sky of the High Plains moved her as the beauty of the Oklahoma countryside had moved her mother years earlier. Frustrated that she had little time after meeting the myriad demands of the college and increasingly aware that Sheffy meant to keep her in academic limbo, Debo was determined to change her prospects.

In her late thirties, she was willing to sacrifice to fulfill her goal. Above all, she wanted to use her creative talents more fully. She knew that if she failed to break the bonds that constricted her, her life—the only one she had—would be wasted. And "if we waste that," she confided to friends many years later, "we waste everything."

CHAPTER 3

Out of the Pathless Woods

The Making of a Historian

DURING her years at Canyon, Angie often visited her parents in Marshall. After oil was discovered in 1927 on the McCully farm, seven miles southwest of town, other explorations brought in sizable wells. When the boisterous town of Roxana sprang up almost overnight near the Debo family's old homestead, oil crews and their families flocked to the region, now booming with new businesses but short of housing.

The old-timers, remembering that some families had acquired the better land in the runs, saw again that luck as well as perseverance contributed to the making and unmaking of fortunes. The new owners of the former Debo farm located oil on their property. Angie later told a friend that her father never expressed regret over selling the land. Instead, whenever he passed the site, he recalled the family's good times at the old homestead.

Nonetheless, the truth behind the days at the farm was more complicated, for Angie had rejoiced in 1916 that her mother had escaped that "nightmare." Life at the old homestead had never been entirely happy, and the Debos, being human, were undoubtedly disappointed that the oil on that site benefited others. But, in the "spirit of Oklahoma," they accepted their fate with as much outward humor and grace as they could muster.

As streets were paved and residents enjoyed for the first time round-the-clock electricity, many in Marshall built rental units. Although she lived in Canyon, Angie caught the speculative fever. After buying a lot near downtown Marshall, she prevailed on her brother to construct a small dwelling, modeled on the packaged homes sold by Sears, Roebuck. Edwin also made some furniture for the house, including a dining-room table.

43

At the height of the boom, Marshall claimed a population of nine hundred persons. Shortly after, as wells dried up and explorers struck dry holes, operators moved to Oklahoma City. When prospective buyers for Angie's house vanished, Lina and Edward sold their larger home, moved into their daughter's smaller one, and assumed her note.

With little time for researching history, Debo now turned to writing fiction. In 1929, *Farm and Fireside* published "The Right Kind of Wisdom," a "fact story" about farmers that was obviously modeled on Angie's own family.

The heroine of Angie's story, a resourceful, hardworking wife named Ellie, had little education. Nonetheless, as her children advanced in school, she progressed with them. Above all, she wanted to buy her daughter Amy a reed organ since the youngster always arrived at church early to sound out tunes on the piano before Sunday school. Tom, Ellie's husband, was kind, but he thought their money better spent on horses, cattle, and machinery.

One night the couple's farmhouse caught fire. After barely escaping with their children, they examined the ruins by daylight. Rather than replace their furniture, Ellie suggested buying a reed organ, and this time her husband agreed. "I've worked pretty hard to get a little property but last night I wasn't afraid of losing anything but the kids. I realized then there's a good bit more to life than just what you lay up and you can't postpone living until you get a certain amount of money saved," Tom replied.

In the end, Amy learned to play her new organ, and the entire family benefited from Ellie and Tom's more loving relationship. Moreover, their farm flourished as they "began to get on faster." Despite their new prosperity, however, nothing "ever meant as much to them as that organ which they bought when they couldn't afford it. Sometimes," Debo's story concluded, "foolishness is just another name for the highest kind of wisdom."

When Angie received $160 for her story, she immediately submitted others. Unfortunately, they were quickly returned. Obviously her forte was writing history. By fall 1929, Debo had taken her own advice. Putting her deepest wishes ahead of monetary considerations, she obtained a leave from West Texas and enrolled in the University of Oklahoma's doctoral program to study again under Edward Dale. When she received a research fellowship, she extended her leave to two years.

Dale was unrivaled as a graduate instructor. In addition to imparting keen insights, he was "knowledgeable, patient, and generous with compliments." And his classes were fascinating. Angie recalled the time he brought a Choctaw couple into his seminar. As the woman explained her views on Indian life, her husband began singing. Translated into English, the words were "O sun, you remain forever; / O earth, you remain forever; / But I must die." It was the song Satank, the Kiowa warrior, had chanted as soldiers had transported him to prison at Fort Richardson, Texas, in 1871 following his raids into that state. Preferring death to incarceration, he had ended his song by breaking free of his manacles and attacking his captors. The soldiers thereupon shot him and tossed his corpse to the side of the road.

More often, Angie, like others, was enthralled by the humorous tales Dale told in class. Sometimes these included descriptions of the chicanery and corruption that had defrauded Indians. When Debo examined Dale's books and articles, however, she noticed that such unsavory events were missing. Her beloved teacher obviously left out of his writings "anything that wasn't pleasant."

Angie submitted her professor to critical examination in a seminar paper, "Edward Everett Dale: Historian of Progress," which she completed during the winter of 1930–31. This action, unusual for a graduate student, suggests her ambivalence in regard to Dale's views on writing history and his approach to Euro-American settlement of the West, even though her affection and respect for him never wavered. Very likely she was also recalling her visit with Dale en route to Canyon in 1924 when the thought of questioning the inevitability of human progress had amused him. After all, she noted, he had seen prosperous farmsteads replace dugouts and sod houses and frontier hamlets transform themselves into thriving cities. Once a student "sleeping on the prairie," he had become a nationally prominent and respected scholar. Small wonder, Debo wrote, that "imperialism, if [Dale] thinks of it at all, is the march of civilization across the waste places of the earth." Whatever her motivation for writing the paper, Debo was beginning to form her own scholarly identity apart from that of her mentor.

For her seminar papers Angie selected topics on the Comanches, Cherokee John Rollin Ridge, and Cherokee refugees during the Civil War. *The Panhandle-Plains Historical Review,* the *Southwest Review,* and the *Southwestern Historical Quarterly,* respectively, published the papers in 1931 and 1932, as Debo was finishing her coursework. She was already establishing a reputation for her expertise on the Five Tribes.

When Debo lacked a dissertation topic, Dale directed her to a new collection in the University library. Through the generosity of Frank Phillips, an oilman from Bartlesville, Dale had begun amassing an extensive collection of primary sources on American Indians and western history. No one, however, had used the Choctaw files in these holdings, and, taking Dale's advice, Debo began researching their history as a separate republic in Indian Territory.

Dale helped in other ways. He had served as a member of the 1927 Survey of Indian Affairs, a commission headed by Lewis Meriam, a former statistician with the Institute for Government Research in Washington, D.C. Supported by the Rockefeller Foundation, the institute had produced *The Problem of Indian Administration* in 1928, the first extensive survey of conditions among American Indians since Henry Schoolcraft had published his multivolume work in the 1850s.

The Meriam Report, as it was commonly known, uncovered extensive and pervasive poverty among Indians, which it attributed to deplorable health conditions and inadequate educational opportunities in their communities. It also cast blame on the federal government's overreliance on assimilationist policies, which had emphasized Indian ownership of private property as a panacea for recovery following the destruction of their tribal economies. Well received, the report had already led to reforms in the Indian Bureau and its policies. In this new climate, Dale's letter of introduction gave Debo easy access to the government documents that were then located in the basement of the old Department of the Interior building in Washington, D.C.

Debo also investigated the Choctaw files in the Office of the Superintendent of the Five Civilized Tribes in Muskogee, Oklahoma. Here she met Grant Foreman, a lawyer who had served on the Commission to the Five Civilized Tribes from 1899 to 1903. (Chaired by retired U.S. Senator Henry Dawes of Massachusetts, the man who had shepherded the Dawes Act through Congress in 1887, this body from its beginning in 1893 was better known as the Dawes Commission.) Foreman, having embarked on a new career as a historian, was awaiting publication of *Indian Removal: The Emigration of the Five Civilized Tribes of Indians,* which was scheduled to appear as the second volume in the Civilization of the American Indian Series. Joseph A. Brandt, a former Rhodes scholar, one-time city editor of the *Tulsa Tribune,* and director of the University of Oklahoma Press since its inception in 1928, had initiated the series with strong support from William Bizzell, president of the University of Oklahoma. In Brandt's view, this series would highlight the achievements of America's indigenous peoples and their contributions to the state and nation.

Foreman saw the assimilation of Indians into the larger society as the desired goal for Native peoples. Nonetheless, even to him the rampant speculation that accompanied the sale of Creek "surplus lands" in 1904, following the termination of their tribal governments and their communal landholdings, remained a bitter memory. (When their communal landholdings were broken up, the Creeks were forced to accept land ownership in severalty, or as individual allotments.) Undoubtedly Grant shared his sentiments with Debo. Enthusiastic about her project, he directed her to the tribal records, speeches of principal chiefs, court documents, and other files in the Muskogee archives. He also introduced her to his wife, Carolyn Thomas Foreman, daughter of the late John Robert Thomas, former judge of the U.S. Court in Indian Territory from 1897 to 1901. Carolyn Foreman also researched and wrote history, and the couple soon became Angie's close friends.

Initially Debo found her topic only moderately interesting, but the more she researched, the more compelling it became. She felt the full force of the Choctaws' sorrow when they signed the Treaty of Dancing Rabbit Springs in 1830. Only assurances that they would maintain "jurisdiction and government of all the persons and property that may be within their limits west" forever and that "no Territory or State" would ever be allowed "to pass laws for the government of the Choctaw Nation of Red People and their descendants" had persuaded them to exchange their southeastern home for land in Indian Territory. With these guarantees as their "Magna Carta," the Choctaws had reluctantly moved westward.

At first they had prospered in their new homeland by blending their tribal traditions with borrowings from the white world. Many Choctaws had already converted to Christianity, but a larger percentage now followed, and literacy and educational levels increased among them. By blending principles of the English common law and what Debo termed "savage custom," they created a new legal system. Their family life retained one important quality, however; "the laws regarding property and marriage gave the wife complete equality with her husband."

During the Civil War, the Choctaws, along with the Chickasaws, a closely related tribe forced to join them in Indian Territory, had supported the Confederacy. Afterwards, in retaliation, the federal government appropriated their western lands as reservations for the Plains Indians farther west. The Choctaws had also struggled with vestiges of slavery during Reconstruction. Eventually, by adopting their former slaves and awarding them limited citizenship rights, they had overcome much of their racial turmoil.

The greatest threat to Choctaw well-being came, in Debo's view, not from within but from outsiders. Following the Civil War, railroads, mining companies, and ranchers had begun sending growing numbers of non-Indians into Choctaw country. By 1890, the new groups, comprising 75 percent of the population, had formed their own institutions, and increasing numbers now clamored for an end to tribal government and the breakup of communal lands.

The Dawes Commission assisted the newcomers by painting a dire picture of conditions within the Choctaw republic. In its annual reports, dating from 1893, it depicted the Choctaw government as dominated by a mixed-blood elite that exploited full-bloods, cared little for the non-Indians within their midst, and ruled through violence and corruption.

Although Debo rejected these sweeping allegations, she admitted that problems had existed. A small office-holding group, which resorted at times to corruption and bribery, had dominated the republic, and the resulting frustration spawned political violence. The Choctaws also contended with high crime rates, brought on in part—but only in part—by unruly outsiders. And even though they valued education highly, neighborhood schools for the children of outsiders were poorly funded, while Choctaw boarding schools "maintained scholastic standards that would be a credit to any school system."

Overall, Debo noted that for its own people the republic had increased the standards of public health and education—areas that lagged seriously among contemporary Indians, according to the Meriam Report. Moreover, although members of the Dawes Commission saw tribal ownership of land as the means by which leaders exploited the full-bloods, Debo viewed all Choctaws as universally attached to communal ownership.

Faced with the Curtis Act of 1898, congressional legislation that swept away the laws and courts of the Five Tribes and brought all residents of Indian Territory under federal jurisdiction, Choctaw leaders had bowed to the inevitable. Despite resistance among conservative full-bloods, the majority of Choctaws, and most of the Chickasaws as well, had ratified the Atoka Agreement giving them individual allotments of 320 acres. In 1902 a supplementary agreement had created a citizenship court and had established procedures for selling mineral lands, with the proceeds going only to those who had registered their allotments.

Choctaw representatives, as well as delegates from the other Five Tribes and progressive reformers like William H. Murray and Charles N. Haskell, had met at the Sequoyah Convention in 1905 and had petitioned Congress for permission to form a separate Indian state. Their request had been denied. Two years later, Indian Territory and Oklahoma Territory were merged into the new state of Oklahoma.

Debo had known some of this history earlier, but the evidence she now compiled altered her understanding of the relations between Indians and white authorities. In the past, Oklahoma historians like Roy Gittinger, accepting the conclusions of the Dawes Commission reports, had viewed allotment and termination of the Choctaw protectorate as "a distinct step toward the solution of the Indian question." Debo, by contrast, saw the Choctaw republic as supported by its people and enjoying its share of successes. By requiring its members to accept allotment and termination, the United States had forced them to give up more than just a portion of their homeland and their autonomy. It had compelled them to give up their way of life, a loss beyond calculation.

As Angie worked through the summer and fall of 1931, she struggled with her own impending loss. After three years of happy marriage to Ida Elizabeth Henneke of Enid, her brother, Edwin, was terminally ill with Hodgkin's disease. Angie helped her sister-in-law and parents care for him until he died on October 3, 1931. Then, with her dissertation partly finished, she returned to her West Texas classroom.

Dale's initial response to Angie's first two chapters of the thesis set off a dispute of sorts between him and his student. Debo refused to accept his view that her first chapter was too long and relied on too many secondary rather than primary sources. (According to Debo's calculations, the secondary sources represented one-seventh of the total.) Although Dale informed her that he could not conceive of having challenged the comments and suggestions of the director of his doctoral thesis, Frederick Jackson Turner, the dissertation was, after all, her work, to be done her way. She should accept his criticisms only "for what you think they are worth." At the same time, Dale reminded her that the other members of her committee agreed with him, and her work had to pass their scrutiny.

By now the Great Depression, ravaging the economy since 1929, had deepened throughout the United States. As legislative funding for higher education plummeted, the regents of the teachers' colleges in Texas cut spending by 25 percent. They also discussed transforming West Texas State Teachers College into a two-year school.

During the fall of 1932, with one of the history professors on leave, Angie was assigned to the college faculty for the first time. It was a mixed blessing, for her workload included teaching six days a week. Simultaneously her declining salary left her increasingly hard-pressed to pay for living expenses and dissertation credits. Shortly before Thanksgiving, she learned to her immense relief that, despite her earlier disagreements with Dale, her doctoral thesis was approved.

During the winter of 1932–33 Debo looked for another position. Although she had enjoyed her work at West Texas, teachers colleges were now under legislative scrutiny, deservedly she thought, given their academic standards. Simultaneously, she applied for various fellowships and grants, for she hoped to investigate a new topic—the process of liquidating the landholdings and governments of the Five Tribes following allotment.

Dale promised to notify Debo if openings arose and wrote recommendations to granting agencies in support of her proposed study. Still, given the increasing severity of the depression, teaching vacancies were almost nonexistent. Above all, he advised her not to leave West Texas "until you are positively certain that you have something better elsewhere."

Early in May 1933, Debo defended her dissertation, "History of the Choctaw Nation from the End of the Civil War to the Close of the Tribal Period." When she returned to Canyon, a flood of congratulatory notes from female colleagues awaited her. They rejoiced that one of them had finally earned the terminal degree.

Soon after her thesis defense Debo learned that West Texas might not renew her contract. Another cut of 50 percent in state appropriations for higher education necessitated the elimination of many positions. Remaining faculty sustained a salary loss of 25 percent, the second reduction in less than two years. In addition, tensions now increased between Debo and Lester Sheffy.

Because Debo once vowed never to discuss the issues between them, the full story will never be known. Nonetheless, some clues remain.

Debo undoubtedly transmitted her dissatisfaction with academic standards at West Texas State to Sheffy, for such attitudes are never easily masked. Moreover, she probably irritated him by earning her Ph.D. After he received an honorary doctorate from Austin College in 1937, he was always addressed as Dr. Sheffy, which suggests that the title was important to him. Still, other female members of his department later earned their terminal degrees and experienced no outward difficulties as a result. One of them, Ima Barlow, even collaborated with him in the 1950s to produce a history of Texas.

When President Hill ordered Sheffy to reduce his department, it was, predictably, Debo who was dismissed, while Barlow, employed initially as Angie's temporary replacement while she attended the University of Oklahoma, was retained. After Debo protested against her treatment, Hill appointed her curator of the newly created Panhandle-Plains Museum.

Angie's problems were not over. Sheffy, as secretary of the Panhandle-Plains Historical Society, had worked hard to raise money for the museum and saw himself as instrumental in its formation. In that light, he undoubtedly resented Hill's intervention on Debo's behalf. Relations between Sheffy and his former colleague now became increasingly strained.

At a time when unemployment hovered at 25 percent, Angie earned fifty dollars a month, minus boarding expenses, in her new part-time position. Her duties included holding the museum's Pioneer Hall open on Tuesdays and Thursdays and again on Sunday afternoons and cataloging materials on other days. It was better than nothing, given the economic situation. Putting the best face on her circumstances, Angie wrote Edward Dale that she now had time to research and write.

When Debo learned that the University of Oklahoma Press had accepted her dissertation as a volume in its Civilization of the American Indian Series, she expanded her introductory chapter into three. By relying heavily on travelers' accounts and the work of anthropologist John R. Swanton, especially his *Source Material for the Social and Ceremonial Life of the Choctaw Indians* (1931), published by the Bureau of American Ethnology, she sought to place the Choctaws in a cultural framework.

Debo began by examining Choctaw creation myths to gain a sense of their cosmology. Even though their foremost tradition described their ancestors as having emerged from a subterranean cave beneath a sacred mound, another version told of a leader, similar to Moses, who had led them to their southeastern homeland after a great flood. The latter story, Angie thought, suggested a syncretism of Choctaw traditions and the teachings of Christian missionaries.

Based on Swanton's analysis, Debo interpreted Choctaw culture as a blend of Euro-American and indigenous practices. Their traditional culture was distinctive, however, in terms of burial ceremonies, sports—including their ballgame *ishtaboli*—methods of agriculture, and family life. But where non-Indians often portrayed Indian women as exploited drudges who performed most of the labor while Indian men led leisurely lives devoted to hunting, Angie saw a different situation. Such generalizations, she noted, failed to "take into account the importance and difficulty of the chase." Although it was true that females "performed a large part of the labor of the fields, made the clothing, prepared and stored the food, and carried the burdens; the men," Debo added, "provided the game, built the houses, manufactured the wooden and stone implements, carried on the governmental activities, and protected the tribe in war." Armed with ethnological insights, Debo, viewing Indian sex roles as complementary rather than unequal, was challenging long-standing stereotypes.

Analyzing the speeches and proclamations of Choctaw leaders in the various governmental and tribal documents, Debo concluded that their problems had stemmed from the increasing number of non-Indians encroaching on their land. After the former English colonies had won their independence, the new United States proved the most formidable threat to their autonomy. "Federal officials," Debo wrote, "systematically corrupted and even more systematically intoxicated Indian leaders as an economical method of securing land cessions." Despite such treachery, many of the Choctaws had welcomed missionaries and in 1814 had fought with Andrew Jackson and his Tennessee militia against the Redstick faction of the Creek Indians at the Battle of Horseshoe Bend in present-day Alabama.

Sixteen years later, their friendship availed them nothing. As Debo described their decision to move westward, as the price to be paid for remaining a separate people, she wrote as one who sought to play the role of intercultural broker. "White Americans," she reminded her readers, "with their more mobile habits, have never been able to appreciate the hopeless grief of this despoiled people when they abandoned their ancient homes, and in a strictly literal sense, the bones of their beloved dead."

Decades later Debo was asked why she had chosen to produce a form of ethnohistory, weaving anthropological insights into her narrative and telling her story as fully as possible from the Choctaw point of view. She responded that her study of the Greeks, one of her favorite teaching subjects at West Texas, provided the model. Scholars explaining Greek history invariably began with the myths and legends. "You have the Trojan War, you have Homer, Odysseus and so forth," she explained and "you need to know that." Similarly, one needed to know the stories the Choctaws conveyed to their posterity to explain the ideals that defined them as a people.

Joseph Brandt welcomed Debo's expanded version. Intellectuals like archaeologist Edgar R. Hewett, writer Mabel Dodge Luhan, and, best known of all, John Collier, now commissioner of Indian affairs in the administration of the new president, Franklin Delano Roosevelt, saw Native communalism and respect for nature as antidotes for the ills of modern life. With the competitive, individualistic, and materialistic way of life in economic disarray as a result of the Great Depression, their views found wider acceptance. Oklahoma's Civilization of the American Indian Series had appeared at a propitious time.

In fact, the third and, thus far, most acclaimed volume in the series, *Wah'Kon-Tah: The Osage and the White Man's Road*

(1932), had received glowing reviews. In his diary, Indian agent Laban Miles, a plainspoken Quaker, had chronicled the Osage struggle to maintain their way of life, sometimes by blending their practices and their God with whites' practices and the whites' God. Sadly, as Miles ended his diary, the younger generation, while benefiting materially from the discovery of oil on Osage land, was in grave danger of losing its older spiritual traditions, especially as their wealth attracted non-Indian speculators and developers. Shortly before his death in 1931, Miles had bequeathed his journal to John Joseph Mathews, his close friend.

A mixed-blood Osage, Mathews was the great-grandson of William Shirley Williams, better known as "Old Bill" Williams, the Colorado mountain man. A former aviator during World War I and later an Oxford scholar, Mathews had found himself adrift until he began to delve into his Osage background. With Brandt's encouragement, he transformed Miles's diary into a literary work and, at the same time, assuaged his own restless spirit. When the Book of the Month Club chose *Wah'Kon-Tah* as a main selection, sales reached fifty thousand. Seemingly overnight the University of Oklahoma Press was catapulted into prominence in the publishing world.

Early in summer 1934, Brandt inaugurated a "Centennial of Publishing" to celebrate the hundredth anniversary of the first Oklahoma pamphlet, a document printed in the Creek language in the Creek republic. Debo's *The Rise and Fall of the Choctaw Republic*, which chronicled the successes as well as the problems of another protectorate, appeared almost simultaneously.

All the reviews—save one—were laudatory. But the one negative review rankled. Thankfully, given Angie's emotional state in 1934, she would not read it until its appearance in spring 1935. In the *Chronicles of Oklahoma*, Muriel Wright, granddaughter of the Choctaw chief, Allen Wright, characterized Debo's work as marred by "errors in statement, half-truths and refutations that destroy its value as authentic history of the Choctaws." Moreover, she took issue with the title, since, in her view, which was that of an assimilationist, the Choctaw republic had never fallen:

From its inception over a century ago, it was planned as a training ground for the Choctaw people, in preparation for the time when they of their own volition would become citizens of their protector Republic, the United States. When at the end of almost three quarters of a century they cast a majority vote in favor of such a step by adopting the Atoka Agreement and later the Supplemental Agreement, they as a nation had attained a position where their leaders were counted among the leaders in the new State of Oklahoma organized soon afterward. Thus, the Choctaw Nation as a republic did not fall, it attained its objective.

In addition to disagreeing with Debo's basic premise, Wright found her scholarship "inadequate and superficial in many places," the result of "unfamiliarity with Choctaw affairs and hurried research." Debo had written *Nanih Waya* for the name of the sacred temple mound of the Choctaw in the Southeast, but Wright preferred *Nanih Waiya,* the more common spelling. More emphatically, the term did not mean "leaning" hill, as Debo interpreted it, but instead "productive" or "fruitful" hill.

After seeking to discredit Debo's work by arguing over terms, Wright moved to a more serious point. She denied that Chief Allen Wright, her grandfather, had accepted a kickback. (She made no mention of her relationship to Wright in her review.) When attorney John Latrobe had received $100,000 as a contingency for his services in assisting the Choctaws as they concluded the treaty of 1866 following the Civil War, he had surreptitiously, Debo claimed, given money to the Choctaw delegation. Allen Wright had received $10,000. Muriel Wright agreed that he had accepted the sum, but she viewed it as compensation for living expenses and payment for assisting Latrobe. She was wrong; another scholar, W. David Baird, in his 1972 *Peter Pitchlynn: Chief of the Choctaws* verified Debo's charge, which applied to Pitchlynn as well.

Angie, after reading Wright's review, put it aside, unwilling to waste emotional energy defending herself. She had checked her facts carefully and knew they were correct. Even though, having admired Allen Wright, she regretted her discovery, she had not flinched from revealing his dereliction. Historians, she believed, were responsible for telling the whole truth. As she explained in later oral history interviews: "I feel . . . that if you discover something . . . you ought to tell it all—that you're obligated to do it and that if you leave it out it's just about as bad as though somebody who was carrying on cancer research would leave out some of his findings."

In the spring and summer of 1934, Debo faced other, more pressing problems—namely, issues that still festered with Lester Sheffy. Years later, Angie would recall that when Warren K. Moorehead, a former member of the Board of Indian Commissioners, arrived at the Panhandle-Plains Museum to meet with a group of local patrons, Sheffy, who had excluded her from previous events, despite her position as curator, informed her that she was unwelcome at this one as well. Then, shortly after Moorehead began speaking, Sheffy took her chair to seat a latecomer and left Angie standing as she worked at her desk. Debo is the only source for this account, and it should be noted that others, such as Frederic W. Rathjen, professor emeritus at West Texas and editor of the *Panhandle-Plains Historical Review,* recall Sheffy as unfailingly a gentleman.

Whatever the whole truth of the complicated relationship between Debo and Sheffy, Angie at that time was desperately seeking full-time employment, and an introduction to Moorehead might have given her an important contact. She was also giving strong consideration to investigating the termination of communal landholding among the Five Tribes, and he was an expert in this area. Later, he wrote her expressing admiration for her history of the Choctaws and his amazement that he had not met her at Canyon during his visit.

With her self-regard lessened and increasingly fearful that she would lose even her part-time job, Angie's adherence to the "spirit of Oklahoma"—cheerful equanimity in the face of hardships—gave way, and she succumbed to depression. One incident, which Debo shared with her close friend, Connie Cronley, demonstrates her state of mind at this point. Debo and several other women were traveling by car when they stopped to change a tire. As Angie stood in the road, her companions summoned her away from oncoming traffic. In a "flat voice," she responded, "Oh, it doesn't matter," meaning "it didn't matter to her at that moment if she [lived or] died," though, as Cronley notes, Debo would never have put it so dramatically.

One day, as Angie left the museum, she found herself driving home during one of the many dust storms that struck Canyon in those days. Although she lived only several blocks away, she had no visibility, for the sky was entirely dark. Frightened, she edged her tires to the curb and moved slowly until she saw a dim light shining through the darkness on the porch of her boarding-house. To her immense relief she was safe at home and happy to be alive and unharmed.

As Debo taught summer school at Canyon in 1934, one of her students brought in John A. Lomax's *Cowboy Songs.* Her class knew all the words by heart, for they had learned them from their older relatives, some of whom had even sung the songs to cattle during the long drives. This enjoyable experience served as the catalyst for an important decision. Naturally resilient and deter-mined above all to gain some control over her own destiny, Debo wrote Edward Dale that she had reached a turning point. She now understood that it was futile to waste her life at things that she did not care to do. "I have, therefore," she told Dale, "done what would be considered a very rash thing from any material standpoint. I have definitely quit my work here, and am going to devote my whole time for the next year to writing another book." Although she would continue to search diligently for another teaching position, if none materialized, "it will be just too bad, but I shall have written the book." In the end she preferred "one year of creative work . . . to spend[ing] the rest of an ordinary lifetime just marking time."

At forty-four, Angie Debo stepped into the unknown. Although the uncertainty frightened her, she believed, as she later confided to friends, "each one of us has our life and that's all we have." Sustaining her was a deeply rooted but never publicly discussed faith in a personal covenant with her God, which held "that if we are committed to use that life in the best way that our special talents will permit us to use it . . . we will be divinely guided into the kind of use that we were intended for." For Angie Debo, the best way to use her special talents was as a writer. If that meant that she now depended on the ravens to feed her, then so be it. She would take that chance.

CHAPTER 4

The Long Night

WHEN the women faculty at West Texas gave Debo a farewell shower, the hostess, dressed as a Choctaw, distributed her going-away gifts from an Indian cradle. Afterwards Angie returned to Marshall to live with her parents in the home her brother had built. Not long after her return, early in 1935, she received exciting news. The American Historical Association had selected *The Rise and Fall of the Choctaw Republic* to receive the John H. Dunning Award as "the most important contribution to American historical studies in 1934." Hard-pressed financially, she used part of the two-hundred-dollar prize to pay the premium on her life insurance.

In addition, a grant from the Social Science Research Council permitted Angie to begin studying the project she had identified earlier. She wanted to discover how the Five Tribes had fared in Oklahoma after the imposition of allotment and the termination of their tribal protectorates. The results of her investigation would become *And Still the Waters Run* (1940), although initially the work bore another title. As before, her research carried her to archives in Oklahoma City, Muskogee, and Washington, D. C. Scrupulously honest, she lived so frugally that, in the end, she returned funds to the council.

Debo discovered anew that Henry Dawes, as secretary to the Dawes Commission in the 1890s, had been unalterably opposed to the communal way of life in Indian Territory. In a speech to the Friends of the Indians at the 1885 Lake Mohonk Convention in upstate New York, he had summarized his reasons. Focusing his remarks on the Cherokees, he had explained that they had based their republic on the wrong economic principles:

The head chief told us that there was not a family in that whole nation that had not a home of its own. There was not a pauper in that nation, and the nation did not owe a dollar. It built its own capitol, in which we had this examination, and it built its schools and its hospitals. Yet the defect of the system was apparent. They have got as far as they can go, because they own their land in common. It is Henry George's system, and under that there is no enterprise to make your home any better than that of your neighbor. There is no selfishness, which is at the bottom of civilization. Till this people will consent to give up their lands, and divide them among their citizens, so that each one can own the land he cultivates, they will not make much more progress.

Within the span of a few years, "progress" arrived in Indian Territory for the Cherokees and the peoples of the other protectorates as well. Angie learned that the fate of all the tribes was similar to that of the Choctaws and the Chickasaws. As cities and industries arose in their midst, prompted by the earlier incursion of railroads and mining interests, growing numbers of non-Indian residents, some invited but many intruders, found themselves living under anomalous conditions as American citizens in Indian Territory. In all the republics, they lacked schools for their children and the opportunity to obtain land in fee simple. And they resented paying taxes to governments that left them voiceless. Debo had little sympathy. "Indian tenure," she noted, "rested upon the most solemn commitments by the Federal Government," and, by moving into the territory, these outsiders "had voluntarily subjected themselves to these conditions."

Angie discovered that the Dawes Commission had come down on the side of the non-Indians, publicizing the territory's crime rate and the lack of schools for non-Indian children. It also portrayed the leaders of the protectorates as oligarchs who exploited full-bloods by controlling and monopolizing common property.

Debo heatedly took issue with the commission's claim that communal resources had been monopolized. "[C]ertainly the poor Indian had a better chance to become a prosperous farmer than the landless member of the white man's society," she wrote, noting that restrictions on pastures among the Choctaws and a referendum on proposed enclosures among the Creeks had proved more effective in discouraging land monopolies than any legislation in the various states. Furthermore, "a garbled misrepresentation of the Choctaw's system of public control of natural resources came with especially bad grace from the members of a race that in the short space of a century had seen the greatest natural wealth in the possession of any people pass into private and often rapacious hands."

Debo also contested the commission's statement that only the elite among the Five Tribes resisted allotment, while the large majority of Indians supported it. She maintained that the reverse was true and noted that some full-bloods opposed allotment so strenuously that they never accepted their acreage.

Worse than the erroneous assumptions or unfair charges were the deceptions. At one point the commission charged the Choctaws with mistreating their freedmen and their descendants simply on the basis of statements issued by attorneys who sought larger settlements for former slaves. That was mild compared to an outright lie promulgated by the commission. Despite having received "carefully compiled" information that Isaac Parker, the judge of the Western District Court of Arkansas, which oversaw Indian Territory, had sentenced 172 persons to death in twenty-one years, Dawes told a different story. In a speech he stated that in the space of "ten or fifteen years [Parker had] sentenced something like 1,000 men to be hanged for crimes committed in that Territory." Later this statement was disseminated to the Indian Rights Association and reprinted in *Senate Reports*. Debo understood more clearly than ever that government documents were not always reliable sources.

In the end, allotment left many of the members of the Five Tribes impoverished. Following the liquidation of tribal holdings and governments early in the twentieth century, a "criminal conspiracy" had robbed them of much of their remaining land and its resources. Although Debo had encountered instances of white duplicity in her earlier work on the Choctaws, nothing had prepared her for the enormity of these discoveries.

Through her research, Debo was discovering a period that historians of the westward movement had largely neglected. The subject was important to her, for "the reaction of this process upon the ideals and standards of successive frontier communities is a factor in the formation of the American character that should no longer be disregarded by students of social institutions." Although still indebted to Frederick Jackson Turner, she had moved beyond him and his student, her mentor, Edward Everett Dale. More clearly than either man, she saw the material and spiritual cost that unbridled economic development had exacted from the Five Tribes.

During the years she had taught in public schools, Debo, like other Oklahoma instructors, had assigned her pupils *A History of Oklahoma* (1908), written by Joseph B. Thoburn and Isaac M. Holcomb. This textbook emphasized the accomplishments of the Five Tribes and their governments as the "historic past" for all Oklahomans. As she noted in one chapter of her new manuscript, which she entitled "The Indian's Place in Oklahoma," the sons and daughters of pioneers "accepted Sequoyah and Pushmataha as their ancestral heroes, and the 'Trail of Tears' of the Removal exiles rather than the voyage of Columbus became their odyssey." Now historians publishing with the University of Oklahoma Press were recounting those achievements, and "within a generation their efforts had received national recognition as a distinctive Oklahoma contribution to literature and scholarship."

Furthermore, many members of the Five Tribes, who were more affluent and better educated than the Euro-American newcomers and had "more poise, [and] more of the instinctive grace and assurance of a natural aristocracy developed through many generations of leadership in a small and closely integrated society," held powerful positions in the new state. Simultaneously they maintained their Indian traditions, which Debo perceived as "a mystical appreciation of beauty, strength and depth of feeling, [and] creative artistry."

Although Oklahomans prided themselves on their mixed cultural heritage, the actual story of the Five Tribes, especially that of the full-bloods, remained an unacknowledged tragedy. Baffled by the new land system, which often gave families both a homestead and noncontiguous lands farther away, and confused by the constantly changing legal and bureaucratic systems, they had been easy prey for white and, in some cases, mixed-blood exploiters.

Taking into account the internal divisions within the Five Tribes, which were often based on differences between full-bloods and mixed-bloods, on the varying degrees of assimilation into white society, and on unsettled relationships with the black citizens among them, Debo delineated the responses of these diversified peoples to new conditions and demands. Through the testimony of non-Indians and some acculturated or assimilated Indians on one side and traditional Indians on the other, she described the collision between opposing worldviews. The result was a more sophisticated study than her history of the Choctaws and one that was more chilling in its findings.

In 1908, Oklahoma's congressional delegation had won federal legislation that removed restrictions from land belonging to members of the Five Tribes who were freedmen or mixed-bloods of less than one-half Indian ancestry. Moreover, when the current holders of allotted lands died, remaining restrictions would be removed except for those with heirs "born too late to receive allotments." In other cases, restrictions could be withdrawn under probate court approval and oversight.

Debo found that the way was thus opened for the "grafters," the term applied to those who shamelessly exploited the ambiguities within these complex legal changes. Earlier they had capitalized on Indian naiveté by leasing their land for ninety-nine years at low prices and subletting at higher rents to farmers or mining or oil drilling companies. Now they wrested holdings from "consenting" adults who were confused or intimidated. Sometimes when oil was discovered on Indian land, they kidnapped and held the owners until the latter signed over their possessions. If that failed, some grafters resorted to murder.

They soon discovered that attaining guardianship of orphaned or homeless minors was another way to gain access to Indian land and its resources. After siphoning off royalties from mineral deposits or productive oil wells, many grafters left their charges in dire poverty. But why stop with children when adults who also owned resources, especially oil, could be declared incompetent and brought under "protection"? By levying fees against their holdings for such "services" as depositing or cashing checks, grafters appropriated the remaining possessions of their charges.

In the course of her research, Debo also discovered much about the life of Kate Barnard, the commissioner of charities and corrections and her girlhood idol. She learned, for instance, that Barnard had, at times, displayed "emotional instability" and a willingness "to trade upon her feminity" when fighting her public battles. But, whatever Barnard's weaknesses, "through her sincerity and her sensitiveness to human needs," she had shown, Debo maintained, "greater insight than the most critical thinker among her contemporaries."

Barnard had known nothing of the miserable poverty Indian children endured under the care of some guardians until she learned of the plight of three homeless Indian orphans who were "sleeping in the hollow of an old tree, drinking from a stream, and securing food from neighboring farmhouses." Six weeks after finding the children, Barnard discovered that their guardian was a man who claimed fifty-one additional Indian children as wards. After banking their royalties, he exacted "exorbitant prices for their education and support."

When Governor Lee Cruce vetoed a bill designed to give Barnard the power to protect the estates of minor Indian children, the commissioner sued on their behalf. Unfortunately, limited funds, her own health problems, and an incompetent assistant undercut her efforts. Moreover, by publicizing the sufferings of Indian children in periodicals such as *The Survey,* a national journal for social workers and settlement house workers, she embarrassed the new state. The legislature, unable to abolish her constitutionally mandated office, rendered her powerless by cutting off her appropriations.

The final chapter of Barnard's public career left Debo depressed, but even more disillusioning for her was the record of greed and moral decay she had uncovered. Since youth the tales of pioneers moving to western Oklahoma in successive land runs and eventually merging with Indian Territory to form a state had inspired and motivated Angie. Now she saw another story in eastern Oklahoma quite unlike the celebratory history she had learned from parents, grandparents, and Edward Everett Dale, the "historian of progress."

As she untied dusty old packets in various archives, Debo discovered that the grafters had included well-known officials such as Governor Charles N. Haskell and Senator Robert L. Owen. Returning to her rented room each night, she noticed that the names appearing in the society pages of the newspaper were often those of the wives and relatives of the prominent legislators, lawyers, judges, businesspeople, and developers whose actions she was uncovering. As she explained in later oral history interviews, had she anticipated her findings, she would never have begun her investigation. Once into her subject, however, she felt compelled "to go on with it." She was so intent on finishing her work that she turned down a teaching position at Northeastern Teachers College at Tahlequah. Although Angie presented herself later as victimized by her inability to gain a tenure-track position in a college or university, the truth was more complicated. At critical points in her life, when faced with the decision to devote her energies primarily to teaching or to writing, she invariably chose the latter. She never fully acknowledged that fact to her interviewers. Very likely, she never admitted it to herself.

More than dedication to her current writing project was at work this time, however. As historian Robert L. Dorman notes, Debo was uncovering "on one level, a depression-era parable of the systematic exploitation of the powerless by the powerful, of the 'common man' by 'economic royalists.'" Given her background and her own situation, the dispossession of the Five Tribes was, undoubtedly, a topic of compelling interest. As one imbued with the spirit of Oklahoma, Debo could express her anger over the fate of the Five Tribes in a way that she could never have expressed anger over her own situation. Moreover, she saw in the Indian world qualities that attracted her as an individual. Unlike the majority of Oklahomans, whose values extolled growth and development, most full-bloods of the Five Tribes retained an attachment to tradition and place, priorities that Debo would uphold her entire life.

Throughout most of the summer of 1936, as Angie sat at her typewriter, the intense heat, combined with a seemingly endless stream of days without rain, deepened her sense of foreboding as the story unfolded. The drought-stricken land turned "desolate under blazing sun and fiery wind. Trees died in great numbers along the creeks," she recalled years later, "their limbs standing out gaunt above the tortured vegetation." As the thermometer rose to 113, 114, and even 115 degrees, the frail, the sick, and the aged died in increasing numbers.

With little relief, Angie worked diligently at her desk, sweat trickling down her back. No one, including her mother, interrupted her until her father appeared for the noon meal. After he returned to work, she resumed writing until early evening, when she read her typed pages to Lina. Often her mother shook her head, stating flatly, "nobody will ever publish that." Angie, however, was certain that Joseph Brandt, committed to placing the University of Oklahoma Press at the forefront of Indian history, would publish her work.

In late July, Debo sent her completed manuscript, originally entitled *As Long As the Waters Run,* to Norman. Brandt's response—he judged it to be "one of the most valuable books ever offered the University Press"—left her elated. He acknowledged "some tough problems," since some grafters were still alive and "the wailing walls of Jerusalem will not have a monopoly on tears," but he congratulated her on her "monumental contribution to Oklahoma history."

Angie never knew that one of her readers—scholars chosen by the press to review manuscripts before accepting them for publication—was D'Arcy McNickle, the son of a métis mother, part French and part Cree, and an Irish father. His first novel, *The Surrounded* (1936), would soon be published. Based on McNickle's own experiences, the book dealt with a protagonist who embraced the values of the Indian world after a period of uncertainty and turmoil concerning his heritage.

McNickle was then serving as administrative assistant to Commissioner John Collier in the Bureau of Indian Affairs. In that context, Debo's insights were important to him, for they represented the first in-depth study of the fate of the Five Tribes in the period following the termination of their tribal governments and communal landholdings. Moreover, Debo's description of the ways Oklahoma Indians had lost their land undoubtedly resonated with the writer on a personal level. Earlier he had sold his allotment to finance graduate education at Oxford University in England only to discover that his credits from Montana's state university in Missoula, presently the University of Montana, were not transferable. In light of his firsthand knowledge of the intricate problems facing Indians as they dealt with the white world, McNickle found her manuscript outstanding. "Indian history," he wrote in his report to the press, "has been so neglected by serious students and so overrun by sentimentalists and free-lance commentators of various stripes and colors that it is a real joy to come across a work of such competence." Wholeheartedly, he endorsed its publication.

As administrative assistant to Collier, McNickle hoped that the BIA's victory in winning passage of the Indian Reorganization Act of 1934 would remedy earlier wrongs. Repudiating allotment, which had cost Native peoples 83 million acres, or more than 60 percent of their land, it permitted Congress to appropriate 2 million annually to rebuild their shrunken reservations. Additionally, a 10 million dollar revolving fund would enable Indians to borrow money to purchase livestock and equipment for successful farming. Finally, the revitalization of their tribal organizations would restore Native pride and give them greater control over assets, income, and expenditures.

Oklahoma had been excluded from the 1934 act, largely because Joseph Bruner, a Creek and head of the American Indian Federation, had argued that the Five Tribes had been largely assimilated. Initially, the less acculturated Plains Indians and other tribes in the western part of the state had agreed with Bruner, who was also supported by commercial interests and politicians who objected to removing Indian land and its subterranean resources from taxation rolls. As the debate progressed, however, many Indians of western Oklahoma became convinced that some form of the Indian Reorganization Act would benefit them after all.

By late 1935, Senator Elmer Thomas and Representative Will Rogers had drawn up the Oklahoma Indian Welfare Act, a version more applicable to their state's complicated situation. It allowed the secretary of the interior to acquire land for restoring or enlarging tribal holdings. Held in trust, that land would be exempted from all taxation, save Oklahoma's gross production tax on gas and oil. Moreover, all tribes, save the Osage who requested exclusion, would be permitted to organize and adopt a constitution or charter of incorporation. Once a majority accepted these measures, they would receive access to a 2 million dollar loan fund. Finally, groups of ten or more Indians living in proximity could form cooperatives. Although the act was signed into law on June 26, 1936, as Debo was completing her manuscript, it remained controversial and highly disputed.

The contribution Debo's manuscript would make to the ongoing debate was undoubtedly on McNickle's mind when he suggested that Angie prune unnecessary details to win a wider readership. Brandt agreed. Debo's work on the Choctaws was worthy of high praise, Brandt advised her, but "its audience is necessarily limited." With this manuscript, the subject was "of first rate importance to every intelligent citizen." If she followed the reader's advice, Brandt assured her, this work would attract the attention it deserved.

Angie acceded, but steadfast to the point of stubbornness on issues involving questions of justice, she drew a line. More interested in "sound scholarship" than ephemeral "popularity," she insisted that the extensive Indian testimony in her text remain intact. "For more than forty years," she told Brandt, "nobody has paid the slightest attention to what the Indians themselves thought about a matter so vital to their existence; and I feel that they deserve a chance to be heard."

As she awaited the second reader's report, Angie was already applying for grants from the Guggenheim Foundation, the American Association of University Women, and the Social Science Research Council—in short, any group that might fund her. Without support she could not begin her next project, a history of the Creek Nation.

When no grants materialized, she worked briefly for Grant Foreman on the Indian-Pioneer History Project for the Works Progress Administration office in Oklahoma. After almost three years without a steady job, save for teaching one summer at Stephen F. Austin State Teachers College in Nacogdoches, Texas, she found drawing a paycheck exhilarating. And surviving pioneers responded enthusiastically to her requests for information. As she wrote Edward Dale, the questionnaires they returned, although often "painfully filled out by trembling old hands," provided "an eloquent picture of the life they knew." Finally, her new position also gave her access to Creek testimony, an invaluable aid to her proposed study.

By mid-March 1937, Angie was impatiently awaiting the return of her manuscript from the second reader. Controversy still dogged the Indian Reorganization Act and the Oklahoma Indian Welfare Act, and John Collier and the BIA remained under what she termed "savage attack." Critics in Congress and some clergy accused Collier of advocating paganism by allowing tribal groups to practice their Native religions. Others saw him as a communist, a charge that had haunted him since 1921 when criticism over his support for the Bolsheviks in Russia had forced him to resign as director of adult education for the California Housing and Immigration Commission. Fifteen years later, his continuing attachment to the communal and spiritual values of Indian life sustained those suspicions.

Given the ongoing controversy over current Indian policy, Debo wanted her manuscript published as soon as possible. She was certain, she wrote Brandt in March 1937, that "there is no propaganda in that book for Commissioner Collier or anyone else; but it is the only scientific study that has ever been made of the question about which such a bitter fight has raged for the past four years." She noted that it would please her "to think that sincere people on both sides could have some facts available as a basis for their arguments."

Even more important, she added, her investigations had left her "intensely concerned" for Indian welfare. "If the despoilers of the Indians are going to have their way—as they have always done before, and as they probably will again—I do not want it to be chargeable to lack of knowledge," she informed Brandt. Later that month, after learning that the second reader's report was also favorable, she relaxed. Publication was set for October 1, 1937.

That spring Angie discovered that Professor Morris Wardell, having received his doctorate from the University of Chicago, was leaving the University of Oklahoma faculty to become assistant to the school's president, William Bizzell. Furthermore, another history professor, Alfred B. Thomas, was resigning. Aware that Wardell had been Dale's student, Debo wrote her mentor asking to be considered for one of the two vacancies. She had, admittedly, "one disqualification." She was a woman, few of whom "were employed on history faculties. I have been hoping, however," she added, "that my other qualifications might serve to balance this defect."

Among these "other qualifications" were her academic record, which included all As except for a B in mineralogy. Moreover, she had finished her master's in a year and her doctoral dissertation, when published, had won "national recognition." Debo was certain she "could bring distinction in the field of productive scholarship to any college that might employ me."

Although she had never taught graduate students, she would approach that task as Dale approached it. "When I was a sophomore and you were just beginning your career as a great teacher of history you supervised the writing of our term themes with a seriousness and an attention to method that formed the basis of all my future studies," she told him. Following his example, she had taught students at Canyon to write well-researched history and surely the same would happen at Oklahoma.

She had left West Texas State Teachers College because "it was a little school without standards, and I was working directly under a man who had an unfounded distrust of his own ability and a corresponding fear of people with advanced degrees." Angie added in her letter to Dale that if she remained an uncertain quantity, he could employ her on a temporary or part-time basis and "the future would take care of itself."

Angie was embarrassed by the request she was making; she acknowledged that it brought "a new element into the pleasantest relationship I have found in all my academic career. No action that you might take in the matter, however," she assured her mentor, "would alter the fact that it is to your interest and encouragement that I owe whatever success I have achieved in historical studies. There is therefore no occasion for embarrassment if I have made one request that you do not care to grant."

"To write me a letter telling me about yourself is very much the same as what the lawyers would call surplusage [or excess]," Dale's response began. Yet, though he knew her skills and qualifications better than anyone and was proud of her career, he gave her no encouragement that he would ever bring her into his department. He had to replace Thomas, a specialist in Latin America and the borderlands, he stated, with a scholar capable of directing theses and dissertations in that important area. Dale said nothing, however, about employing Debo as a temporary replacement for Wardell, whose field of study was also Indian and western history. In fact, Wardell's dissertation, scheduled for publication as *The Political History of the Cherokee Nation* (1938), would be the seventeenth volume in the Civilization of the American Indian series. Nor did Dale allude to the possibility of making Angie a part-time or adjunct instructor.

Debo thanked her mentor for explaining his situation. She acknowledged that Dr. Thomas had achieved prominence in Spanish-American studies and that it was important to replace him with another renowned scholar in that area. "I just wrote," she explained, "on the chance that you might be making some rearrangement within the department. I have not kept track of the new men that have come to the faculty since I left, and I thought possibly some of them might have specialized in that field."

In this letter she noted that she was leaving the WPA at the end of the month. Her experience there had been valuable, she told Dale. She had gained a deeper understanding of "the inner life of the people who made this state—Indians, homesteaders, ranchmen, etc.—and it has been a great pleasure to be engaged in work that seems so significant and important." And her deepening friendship with Grant and Carolyn Foreman was a source of great pleasure.

Debo never referred again in writing to this exchange of letters, but it had exacted a heavy toll. She had risked her pride, especially since she surely knew that colleges and universities did not usually bring their own Ph.D.s into departments as faculty members. Still, within six years, Edwin McReynolds would join Dale's department, two years before receiving his Ph.D. from Oklahoma. In similar fashion, Arrell Gibson would return to his alma mater twelve years after receiving his doctorate, again from Oklahoma. Aside from these later developments—which would not have affected the case in 1937—Debo had also asked to be considered for a part-time or adjunct position if a tenure-track position was beyond consideration. In the end, although Dale had responded kindly to his former student, he had rejected her request to be considered for part-time employment by simply ignoring it. Clearly, he did not intend to do for her what he had done for Morris Wardell.

Factors other than prejudice against women and a bias against hiring an institution's own Ph.D. were probably at work here. Dale undoubtedly recalled that Angie had challenged his suggestions for improving her dissertation. He also knew that she could be outspoken and blunt. Despite his genuine affection for her and his pride in her accomplishments, Dale evidently did not want her for a colleague. By contrast, he was totally at ease with Wardell, sharing with him a camaraderie within the department and socializing with him outside the workplace.

Born in 1889, Morris Wardell had obtained his bachelor's from Oklahoma in 1919, a year after Debo graduated. Very likely Dale's recommendations had helped him enter Harvard, where he had earned his master's in 1922. After he had taught at Tulsa Central High School, Dale had brought him to Norman as a summer school instructor in 1923. A year later Wardell was on the university faculty and moving up the ladder. With Dale's support, he was promoted to full professor before he received his doctorate from Chicago in 1936. Dale thought so highly of him that he had delayed Carl Coke Rister's promotion to assure Wardell's continuing seniority. He made that decision even though Rister, who had earned his doctorate at George Washington University in 1925, was a prolific writer in southwestern history from the beginning of his career. On the other hand, Wardell, who eventually coauthored a book with Dale on Oklahoma history, never became a productive scholar.

Dale's attitude toward bringing women on to his faculty cannot be known with any certainty. He had taken an interest in them as students, for the earliest dissertations he directed at Oklahoma were written by women. Anna Lewis's "Early History of the Arkansas River Region, 1541-1800" had been the first in 1930. Debo's dissertation had been the fourth in 1933.

Despite his encouragement of female students, Dale had displayed a bias against women in a 1913 Harvard seminar paper that may still have been coloring his feelings about them as possible colleagues, even as adjuncts. In "Woman's Influence on the French Revolution," he explored the impact of women, both poor women and women of prominence like Marie Antoinette and Jeanne Manon Roland, on the violent actions of crowds. In the end, he thought that women wielded their greatest power by imparting to men some of the attributes he viewed as innately female. "To measure the influence which woman had upon the French Revolution is manifestly impossible, but we can see its results cropping out at many times and in many places," Dale asserted. "The men, even the leaders in the Constituent and the political clubs, seem at times to be imbued with a 'fatal feminism,' a strange sentimentality that causes them to act more like excited, hysterical women than like sober law-givers to whom has been entrusted the task of creating a new form of government for France," he continued. "They waste time on trifles, they talk endlessly, and they show in many ways incapacity for business, sentimentalism, a failure to 'make the head rule the heart,' and other characteristics which we in America usually regard as peculiarly feminine. Thus," he concluded, "not only did the women of France have a large share in the Revolution, but there was also apparently a strain of 'femininity' or at least a lack of masculinity in the men of the period."

To be fair, these words, written more than two decades earlier, may not have reflected Dale's more mature thinking. Still, the passage indicates that as a younger man in his early thirties he associated certain negative characteristics with womanliness. If these prejudices still affected his thinking, it sheds light on his willingness to bring Wardell into his department before he earned his terminal degree, while at the same time he remained unwilling to give Debo even a part-time teaching position despite her postdoctoral achievements. By 1947 when the Oklahoma history department summarized its own history in a brief report, only one woman, Margaret June Mitchell, had taught there since its inception. Although the report never specified her credentials or rank, the *University of Oklahoma Bulletin, General Catalogue, 1926–27* indicated that she held a Ph.D. in education from Chicago (1910) and a master's in history from Oklahoma (1914). From 1917 to 1923, she held the rank of associate professor.

Some sense of the prevailing attitude toward female historians emerges from a later study conducted by William Hesseltine and Louis Kaplan. These scholars noted in an article published in 1943 in the *Journal of Higher Education* that, although women had received about 18 percent of the total number of Ph.D.s in history between 1891 and 1935, only 49 percent, or fewer than half, were employed in academic positions, compared with 74 percent of men. Moreover, when employed, they "taught in smaller and poor schools, held fewer responsible positions, and, presumably, carried heavier teaching loads for leaner salaries."

Even though they acknowledged these hardships, Hesseltine and Kaplan pointed to another factor that limited female advancement—women's lack of productivity in research. "[T]hey wrote but 13 per cent of the books and 7 per cent of the articles. Whatever discrimination might exist against women as teachers or administrators," the authors concluded, "there were none against them as productive scholars."

Since granting agencies were not misogynists, and since men and women faced the same problems in conducting research and writing, the authors concluded that, after half a century, "the record of the average woman who persevered in academic study until she attained the doctorate is not impressive. She has seldom held high or responsible positions in the teaching profession, and she has not proved a productive scholar." Exactly how the authors thought this hypothetical woman could engage in extensive research and writing when she was 50 percent less likely to find academic employment and thus more likely to earn her living at another occupation never entered their calculations. Nor were they concerned about her lesser pay and heavier teaching loads, both of which provided obvious impediments to archival research and writing, even when she was fortunate enough to be employed in a teaching position or win a grant. In Hesseltine and Kaplan's view, she had not yet proved productive as a scholar, and that was the major impediment. They could not foresee that expanding her opportunities or improving her working conditions would change her status within the profession.

Debo was now concerned about issues beyond Dale's unwillingness to bring her into his department. As she completed her work for the WPA project, a new anxiety plagued her. Increasingly she worried about the potentially explosive nature of her forthcoming book. Finally, in mid-July, she voiced her fears to Joseph Brandt; the legislature might cut off funding for the press after her new work appeared in print. After all, that had been its response to Kate Barnard following her outcry over the fate of Indian orphans.

Brandt at first assured Debo that, given her diligent research, he was obliged to publish her work. His staff, however, overheard the conversation and expressed concern. Brandt's equanimity vanished. He had to safeguard the interests of a press that was one of the few outlets for scholarly works on American Indians, as Angie herself had stressed. He would submit her manuscript to President Bizzell, he told her.

Bizzell in turn gave Debo's work to his assistant, Morris Wardell. "I feel sure that if the book is published as it is, there will be abundant adverse criticism with reference to personalities," Wardell warned. Although he found the manuscript praiseworthy, especially since it was "fearlessly written," he predicted that "some critics would discount the author's ability to weigh all materials used." Debo's story needed telling, Wardell admitted, but "such personal facts as to make it objectionable" should be omitted for they invited libel suits. Moreover, many of those named were "friends of the University," and in the background loomed the ongoing depression and Governor William H. Murray's threats to cut funding for higher education. In that context, Wardell added, "we are in no position at the present time to invite criticism."

Even if all personal and nonessential facts were deleted, Wardell held reservations about the manuscript as a whole. Citing specific examples, he noted that the word "grafter," used in the heading of a chapter entitled "The Grafter's Share," could mislead readers unaware of how loosely the term had been used twenty years earlier. As for Debo's description of the various methods individuals like the former senator, Robert L. Owen, had devised for exploiting the allotment process, Wardell cautioned greater discretion. "The book is history, and the facts are there, but it is dangerous to write in a book about it." After questioning Debo's judgment on a number of minor points, he objected to her willingness to name individuals who had cheated the Indians. "This gentleman," he noted of one person (a former college president who had exploited Indian generosity to raise money), "is a good friend of the University of Oklahoma. Why should we go out of our way to rehash something that he no doubt would like for the public to forget?"

Shortly after Wardell filed his report, Bizzell informed Brandt that Oklahoma could not publish Debo's manuscript "without thorough revision." Otherwise it could generate "considerable ill-will" and "disagreeable litigation." Furthermore, Wardell's report had convinced Bizzell that it contained "errors as to fact" that diminished its usefulness to professional historians.

As soon as she read the unsigned copy of the report, Debo knew she needed another publisher. Soon after, her contract marked "cancelled by mutual consent" arrived in the mail. Not suspecting Wardell's role, she concluded that Dale was responsible for the negative appraisal. Although she never acknowledged that she harbored anything but gratitude toward Dale, the recent exchange of letters between them may have generated unconscious resentment within her that expressed itself in her hasty judgment. More likely, however, she arrived at her conclusion on the basis of past experience. Although Dale had often told his classes about the duplicity whites had practiced against Indians, he had deleted such incidents from his publications. When Angie had pressed him outside of class on this point, he had warned her that it was too soon to publicize such facts. In that light, her assumption that he had written the unsigned reader's report was understandable.

Despite this setback, Angie, bolstered by a grant from the Social Science Research Council, was now at work on her history of the Creek Indians. Although travelers and missionaries had described them in their accounts, and anthropologists like John Swanton had analyzed their culture, historians had not dealt impartially with their life east of the Mississippi River. And even though Annie Abel and Grant Foreman had delineated the removal of the Creeks westward, Debo wondered how that event had affected "the internal life of the tribe." Finally, no one had examined Creek life in Indian Territory before passage of the Curtis Act destroyed their protectorate.

As she had done in studying the Choctaws earlier, Debo began by examining the tribe's origin myth. The Creeks traced their beginnings to a land of high mountains, "the backbone of the world," from which they had moved eastward across a great river. Beyond the Mississippi, they formed themselves into a large confederation consisting of two parts—the Upper Towns along the Coosa and Tallapoosa Rivers and the Lower Towns along the Flint and Chattahoochee. Although the Creek Confederation probably antedated the coming of European invaders, it acquired greater strength after their arrival.

Debo, assuming at first that the Creeks were more warlike than the Choctaws, learned eventually that these proud warriors and astute diplomats were simply more determined to preserve their way of life. But while they clung tenaciously to their traditions, they lacked the guile to withstand white ruthlessness. As Creek trust was repeatedly betrayed, their landholdings shrank. Eventually they were "dragged from their ancient homes and flung down upon a raw western frontier to conquer it or die."

In narrating the story of their removal and their early years in Indian Territory, Debo drew on the testimony of "old-time" Creeks, compiled from Grant Foreman's WPA project on Indians and pioneers. These accounts, based on oral history passed down through several generations, proved invaluable for purposes of interpretation. From them Debo also learned an astounding fact. In checking Creek statements against other documentary evidence and Foreman's 1932 *Indian Removal*, she discovered that their oral history accounts were accurate over a period of one hundred years. Beyond that, there were discrepancies, and Debo, as a historian, demanded strong and verifiable evidence as the basis for her conclusions.

In Indian Territory the Creeks had rebuilt their lives and over time had eased the tensions between themselves and neighboring western tribes. Turning inward, they began to prosper until the American Civil War intervened, reviving old animosities and exacerbating dissension among them. When the "White Man's War" ended, the Creeks faced "the encircling menace of a new frontier." Nonetheless, they had remained fiercely attached to their old ways. Even after they were compelled to accept allotment, a group of full-bloods under Chitto (Snake) Harjo had resisted. Not until the federal government brought its leaders to trial in 1901 was the so-called Snake Rebellion broken.

Eventually Debo entitled her new work *The Road to Disappearance: A History of the Creek Indians* (1941), largely because she thought that no one would read a book called *A History of the Creek Indians*. Her choice proved unfortunate, for even though she chronicled the end of their separate existence, she noted at the beginning of her work that the Creek spirit survived in "native steadfastness" and in "the unyielding tenacity of their native traits." Moreover, she saw their influence on the history of Euro-Americans as "profound and permanent." Thus, although the republic had disappeared, the Creeks themselves endured.

The words of Chief Pleasant Porter conveyed that message. In addition to proving himself a farsighted and skillful negotiator for his people after the passage of the Curtis Act, he understood the contributions they had made to the new state that was envisioned and to the nation as a whole. His ability to find enduring meaning,

while relinquishing his fondest hopes, undoubtedly sustained Debo
as she struggled against her own poverty and a growing sense of
marginalization in her profession. She ended her work with his
moving 1900 peroration to the Creek Council:

> The vitality of our race still persists. We have not lived for
> naught. We are the original discoverers of this continent, and
> the conquerors of it from the animal kingdom, and on it first
> taught the arts of peace and war, and first planted the institu-
> tions of virtue, truth and liberty. The European Nations found
> us here and were made aware that it was possible for men to
> exist and subsist here. . . . We have given to the European
> people on this continent our thought forces—the best blood
> of our ancestors having intermingled with [that of] their best
> statesmen and leading citizens. We have made ourselves an
> indestructible element in their national history.

Porter concluded with this assurance: "The race that has rendered
this service to the other nations of mankind cannot utterly perish."

While Debo worked on the history of the Creeks, Brandt sent
As Long as the Waters Run to Bobbs-Merrill and Simon and
Schuster, among other publishing houses. No one was interested,
although Brandt considered it worthy of a Pulitzer Prize. Even
though editors and readers praised Debo's thorough research,
they saw it as having little appeal for a popular audience.

In 1938 Angie was passed over when she applied for a teaching
position at Texas State College for Women in Denton. Now forty-
eight, she worried increasingly about her future. That same year,
in July, Brandt left the University of Oklahoma Press to become
director of Princeton University Press. Soon after, he solicited
Debo's manuscript and, by summer 1939, had received a favorable
report from John Joseph Mathews. Although the well-known
writer praised the work, he, like others, warned that its publication
could bring lawsuits. Brandt assumed responsibility for deleting all
potentially libelous material from the work. Since his duties at
Princeton were even more demanding than those at Oklahoma, his
painstaking efforts on Debo's behalf proceeded slowly.

Months passed and as Christmas 1939 drew near, Angie was
in despair. "Since you have not been able to snatch any spare

time in the six months that you have been earnestly trying to find it, can't you take some time off and do it?" she begged her old friend. She also reminded Brandt of the compliments the work had received. Although she appreciated the interest and support he had shown in her work over the past three years, she now found herself "completely at the end of my financial and spiritual resources."

Debo had finished her book on the Creeks in May that year and since then had been "desperately trying to find something to do—teaching, lecturing, research, *anything*—but I have dropped completely out of the world, and there is no possible way of getting back until I can publish something." With uncharacteristic self-pity, she noted, "it seems to me that I have qualities of mind and spirit that should not have been discarded by the world. But that," she added,"is off the subject."

Her latest manuscript—*The Road to Disappearance*—was now with Savoie Lottinville, Joseph Brandt's former assistant and his successor at Oklahoma. Since the depression lingered, the press, faced with a restricted budget, had postponed the publication date for her latest work indefinitely. Five years had passed since *The Rise and Fall of the Choctaw Republic* had appeared, and Angie feared she had been forgotten.

The recent years had taken their toll. Earlier, Debo had always summoned strength from her vast reservoir of grit and determination. Through conscientious and painstaking labor she had won her terminal degree. Then she had transformed her dissertation into a book that won one of the most prestigious awards given by the major historical association in America. Surely, if merit and diligence alone were determining factors, she would have by now been tenured at a college or university. Instead, she was living a hand-to-mouth existence marked by unremitting anxiety. What the future held as she neared her fiftieth birthday in January 1940 remained an open and troubling question. When the winter solstice fell in December 1939, Debo was experiencing the long night of the soul. She had nothing save her faith in her God and in herself to sustain her.

CHAPTER 5

New Opportunities Beckon

AFTER rereading *As Long as the Waters Run* and consulting an attorney, Joseph Brandt informed Debo that, to protect Princeton University Press against libel suits, the names of all characters unknown outside Oklahoma should be deleted. Assured that she could still identify prominent individuals such as Robert Owen and Charles Haskell, Angie agreed. Brandt now knew, however, that anthropologist Oliver La Farge, author of the Pulitzer Prize–winning novel, *Laughing Boy* (1929), would soon publish *As Long As the Grass Shall Grow* (1940), a book on Indian-white relations. Thus Debo renamed her work, scheduled for publication late in 1940, *And Still the Waters Run.* In the meantime, since the University of Oklahoma Press still lacked the funding to publish *The Road to Disappearance,* she circulated it to other presses.

In the winter of 1940, Debo was reduced to taking out a loan against her life insurance. When she learned that the directorship of the Federal Writers' Project for the State of Oklahoma was open, she borrowed the train fare to Oklahoma City. Arriving in town early in March, she rented a room at the YWCA for fifty cents a night and staved off hunger with sandwiches from home.

After an encouraging interview, Angie returned to Marshall. But as weeks passed with no word, her anxiety mounted. To relieve tension, she worked in her mother's garden, helping Lina set out chrysanthemums and irises. She also gave her parents' home a thorough spring cleaning. It raised her spirits: Whatever happened, she decided, "I can accept it and go on."

When she learned on April 19, however, that the Macmillan Company had rejected her history of the Creeks, she confessed to "suffering seriously from crushed wormery." A day later came the letter informing her that she was the new head of the state's Federal Writers' Project.

In Oklahoma City, Debo discovered that she would oversee the production of the state guide, which had been in limbo for several months. The former director, novelist William Cunningham, whose *Green Corn Rebellion* (1935) remained a powerful work on rural socialism, had been dismissed following congressional investigations into allegations of waste and mismanagement in the WPA.

As she began her duties, Debo realized that preliminary drafts completed by the former state workers required, in her words, "drastic revisions." Lacking adequate knowledge and the skills to interpret facts, they had approached their task as if they were describing Oklahoma for a "Western Story" magazine. (One of Cunningham's assistants had been Louis L'Amour. Then a short story writer, he later became one of America's most prolific western novelists.) Moreover, with the exception of Dorothy Holcomb, none of her staff could write well. Only Dale's agreement to furnish an interpretative essay and the inclusion of a historical essay she herself was writing could, Angie thought, bring depth and realism to the projected volume.

Within weeks Debo was disillusioned with the job she had viewed earlier as her salvation. Attending meetings, submitting reports, and correcting the mistakes of her staff—many fresh from relief rolls and poor at following directions—left her frustrated and tense. Irritated by conflicting bureaucratic demands from Washington, she approached her managerial responsibilities as if she were a schoolteacher instructing children. Certain that she knew the best way to accomplish tasks, she issued a memorandum and directives that told her staff exactly how to perform simple tasks: "Use the heading . . . you will find on your assignment, . . . Do not make any other heading," she decreed. She admonished them to locate their own books in card catalog and not to bother the librarians. Adult workers, competent or not, undoubtedly resented her orders, and the resulting undercurrent in the office could only have added to her burdens.

Debo's difficulties lightened somewhat when J. Stanley Clark of Muskogee joined her staff as her assistant. A skilled writer, he had worked as an editor under Grant Foreman on the WPA project on Indians and pioneers. He was also an excellent researcher, having recently completed his dissertation at the University of Wisconsin on the history of the Ponca Indian Agency. Although he and Angie became close friends, he stayed only a month before accepting a higher-paying position elsewhere.

More disappointments were in store. After all the hardships Angie had experienced in getting *And Still the Waters Run* published, the work received little attention when it arrived in bookstores late in 1940. There were brief reviews in *Christian Century* and *The Nation,* but only one national newspaper gave it notice. In the *New York Herald Tribune,* Stanley Vestal (who was actually the Oklahoma writer, Walter Campbell), best known for *Sitting Bull: Champion of the Sioux* (1932), praised Debo as "a scholar of honesty and courage," who exhibited "a talent and skill, which many a literary man might envy."

Fundamentally optimistic, Debo never lost confidence in her ability as an author. Instead, she concluded that public concern over the outbreak of World War II was diverting attention from her work. In a sense she was correct. The United States, as the "arsenal for democracy," was enjoying renewed prosperity, a fact that lessened the potential impact of *And Still the Waters Run.* During the depression, writers and intellectuals who saw Indian communalism as an attractive alternative to the intense individualism and materialism of American society had commanded a larger and more receptive audience for their views. Now, with prosperity returning, the tide had shifted.

In March 1941, Debo turned her directorship of the state writers' project over to J. Stanley Clark, who replaced her even though his former stint with the agency had been brief. In explaining to Dale her decision to give up her job, Angie blamed the bureaucratic system rather than her own managerial style. The idea of hiring unemployed writers was, she maintained, "an economic fallacy," for she had met "few, if any, unemployed writers in Oklahoma." Among the "forty people assigned to my project, most of them intelligent and conscientious, and capable of performing acceptable research under supervision," only one person had demonstrated writing ability. "The piling up of research which could not be used was completely repugnant to my standards of thrift in the use of public funds," she noted. "Badly as I needed my salary, I did not think it important enough to tempt me to continue at work that I considered socially indefensible."

Although *And Still the Waters Run* received little attention, its appearance revived Debo's hopes for a teaching position. She asked Dale to look for vacancies when he attended the Mississippi Valley Historical Society meeting in April 1941. If her specialization in American Indian and southwestern history rendered her unattractive to most institutions, her abilities in the classroom, she thought, would set her apart. She was certain that "people who can hold the attention of a college class and inspire people to enter into research and writing are not too plentiful even in the overcrowded history field, and it seems to me there should be a place where my talents would be used."

With the economy improving, the University of Oklahoma Press scheduled *The Road to Disappearance* for publication. As Debo meticulously double-checked her facts, she wrote Dale, asking him about the population of a Creek town. His reply left her overjoyed—not because of the information it carried, but because of its salutation: "Dear Angie," Dale began, not "Dear Miss Debo," as always before. She considered "framing the letter. You used to call me by my given name—I have been in your classes since I was a freshman taking Government out in Park Row." she wrote him. "I hope you will continue the good habit."

Dale's response was equally cordial: "[A]fter all, why should I not call you Angie. You see I always think of you as Angie and besides, am I not your academic godfather since your freshman days. You even," he added, "returned to me after testing the intellectual flesh pots of the great University of Chicago and I have always taken to myself some crumbs of credit for your rise to fame as a writer and historical scholar." Significantly, although "Miss Debo" became "Angie," "Dr. Dale" never became "Edward."

As the United States entered World War II following Japan's attack on Pearl Harbor on December 7, 1941, Debo's history of the Creeks arrived in bookstores. Her pleasure in holding her third book on American Indian history was marred, however, by the appearance early in 1942 of *Oklahoma: A Guide to the Sooner State,* the product of the Federal Writers' Project. To her chagrin, someone had substituted another essay for the one she had written on Oklahoma history. It contained errors and, more important, a different interpretation of Indian-white relations. Debo's original essay had begun by noting, "Although Oklahoma is young as a state, the region came early within the scope of the white man's imperial ambitions." It then described the cavalcade of explorers, priests, and traders who had named (in various languages) the state's geographical features. However, her essay continued, "the real colonization of Oklahoma by a civilized people began with the arrival of immigrant Indians from the Southeast."

The essay that appeared in the volume instead never referred to "imperialism." Moreover, the termination of the Five Tribes of Oklahoma was described with little passion and as part of a larger cautionary tale. Reflecting the animosity many intellectuals harbored against big business during the New Deal, the account centered on the political transformation of Oklahoma from "a Bryanesque commonwealth, controlled by farmers and small business men, to a modern industrial state dominated by the 'big money' which the pioneers had so greatly feared."

Angie struggled to overcome her disappointment. Most people, she wrote Dale, would not catch the errors. "I think they will not even detract much from the book's usefulness. But I do regret that I allowed my signature to be used." Even though she was violating her own principles by exposing "the inner workings" of an organization that had employed her, she had the right, she told Dale, "to explain that the book was changed without my knowledge."

Still hoping for a teaching position in a college or university, Debo published rapidly. With information left over from her book on the Creeks and additional insights from WPA interviews under the project on Indians and pioneers, she soon produced a history of Tulsa, a city that had intrigued her since she had first visited it as a college student in 1916. Although she had moved beyond Frederick Jackson Turner and Edward Everett Dale in her understanding of the impact of non-Indian settlement on the well-being of Native peoples, she still applied Turner's model to her urban biography. Tulsa, which arose on the last frontier, was "the most American of American cities," she wrote. "All the forces that have gone into the making of the Republic have been intensified there. The successive stages," Debo emphasized, "through which the country as a whole has passed during three hundred years of history—Indian occupation, ranching, pioneering, industrial development, and finally disillusionment and the recasting of objectives—have been telescoped within the single lifetime of some of the older Tulsans. The result," she concluded in a passage that paraphrased Turner's conclusions concerning the impact of the frontier on American character, "has been the quintessence of Americanism—its violence and strength, its buoyant optimism, its uncalculating generosity, its bumptious independence."

Many writers had traced the roots of Tulsa to the coming of the railroads. Angie disagreed. In 1836 the Creeks in Indian Territory had built a new version of Tallasi, an old governing center on the Tallapoosa River in present-day Alabama. In time it became known as Tulsa. The story Debo told was by now familiar. After the town was incorporated, non-Indian speculators siphoned off the greater share of profits. Nonetheless, Tulsa remained a relatively quiet cattle town until the Red Fork oil strike inaugurated its boom era in the early 1900s. With the opening of the Glenn Pool on November 22, 1905, "the richest small field in the world," the town soon emerged as one of the great oil capitals of the world.

With this manuscript in Savoie Lottinville's hands at the University of Oklahoma Press, Angie started another book. This time she was working on the history of a town she named Prairie City. Basing it largely on Marshall, she included events that had occurred in Hennessey and other nearby towns as well. By giving

88   ANGIE DEBO

her actual characters fictitious names but using statistics and historical facts from Logan and Kingfisher Counties, she was determined to produce history less likely to generate libel suits.

Even though the town itself remained inconsequential, "its
development spans in time and space most of the life of the
American people," Debo wrote Dale, early in winter 1942. With
Dale's enthusiastic assurance that her projected work was indeed
a work of history, Debo obtained a grant from the Alfred A.
Knopf publishing house and was soon immersed in her writing.

Angie had received outside funding before but never a grant
paying a hundred dollars a month, and she was elated. "I have
had a pretty hard time holding on since I lost my position at
Canyon," she wrote Dale. But all her past tribulations now seemed
"the best thing that ever happened to me." Thus far, her publications had produced little income. Although a history professor
in a department somewhere might publish books and articles
that paid little or nothing, it was all "a part of his service to his
college." For years Angie had had no salary to rely on. Now, in
addition to a generous advance, "the resources of an important
publisher will be devoted to making my work popular." She
might even earn substantial royalties.

Here Angie's optimism reflected the insights she had gained
from an old friend. Mary Smith, formerly Mary McLean, her colleague from West Texas, was now dean of women at the college
in Canyon. After reading *And Still the Waters Run*, Smith had
learned about the Knopf fellowship. Although she had never
understood the source of Debo's earlier hardships, Smith now
pointed out that "perhaps the time will come when you will see
it was the adversity that hastened your achievement." She had
been such a conscientious teacher, Smith told her, that had she
stayed at Canyon, she would never have written as much. Either
that or she would have wrecked her health attempting to teach
and publish at the same time. Instead, she had produced works
that were, Smith believed, "to the Indian race what Plutarch's
Lives or Gibbons Roman Empire have been to their times."

Reinvigorated by the faith and affection of her friend, Debo was
hard at work on the new book, interviewing old-timers in Marshall,

including the widow and daughter of Sylvan Rice, the owner of the original crossroads store that had marked the town's beginning. She also interrogated local figures like Billy Fox, an old buffalo hunter, and his wife. Later she checked her facts with longtime resident George Beeby, whose diary proved invaluable. The documents would keep, but "the old people," Debo wrote Dale, "are dropping off pretty fast." Although her sources often ran events together or remembered them out of sequence, their recollections, like her parents' memories, accurately described their farming life and their ways of coping with challenges and setbacks.

After consulting the *Kingfisher Free Press* and completing painstaking research into census data, land costs, and producer and commodities prices, Debo searched for incidents that demonstrated the "spirit of Oklahoma." She was looking for instances in which the "free-masonry of shared experiences" had contributed to the pioneers' resiliency and perseverance.

Briefly she considered describing her parents' good-natured response when she and her brother had spilled kerosene on the family's supply of flour. She also thought of using the experiences of a family from Greer County who suffered similar misfortune after a skunk wandered into their cellar—even when they ate outside, a sickening odor permeated their biscuits and bread. Even the birds rejected the crumbs. In the end, Debo emphasized the spirit of Oklahoma by incorporating the story of a dog that jumped into a barrel of sorghum. The pioneers had used the syrup anyway, arguing that any contamination would have clung to the dog's hair when he bolted from the barrel.

Late in spring 1943, the first edition of *Tulsa: From Creek Town to Oil Capital* sold out soon after it arrived in bookstores. Heartened by her regional popularity, Angie moved quickly to complete *Prairie City*. The book, a "history of the United States in microcosm," was based on the idea put forth by "Big Jim" Murphy, a farmer on Horse Creek. According to the Irishman, "Ev'rything that iver happened annywhere has happened at Marrshall, Oklahoma." A "typical, rather than an actual community," its story was "essentially true historically; for it is not the actual little town that matters, but its universal significance."

Dedicated to Edward Everette Dale, "who has taught the children of pioneers to love the story of their origins," the book opened with the pioneers who made the first land run in 1889 and a year later planted their crops. The following winter, after a summer drought, they endured their "starving time" as they barely survived on kaffir corn, turnips, wild game, and plums and grapes women found by the creeks. Many of the men left home in search of work, and almost all families relied on credit at the country store. One woman, driven mad by the poverty, hunger, and stress, reportedly summoned a traveler, "Look here! We're goin' to have some fried chicken. I'm dressin' it now." So saying, Debo added, "*she held up the dismembered body of her infant.*" Frontier experiences broke some of Prairie City's residents, but others rose to the challenge, becoming in the process hardier individuals.

These struggles notwithstanding, the sodbusters founded their churches and established public education in a primitive structure known as Union School. Undoubtedly Angie was thinking of herself when she wrote that, whatever its inadequacies, some children "found in their tattered books a mystic summons to a realm beyond the boundaries of time and space and the urge for further schooling became with them a consuming flame."

At first the residents of Prairie City endured pleasures and sorrows together despite ethnic, religious, and political differences. Their sense of participating in a significant movement bound them together, "the white light of history converging upon their everyday acts." Every April 22 they celebrated the anniversary of the first great land run in 1889.

At those communal events, Prairie City residents sang their well-known hymns, old country ballads, or "lighthearted ditties of their own that were already springing up from the fresh Oklahoma soil." At the center of their social lives, however, were their church services. Two clergymen, one Baptist and the other Methodist, assisted each other and shared the same building during the early years.

Although Debo described early cohesiveness, she also saw the dark side of pioneering. The new land attracted the ne'er-do-wells, the shiftless, the emotionally unstable, and the violent. For many of them, the hardships and exigencies of frontier living only magnified their inadequacies and failures.

Angie found, moreover, that Prairie City's leaders sometimes floundered. After the residents bonded themselves to bring the railroad to town, promoters sold narrow twenty-five-foot plots of unsettled land, chosen by lottery, to unwary outside investors. Later, those wanting to purchase adjacent lots or seeking to move to other parts of town were forced to search for strangers who had lost interest in the hamlet. Eventually some farmers acquired the useless lots for back taxes and turned them into city gardens. "Thus," Debo noted, "in selling patches of raw land to deluded buyers the promoters had unwittingly set limits—physical and spiritual limits—to the future of Prairie City."

In the twentieth century, Angie observed, international events shaped the town's destiny more directly. The Great War, by destroying much of Europe's food production, sent commodity prices soaring. After 1921, their decline left the heavily mortgaged struggling to survive. Meanwhile, the discovery of oil, later in western Oklahoma than elsewhere in the state, increased economic disparity among families. During these years, the rise and fall of the local Ku Klux Klan exacerbated tensions and divisions until at last the town regained its sanity. Frederick Jackson Turner's 1893 "Significance of the Frontier in American History" had identified individualism and American exceptionalism as traits arising from frontier conditions. Debo's study of a pioneer town told instead of the erosion of an earlier sense of community in a place increasingly affected by technological change, economic periods of boom and bust, and national and international cataclysms.

Prairie City brought the composite town through the Great Depression and New Deal policies that compelled farmers, who had always sought abundant harvests, to limit production. By the late 1930s, residents, remembering that World War I propaganda had exploited their credulity, dismissed accounts of German atrocities and clung tenaciously to isolationism. Then the Japanese attack on Pearl Harbor brought an abrupt turnabout in public opinion.

As she ended *Prairie City,* Debo noted that World War II had hastened the town's decline. Few of the young people who had gone overseas or located higher-paying jobs in defense-related industries in larger cities would ever return. Agriculture, increasingly mechanized, needed fewer hands. Nonetheless, Prairie City would endure, "since the fields still produce and the world still eats," and one day the town might find itself part of a larger global community. "Why not a new village of farmers, citizens of the world through schools and radio and space-consuming transportation, grouped together in friendly sociability, building directly upon the soil?" Debo wondered. In her opinion, "the history of Prairie has been shaping itself toward some such end."

Angie viewed *Prairie City,* which appeared early in 1944, as her gift to her family and community. It came none too soon, for that spring, eighty-one-year-old Edward Debo fell gravely ill. For the past few years he had seemed almost indestructible, as he operated a produce plant where he collected chickens, eggs, and other dairy products for resale to larger warehouses. When he died in an Enid hospital on May 15, 1944, he was, to Angie's regret, only halfway through her newest book.

After Edward's funeral, Angie and her mother gave away his belongings—except for the decorative mustache cup Lina had bought him early in their marriage and which he used only for special occasions. Angie also moved Edward's looking glass into the kitchen, where it faced another mirror. Each day, as she arranged the back of her hair, thoughts of her father flooded into her mind. Years later, in oral history interviews, Debo's most vivid recollection of Edward concerned the day that she had watched him transplant trees from the creek in back of their house to the front yard. As he rocked the roots gently into place, it seemed to her as if he were tucking the trees into bed. She knew then that, despite his undemonstrative nature, he was a man of strong and tender feelings. Later, his example in remembering only the good times his family had enjoyed on the homestead where another family later discovered oil had taught her the value of appreciating the nonmaterial benefits of life. In time, as she adjusted to his absence, Angie's grief subsided, and she was left with memories of his steadfast faith in her abilities and his enduring love for his wife and children.

Angie had, at times, fretted that her lack of a steady job had left her dependent on her parents' help well into middle age. But if the Great Depression had contributed to Debo's unemployment in the 1930s, World War II now opened new opportunities for work. This change was common for many middle-aged women in America, as those over thirty-five became one of the fastest-growing segments of the labor force during this period. Since Marshall had lost many of its instructors to military service or defense industry work, Debo, in her mid-fifties, returned to the classroom to teach history in the local high school.

Hugh O'Neill, who later became her neighbor, was one of her students. After the class discussed the Protestant Reformation, Angie noted that they had studied the movement from the Protestant viewpoint. There was another perspective. Since O'Neill had been raised a Catholic, she asked him to share his interpretation so that all sides would receive a hearing. In this way she taught her class that history depends, not only on the facts and evidence one marshals, but the position one takes and the questions one asks.

As 1944 drew to a close, Debo could look back on the past five years and see that much had been gained. *And Still the Waters Run* had garnered no awards and enjoyed few sales, but she knew that it was the most important work she had written. Besides, it gave her a sense of completion, for she had answered to her satisfaction every question her research had raised. Shortly after, *The Road to Disappearance* had appeared, taking its place beside the other tribal history, *The Rise and Fall of the Choctaw Republic*. More recently, *Tulsa* and *Prairie City* had been published, and the first had been well received by the public. The latter, however, was not selling, and the excess inventory would soon be remaindered (sold by the publisher at much reduced rates). Undaunted, Debo was determined to continue writing.

She had also taken on another job. On November 21, she filled a vacuum by becoming the lay pastor of the Methodist Church, which had lost its minister during World War II. Years later, when asked to explain how she had become a lay minister, she responded with some embarrassment, "I volunteered." She was a popular pastor. Her parishioners recalled that during burial services she often sprinkled dirt over a farmer's casket, intoning, "With this loved soil of Oklahoma which you tilled for so many years, I bury you." She also performed marriages, and one couple, Brian and Louise Harpster, always celebrated their anniversaries by sending her cards or letters and occasionally paying her a visit. Finally, Debo's parishioners were moved by her generosity. Despite years of poverty, she spent her salary of $165 (all the small congregation could raise) on liberty bonds for the war effort. Later, she donated them to the church.

Although her youth was gone, Miss Angie, as the townspeople called her, now owned a fur coat, probably purchased with royalties from *Tulsa,* and she dressed with panache. Photographs of her from this period reveal a well-groomed woman who seemed at peace with her life and content with her work. She still missed her father, but she treasured Lina's companionship and their shared memories of the trials and triumphs they had endured together. Most comforting, Debo drew solace from Marshall, the community she had served in so many ways. Its residents appreciated her more than ever since she had brought their small Oklahoma town—the major inspiration for *Prairie City*—before the larger world. Although sales of that book had slowed to a trickle, time would prove that she had given the town a kind of immortality.

The Debo family, dressed in their Sunday best, had their picture taken by a traveling photographer in 1899. Obviously, as Angie wrote later in *Prairie City*, they felt the "white light of history." From left to right: father, Edward; son, Edwin; daughter, Angie; and mother, Lina. Courtesy of Angie Debo Papers, Oklahoma State University Library, Stillwater.

Students and teacher at the one-room Rosenberg schoolhouse, District No. 97, southwest of Marshall, Oklahoma Territory, about 1901.

Even in this modest building, with few resources, Angie found "a mystic summons to a realm beyond the boundaries of time and space and the urge for further schooling." Angie is the young girl at the far right, standing with her hand on her pony, Queen. Her brother, Edwin, stands on the other side of Queen. Courtesy of Angie Debo Papers, Oklahoma State University Library, Stillwater.

Angie Debo developed an unusually strong and affectionate relationship with her mother, and this picture, taken about 1904, captures the bond between them. Note how Lina Debo has changed in the five years or so since her family had their picture taken by an itinerant photographer. Although she loved the new land, adapting to the rigors of life in Oklahoma Territory obviously took its toll. Courtesy of Angie Debo Papers, Oklahoma State University Library, Stillwater.

By age seventeen, Angie Debo had her own one-room schoolhouse in rural Oklahoma. She is shown here with her class of students of varying ages. The little girl at Debo's right arm is Agnes Semrad; too young to attend school, she nevertheless wanted to be included in the picture. Courtesy of Angie Debo Papers, Oklahoma State University Library, Stillwater.

To
Walter Ferguson
with Best wishes
?
Edward Everett Dale

Edward Everett Dale, a former student of Frederick Jackson Turner. Angie Debo recalled him as being different from any of her other teachers. He strode into his University of Oklahoma classes, she said, with his "cowboy walk, his soft voice, and his alert far-seeing eyes." Throughout the rest of Debo's long life, she remembered him as the person who had the greatest impact on her scholarship. Courtesy of Walter Ferguson Collection, Western History Collections, University of Oklahoma Libraries, Norman.

Angie Debo during the period she taught at West Texas State Teachers College in Canyon, Texas. Her irrepressible quality is evident in this picture. Taken probably in the late 1920s, it shows her dressed for hiking, most likely in Palo Duro Canyon where she often took student groups. Courtesy of Angie Debo Papers, Oklahoma State University Library, Stillwater.

Angie Debo in Canyon, Texas, in the 1930s. Although her car was notably unreliable, she cherished it as a source of freedom and mobility. Courtesy of Angie Debo Papers, Oklahoma State University Library, Stillwater.

Taken in 1940 about the time that Princeton University Press published *And Still the Waters Run,* this picture shows Angie Debo in a calm state after a turbulent period. Since 1934, she had experienced dismissal from West Texas State Teachers College and a period of turmoil at the Panhandle-Plains Museum, followed by a long stretch of unemployment during the Great Depression. Courtesy of Angie Debo Papers, Oklahoma State University Library, Stillwater.

Angie and Lina Debo in 1947. By then, Angie was working as the curator of maps for Oklahoma A & M College in Stillwater (later Oklahoma State University). She was also working on *Oklahoma: Foot-loose and Fancy-free,* which was published the following year. Lina Debo, who was almost eighty, was becoming increasingly frail, but the bond between mother and daughter was still strong. Courtesy of Angie Debo Papers, Oklahoma State University Library, Stillwater.

Angie Debo in 1948. Courtesy of Angie Debo Papers, Oklahoma State University Library, Stillwater.

Although Angie had retired from her position as curator of maps at Oklahoma State University by 1956, she was especially pleased with the university's new Edmon Low Library. Here, as she stands in front of the library, her body language indicates her pride. Courtesy of Angie Debo Papers, Oklahoma State University Library, Stillwater.

Angie Debo's friend, Lois Clark, the widow of J. Stanley Clark, historian and colleague from the days of the Federal Writers' Project for the State of Oklahoma, took this picture of Angie Debo in 1977. She is standing on her front porch and is wearing an 1890s dress and her grandmother's hat as part of her role as participant in Marshall's Prairie City Days celebration. Courtesy of Carter Blue Clark.

By 1982, Angie Debo was ninety-two and giving oral history interviews to Gloria Valencia-Weber (left), Glenna Matthews (back), and Aletha Rogers (right). Although Debo suffered from the often excruciating pain of osteo-porosis, her engagement with these younger women, whom she admired and respected, gave her a renewed sense of purpose. She also expressed appreciation for the support of her friends and neighbors as she became increasingly frail and incapacitated. Courtesy of Angie Debo Papers, Oklahoma State University Library, Stillwater.

Charles Wilson, famous for his paintings of Oklahoma Indians and his *Roots of Oklahoma* murals in the capitol building, was the artist who painted Angie Debo's portrait, which now hangs in the capitol rotunda in Oklahoma City. This photograph, taken by an Oklahoma State University employee in 1985, shows Wilson as he completes the painting, with Angie sitting in a chair in her living room. Debo said that Wilson had captured her essential characteristic, which she defined as "drive." Courtesy of Angie Debo Papers, Oklahoma State University Library, Stillwater.

CHAPTER 6

Years of Frustration and Loss

BY September 1944, Debo had edited a cattleman's memoirs. Oliver Nelson, a teamster on the Chisholm Trail, had served as a cook in the Cherokee Strip and later participated in the No Man's Land (the Oklahoma Panhandle) Roundup before opening a stagecoach station in the Texas Panhandle. Angie entitled the work *'Light Up and Fill Up,* or, as she noted, "the characteristic invitation to every passing stranger to dismount and share a meal."

After sending the manuscript to Alfred Knopf, the New York publisher, Debo gave thought to the foreseeable future, conditions at the end of World War II. Scholars and pundits were questioning the role the United States would assume in areas of the world still under European domination. Would the nation support Great Britain and France as they struggled to retain their possessions? Or would the country that had once been a collection of colonies ally itself with those who would seek independence after the war?

In that context and in light of her ongoing interest in American Indian policy as a form of imperialism, a subject she had been discussing in correspondence with the Commissioner of the Bureau of Indian Affairs, John Collier, since 1941, Debo wrote Savoie Lottinville at the University of Oklahoma Press. Would he welcome a work on America's "real imperialism," its treatment of its Native peoples? "If we succeed, in spite of mistakes, in solving this problem we will have demonstrated our capacity to guide a subject people into citizenship and cultural assimilation," she told him. If not, "we may as well admit that the colonial problems that will be left from this present war are beyond our solving. Anyhow," she added, "I think that a serious evaluation of our dealings would be a serious contribution to modern thought, and that it must be traced historically."

Lottinville, believing such a work would not sell the two thousand copies required to recoup production costs, was not interested. He suggested that, instead, Debo should write a history of the Indian tribes of North America, a book the press had long desired. Earlier, without success, he had approached the WPA about this subject. But he was convinced that a single writer could produce a more "integrated" study, and no one was "more abundantly equipped for such an undertaking" than Angie Debo. Although she believed she would need to study many Indian tribes intensively before attempting such a project, Debo was intrigued. She told Lottinville that if she could confine herself to Indians of the United States, she might undertake such a work one day.

In the meantime, Angie applied for a Rockefeller Foundation fellowship offered through the University of Oklahoma Press. The chosen scholar would produce a study of Oklahoma modeled on George Sessions Perry's *Texas: A World in Itself* (1942). The latter, an interpretative work, breathed life into the history of the Lone Star State through a series of seemingly artless essays that explored such topics as the economic importance of raising turkeys in farm households.

In her proposal for the fellowship Debo presented Oklahoma as "America in microcosm," a place where "history telescopes, within the lifetime of men now living, the whole story of the United States." Here, in quick succession, had passed Indians, cattlemen, pioneer farmers, manufacturers, and academics and educators. Many of these figures were still alive. It was as if "Pocahontas and Thomas Jefferson and Carter Glass were all living in Virginia at the present time," Debo observed. A study of the state would shed light not only on "the forces that shaped America" but on "the spiritual equipment that this nation now has for its present rendezvous with destiny." In short, an analysis of a uniquely American society, whose dominant trait was "the individuality that makes every Oklahoman stand alone," would illuminate the nation's character as it faced unprecedented post-war responsibilities.

When she received the fellowship, Angie resigned from teaching to meet the one-year deadline. As soon as the Marshall Methodist Church found a resident minister, she also stepped down as lay pastor. Only one other responsibility remained: No one else could care for Lina, now eighty-one and increasingly frail. To assure herself that her mother was close by when she was involved in research at the Oklahoma A & M Library, she rented an apartment for the two of them in Stillwater.

As Angie began her new study, her sense of indebtedness to Edward Everett Dale only increased. Since her days as a college freshman, his statements and writings had penetrated so deeply "that I repeat them unconsciously," she wrote him at one point. In *Prairie City*, one of her sentences sounded very much like a statement he had made in his *A History of Oklahoma* (1924), coauthored with James Shannon Buchanan. "'He saw his rude sod house transformed—.' Of course," Angie observed, "I had read it many times before and forgotten it—or rather remembered it so deeply I thought it was my own idea. And I quoted it almost word for word on page 11 of *Prairie City* without once realizing I had 'borrowed' it. And," she continued, "I named my first book, *Choctaw 'Republic'* thinking it was my own idea—and it was yours, too. Well, there just isn't any thing I can do about it, for I do it unconsciously," she concluded. "I guess you taught *too* well, and I learned too deeply. Anyhow I am grateful for this continuing influence."

Dale, "flattered" that she found herself "unconsciously using" his words in her writing, assured her that he had "borrowed from Turner again and again" and more than he knew. She owed him no apologies, for she was his "outstanding student in the field of historical literature," and he was proud of her achievements. Besides, the day was coming when she and others would carry the torch, and "if I have contributed a little of a fire which has lighted it," Dale noted, "I shall be most happy."

With large numbers of World War II veterans entering colleges and universities, the demand for instructors was higher than ever. To help meet that demand, Debo had been teaching courses intermittently at Oklahoma A & M College since 1945. Then, at about the same time she heard that she had received the Rockefeller Foundation fellowship, T. H. Reynolds, the chair of the history department at Stillwater, had offered her a teaching position that, as LeRoy Fischer, professor emeritus of the school, recalls, would have placed her on a tenure track. But Angie declined the offer in favor of other employment. Recently, Edmon Low, the chief librarian at Oklahoma A & M, had asked Debo to become curator of maps at that campus. She accepted the offer. As she wrote Carolyn Foreman, it "is better for me than teaching because it fills certain hours and that is all." "[T]he administration," she added, "wants me to write." Henry Bennett, president of A & M, assured her she could take summers off for research and still remain on the payroll. However much Angie claimed to love teaching, writing was more important to her, a fact she demonstrated consistently throughout her life. She never found it easy though, and years later she confessed, "I enjoy writing a book just as a galley slave enjoyed rowing."

Readers' reports on Debo's completed manuscript on Oklahoma arrived at the press shortly after New Year's 1948. The first unsigned reader—actually Edward Dale—found her interpretation of Oklahoma disappointing. The second reader—who was never identified—castigated her manuscript as "chatty, colloquial, and undistinguished," possibly because she feared being thought "too literary." Worse, her massive data remained undigested. Even though she noted the "many shortcomings of the State and its people," she conveyed these faults, the second critic added, with "a tone of so what? [S]o long as these are our faults, they are better than the virtues of other people." Soon thereafter Lottinville informed Debo that three other scholars also considered her manuscript unsatisfactory. Lacking objectivity, it exuded an "unconscious chamber of-commercialism—a home town point of view which will miss the mark of satisfying the home towners and the out-of-towners equally."

With an unidentified but trusted friend's evaluation that her manuscript was "the best writing" she had ever done, Angie's prickly sensibility concerning criticisms of her work came to the fore, stronger than ever. Although five readers disliked her work, she would not discard "what satisfies me." If the press insisted on major revisions, she would find another publisher. At a minimum, she would not write another book.

By early spring, Debo was revising her manuscript, "not to please the critics but to please myself." She was relieved when she received a letter from Dale, "not as a member of the so called Rockefeller Committee but as your old friend and former teacher." Her dispute with the press troubled him since he had suggested her for the fellowship in the first place. If she would acquire the necessary "humility" and agree to substantive changes, he would critique her manuscript carefully. Properly revised, it could "add much to your reputation as an author." A chastened Debo accepted his offer and spent the spring recouping her depleted energy by devoting weekends to rest and church. After teaching her Sunday school classes, she often drove Lina into the countryside to see the redbuds and other flowering trees in bloom.

In June she received her manuscript, "with a very careful conscientious criticism by Dr. Dale. I will follow all his suggestions—whether or not I agree—except in matters that seem vital to the integrity of my interpretation," she noted in her diary. Among other suggestions, he advised her to avoid the issue of race relations. In his view, although Oklahoma was southern in attitude, racial lines were not as rigidly drawn as in Mississippi or Alabama. "The Negro question is nationwide and very hot. I'd steer clear of it so far as possible," he warned.

Debo refused, seeing this issue as "vital to the integrity of my interpretation." There was one glaring exception to the old adage that Oklahomans "never see a stranger." "Only the Negroes," she noted, "are held outside this general neighborliness." And although blacks had achieved legal victories, including the right to enter the University of Oklahoma, their inability to compete economically left them seriously disadvantaged. At the same time, she admitted that blacks had made some progress:

No respectable editor would now place the story of a fatal accident to a Negro citizen under the heading "Another Dead

Nigger," which I found in a county-seat newspaper of about
the time of statehood. No corporation involved in a gasoline
explosion would now make a death settlement of $7,500 each
for white victims, $2,500 for Negroes, as happened in a disas-
ter that shattered Ardmore in 1915.

Debo was also unwilling to delete, as Dale suggested, the term
"Holy Rollers" from her description of various religious denominations and their practices. In her view, she had described them
accurately and, "unable by nature and training to tell what seems
to me a partial truth," she would forgo publication if the term
was not accepted. She did agree, however, to revise her chapter
on athletics and eliminate her opening chapter, which dealt with
the origin of common stereotypes concerning Oklahoma. In
addition, she would follow editorial advice on various terms and
references that dated her text.

Although outwardly cordial in his letters to Angie, Dale voiced
his disappointment to others. The revised manuscript was "very
much improved" and "publishable" with good editing, "but it will
never be quite what you and I had hoped," he wrote Lottinville.
The disagreements between Debo and the press had threatened
to become an immense problem—or, as Savoie himself phrased
it, "a lulu." Although she acknowledged her indebtedness to the
Rockefeller Foundation, which indicated her willingness to repay
the agency for funding the project, Debo suggested that the
press send the manuscript back to her to dispose of as she saw fit.

The whole situation, which showed once again Angie's great
sensitivity to criticism, did not represent her finest hour. Nevertheless, the final manuscript Angie submitted was better than her
critics contended. In 1987, almost four decades later, historian
Anne Hodges Morgan, who coauthored with her husband, H.
Wayne Morgan, the 1976 bicentennial publication, *Oklahoma: A
History,* noted that she found it invaluable for her research. It
was, in her estimation, "The best and most accurate interpretation of the state ever written."

That is not to dismiss its shortcomings. Because Debo came
from a family that was midwestern in origin and lived in the
region north of the Canadian River, she had less of a feel for the

southeastern portion of the state. Southerners from neighboring states had settled "Little Dixie," and cultural differences clearly divided that portion of the state from other areas. But Debo devoted little attention to evidence of Oklahoma's continuing sectionalism.

The major problem with the book, however, was not of Angie's own making. Originally, she had planned to juxtapose popular myths against realities and to that end had originally entitled the manuscript, *Oklahoma: Where the Tall Superlatives Grow.* She had devoted her first chapter to discussing the work of two prominent authors, John Steinbeck and Edna Ferber. Both, she contended, had written about Oklahoma without bothering to check historical and geographical facts. Unfortunately, given their reputations and popularity, their errors were fixed in the public mind. Although Debo's opening chapter was omitted from the first edition, the issues she raised were important to her and to Oklahomans in general. When the University of Oklahoma Press reprinted the work as a paperback in 1987, the deleted chapter reappeared as a conclusion.

In that chapter, Debo noted that Steinbeck's *Grapes of Wrath* portrayed tenant farmers in eastern Oklahoma as driven off the land by the mechanization of agriculture and the dust bowl. The dust bowl, she explained, had affected only the state's western Panhandle and a small contiguous area. Other states, especially Kansas, had lost a greater percentage of their population to the calamity. Yet, because *Grapes of Wrath* was so well known, the public identified the nation's most sustained and serious ecological disaster with Oklahoma.

As for Ferber, she had spent thirteen days in Oklahoma conducting reserach for her novel, *Cimarron*. (Later in a speech before the Writers' Federation, Debo noted that Ferber should have learned more in thirteen days. But, she added sardonically, perhaps she was a "slow learner.") In describing the weather as dry and parched on April 22, 1889, the day of the first opening, the novelist had ignored facts entirely. Spring rains had left the land green, and water was plentiful. Worse yet, Ferber described Yancy Cravat, her hero, as a *"champion of the red men."* In the novel he lost his chance to become governor when he spoke out against Indian reservations. His wife, the heroine Sabra, later expressed hope that one day Congress would free the Indians from their imprisonment. In that story line, Debo stated, Ferber displayed her ignorance of Indian policy. Instead of confining them to reservations, the federal government, acting on behalf of the Oklahoma "boomers," had opened unassigned lands in Indian Territory to outside settlement over vehement Native protest. "Otherwise," Angie maintained, "there would have been no state of Oklahoma; it would have remained Indian Territory." In reality, the hero's efforts to end the reservation system were "about as daring and revolutionary as an editorial in Hitler's Germany advocating the annihilation of the Jews."

With the opening chapter deleted, Debo renamed her manuscript *Oklahoma: Foot-loose and Fancy-free*. Although shortened, the final version was unmistakably hers. Following her description of the state's physical setting, Angie used the discarded historical essay written for *Oklahoma: A Guide to the Sooner State* as her second chapter. Presenting the Trail of Tears as "an Oklahoma epic," she underscored the Indian's vital role in creating the culture of the state. When she had taught occasional courses at Oklahoma A & M, students from other states had told her, "You have a new concept of history here. In my state we start with the first white settlers and tell how they drove out the Indians; here you tell what the Indians built and how the white people came and joined them."

If the University of Oklahoma Press through its Civilization of the American Indian Series, Debo reflected, was now giving the state's Indians "an equal hearing before the bar of history," they still suffered "before the bar of justice." Non-Indians thought that they had solved the problems of Native peoples simply by terminating their communal holdings and awarding them United States citizenship. Although some scholars had described the way that Indians had lost their holdings, few Oklahomans had any idea of "what the process did to their spirit. The hardest hit were the full bloods of the Five Civilized Tribes," Debo wrote. "The most fortunate of all were the hunters of the Southwest."

Debo leveled other criticisms as she wove into her narrative the warnings of environmentalists. In a chapter called "Plowman's Folly," which was based on Edward H. Faulkner's book (1943) of that title, she identified the sodbusting plow as a major cause of the Great Plains dust bowl in the 1930s. She also reiterated the warnings Paul Sears had sounded in *Deserts on the March* and *This Is Our World*. Published by the University of Oklahoma Press in 1935 and 1937, respectively, these works predicted environmental disaster unless the United States ceased exploiting its resources, especially those in the public domain, for immediate gain.

For Angie, many of these resources had already been irrevocably lost. "To the Oklahoman who loves his state, the salient agricultural fact is that much of it has already gone down to the Mississippi delta," she wrote. Given the "light, thin soil; large areas too rough for agriculture; and violent extremes of flood and drought," the usual "method of settlement, although in the American tradition, was the worst possible method for the land." As the last area opened to settlement, "All the bad practices inaugurated at Jamestown and repeated on successive frontiers were intensified in Oklahoma." Later, oil drilling added to the devastation.

These tendencies, Debo observed, had originated in "the pioneer psychology" at the heart of the frontier process. "For nine generations the process had been repeated in the United States, gaining momentum, gaining dignity by association with the noblest of human motives. To establish a family on the land, to build a new society—this was the American ideal." Unfortunately, she added, "slashing the timber, destroying the grass, mining the soil—this was noble, too; this was a part of the process."

With her interpretative work on Oklahoma scheduled for publication in late spring 1949, Angie turned her full attention to other matters. She fretted that several presses, including Knopf, Oklahoma, and others, had rejected her edition of Oliver Nelson's reminiscences. Nonetheless, she prepared for her next project—a survey of full-blood settlements of the Five Tribes in Oklahoma for the Indian Rights Association. For years the fate of these Indians had haunted Debo, and she wondered if the hotly contested

Oklahoma Indian Welfare Act of 1936 had actually reversed the drain on Indian land and resources. If so, were the full-bloods better off; if not, what more was needed?

After leaving Lina in the care of a reliable neighbor in June 1949, Debo stopped at the Union Agency at Muskogee to review available statistics. Then she traveled to out-of-the-way places in eastern Oklahoma, "visiting remote cabins in hidden valleys back from the almost impassible roads that wind through the mountains, or in the brushy tangles that break the plains." In her journeys that summer she came to know, as she later recalled, the location of every "bad bridge" and "all the bad roads in the hill country." The Indian Rights Association could not compensate her, but Oklahoma A & M's president, Henry Bennett, honoring his promise to support her scholarly activities, paid her salary year-round.

Initially, clergy or agency fieldworkers introduced Angie to Indian families. Interviewing members sometimes "on rustic porches or inside rude dwellings where chickens wandered in and out through unscreened doors, or sudden showers dripped into every available vessel through leaky roofs," she wondered if they would respond to her questions. Her misgivings vanished when she found them cordial and forthcoming in their answers.

By late summer, Debo concluded that the problem the full-bloods faced was simple; they were destitute. Once owners of half of Oklahoma, they now existed in "appalling poverty," with the Cherokees suffering the most. Nonetheless, they retained their dignity and demonstrated deep love for their families. The women, despite the lack of running water and other standard conveniences, "keep their dilapidated houses surprisingly neat. The washings that hang on their lines are clean, their beds are clean, and there are flowers blooming in their yards." Most telling, "their sleeping babies are invariably protected with mosquito bar." Certainly, Debo noted, such habits constituted "an important asset to be used in any attempt to improve their condition."

Restoring prosperity would not be easy, Angie knew. Statistically, the full-bloods owned some twenty acres per person, about the same as other rural Oklahomans. Much of what they possessed, however, was located in the Cherokee Ozark counties, the "cut-over pine area of the Choctaw mountains," or the "blackjack-postoak jungle that covers the belt of ragged hills stretching between the rivers to the west"—all of which was unfit for farming. Even though some Choctaw and Cherokee "hill dwellers" held land to the west, these acres were almost useless, for "the idea of migrating to that distant region is as foreign to their experience as it would be for a white Oklahoma farmer to settle among the Eskimos." Finally, since most of the land remained in the hands of an aging population, which was losing thirty-five thousand acres annually through death and the removal of restrictions against sales, the possibility of bequeathing enough to younger Indians to give them a foothold was declining with each passing year.

Surely, Debo argued, federal and state policies that allowed this continuing impoverishment should be reversed and replaced by the systematic purchase of additional tracts. Moreover, expanding the highly successful 2-million-dollar revolving loan program, part of the Oklahoma Indian Welfare Act, would give the full-bloods greater access to credit and help them rebuild their holdings. Already, through the program Cherokees had established strawberry farms, Choctaws had entered cattle raising, and Creeks had added sufficient acreage to transform their farms into profitable enterprises. Additionally, most members of the Five Tribes had repaid their debts in a timely manner.

If alleviating economic distress among the full-bloods was the first step, easing social problems was a necessary second. Although decades had elapsed since the publication of the Meriam Report, tuberculosis remained the foremost killer of Indians, and their infant mortality rate surpassed that of any other group. True, public health services lagged throughout Oklahoma, but some Indian counties had none whatsoever, a condition that required immediate attention.

Debo also called for educational improvement. Perhaps doctoral students seeking dissertation topics in colleges of education could investigate the effectiveness of various programs among Indian children as a prelude to identifying those that were most promising for future implementation. Finally, even though churches had compiled a "heroic history of mission work for the Five Tribes," Debo found ministers often "oblivious to the Indians' economic life." Sparing no feelings, she pointed to the "superficiality" of the churches' efforts and asked for new programs that would attack root causes of suffering. "More than the welfare of a few thousand Indians is at stake," she reminded her readers. "It is a matter of national good faith."

On November 8, 1949, exactly fifty years after the Debo family had first arrived in Oklahoma, *Foot-loose and Fancy-free* was published. As she read it to her mother, Angie was disappointed. Too much had been changed, she wrote Savoie Lottinville, and "all the revisions fall into a simple formula: delete everything that sparkles. The facts and statistics remain, but the interpretation is gone." Although she was grateful to the press, the Rockefeller Committee, and Edward Dale, "who out of his simple goodness undertook the thankless task of composing our differences," she vowed she had written her last commissioned work.

Nonetheless, when Oklahoma A & M honored her for her newest publication and her contribution to Oklahoma history in general, Angie enjoyed the evening. Dale lauded her in his address and Savoie Lottinville and Mary Stith, his editor-in-chief, were among the smiling guests. The collegiality of the event erased much of the earlier rancor.

Later, Dale wrote Debo noting that he had sensed Lina's pride in her daughter when he had met her at dinner. "I am equally sure that you must be very proud of her, for though I claim in some sense to be your academic godfather, I know that you owe any success you ever attained far more to your mother than you do to anybody and everybody else." Intuitively, he had grasped the truth of Lina's role in her daughter's life.

Joseph Brandt, to whom the book was dedicated, now chaired the graduate program in journalism at the University of California at Los Angeles. In 1941, he had left Princeton University Press to return to Norman as president of the University of Oklahoma. During his two years in that office, he had encouraged faculty governance and a restructuring of the freshman and sophomore years before students selected their majors. When faced with faculty resistance and a legislative cut in appropriations, he had resigned. Despite his disappointments, he harbored fond memories of growing up in Oklahoma and his earliest years in journalism and publishing within the state. He also saw Debo's new work as "an entirely fresh approach to Oklahoma." Although her style had changed and no longer showed "the delightfully free manner of *Prairie City*," he congratulated himself for having published both *The Rise and Fall of the Choctaw Republic* and *And Still the Waters Run*. Someday, he predicted, the public would understand that the latter was among "the most significant histories to be published in this century." That would not happen, however, he added, until Americans understood "that the Indian is as important to our knowledge of ourselves as Greek or Roman civilization."

As Debo doggedly pursued a publisher for her cowboy memoirs and assisted the Indian Rights Association as it sought a publisher for her report on the Five Tribes, she also worried about her country and the developing cold war between the United States and the Soviet Union. "Ominous news!" she wrote in her diary on June 25, 1950, when North Korean troops from the Communist People's Democratic Republic moved into the territory occupied by the United States–backed Republic of Korea in the south. "North Korea declared war on South Korea, which means Russia has finally attacked the U.S. We may bluff them off. Otherwise World War III has started." Instead, it turned out to be, Americans were told, an "international police action." But whether referred to as a police action or a war, soldiers were dying in combat.

Fall of 1950 brought additional frustrations as other presses rejected her Nelson manuscript. She found little to lift her spirits. On November 16, when she was inducted into the Oklahoma Hall of Fame, she described the ceremony as disappointing and "tawdry." It was probably not the actual event, but rather Angie's frame of mind that led her to this conclusion. At this point, nothing seemed to be going well. With her recent difficulties in publishing her Oklahoma book still fresh in her memory, the rebuffs she was sustaining from publishers threatened her self-confidence as a writer, one of her major sources of self-esteem. Even worse, with Lina's health rapidly declining, Angie was finding it hard to sleep at night.

Her country's deepening involvement in Korea also troubled her during quiet moments of the day or late at night as her insomnia grew worse. As Christmas approached, she placed herself and her ailing mother at the top of her shopping list. After purchasing a portable record player, she spent an equal amount—$29.95— for Handel's *Messiah,* one of her best-loved pieces of music. On Christmas Eve and throughout the next day, she and Lina listened to it repeatedly. A month later they were still playing excerpts before retiring. "I find I can sleep in spite of what is happening in Korea," Angie wrote in her dairy. Even though "the Communists would call [the music] an 'opiate,'" it served no purpose to "lie awake at night."

The winter of 1950–51 seemed interminable, but Angie knew that spring had arrived when she awoke one morning to the mockingbird's call. Soon after, she received copies of *The Five Civilized Tribes in Oklahoma,* issued by the Indian Rights Association as a brief pamphlet.

In May Debo again left her mother with a trusted neighbor to attend the annual conference of the Oklahoma Historical Society at the old Cherokee capital of Tahlequah. Simultaneously, the Cherokee Seminary Association was celebrating the centennial of the founding of the Cherokee Female Seminary. Modeled on Mary Lyon's Mount Holyoke Female Seminary, it had disseminated Euro-American middle-class ideals of genteel womanhood among the daughters of the Cherokee elite before closing in 1909. After members of the historical society and the seminary association toured the Heritage Center, including the reconstructed Tsa-La-Gi Ancient Village, where Cherokee artisans demonstrated their crafts, Debo read the assembly Grant Foreman's final report to the board of the historical society. Now bedridden with heart disease, he urged fellow members to preserve Oklahoma's historical legacy.

Throughout that year and into the next winter, Debo visited the Foremans whenever possible. Each time she arrived at

Muskogee, she found Grant visibly weaker and Carolyn thinner and more fatigued. Angie knew that never again would the couple guide her around their yard, examining the various trees and shrubs from their global excursions. And never again would the three of them visit nearby woods and meadows to identify the region's songbirds and their calls.

Despite Angie's sorrow over the imminent loss of one of her best friends, her spirits received a much-needed boost in April 1952. After seven years of sending Oliver Nelson's memoirs to various publishers, she finally received a contract from Arthur C. Clarke. The work was now entitled *The Cowman's Southwest*, and its publication within the next several months would bring her name before the historical profession again. Debo was relieved. She knew that she would have little time for writing in the foreseeable future as she struggled with the growing demands of caring for her mother. Although an attendant stayed with Lina during the day, her diabetes and dementia, the latter brought on by atherosclerosis that reduced the flow of oxygen to her brain, compelled Angie to prepare special meals and supervise her mother's activities constantly whenever she was home. Debo could produce a column, "This Week in Oklahoma History," for the *Oklahoma City Times* and review books, but more ambitious projects were at least temporarily beyond her capacity.

Late in April 1953, Debo struggled against despondency as she learned of Grant Foreman's death and admitted to herself that Lina had now lost all hold on reality. The unusual number of electrical storms that season awakened the frail woman almost nightly and brought on hallucinations, which, in turn, made it more difficult for Angie to enjoy uninterrupted sleep for even three or four hours. By early June, Angie was exhausted as she moved her mother back to Marshall, in hopes that more familiar surroundings would soothe her. Instead, Lina's terrors increased. When she sobbed inconsolably one night that a baby had died, Angie decided to seek long-term care for her mother.

Once Lina entered a Stillwater nursing home, her condition improved. For some strange reason, the attending physician explained, it was her daughter's presence that had triggered many of her nightmares and hallucinations. "Our interests are identical," Angie wrote in her diary, as she enjoyed her first full night's rest in years. "I could not have accepted relief at the expense of her suffering, but she is better off, too."

Shortly before Christmas, Debo, feeling lonely and adrift, attended a wedding at the Marshall Methodist Church. The bride, Jane Bryson Burchart, was the daughter of her old friends, Raymond and Mabel Bryson. They and their guests responded to Angie with such warmth that she made an important decision. She would return to Marshall to live after she retired from Oklahoma A & M.

Late in the evening of June 10, 1954, Debo was summoned to the nursing home. Her mother's condition had drastically worsened. As Angie was dialing the physician shortly after midnight, Lina slipped quietly away. Two days later, before the funeral, Angie caressed her mother's hands. Later she wrote in her diary, "I do not grieve much. It is so comforting to have her long nightmare over."

In writing her mother's obituary, Debo reflected on her eighty-eight years of life. Although Lina's schooling had been brief and her calloused hands had testified to her early work in the fields, she had exhibited "a keen intellect, great sensitivity to beauty in nature and the arts, and strong affection for friends and family." When she had children of her own, she had taught them to value education. Angie paid her mother high tribute in summarizing the meaning of her life: "Every place in which she has lived since her childhood has been better because of her quiet influence."

At sixty-four, Miss Angie, having lost all of her immediate family, found that her friends and neighbors in Marshall were more important than ever. Still, as she had counseled Carolyn Foreman following her husband's death, creative work was "the only antidote to grief and loneliness." Angie would also find that a political cause could be as therapeutic as creative work.

John Collier, facing continuing hostility in Congress, declining appropriations for Indian programs, and the threat of even greater cuts, had resigned as commissioner of Indian affairs in 1945. In the years since, Indian policy had taken another turn, and this new direction—"termination"—seemed to Debo a return to the assimilationist policies embodied in the Dawes Act. Many factors had contributed to this development, including an ongoing view that Collier's policies, with their respect for communalism and Native culture, were "un-American" in this cold war era that stressed personal rather than group initiative. During President Harry S. Truman's administration, moreover, Commissioner of Indian Affairs Dillon S. Myer, former head of the War Relocation Authority, viewed Indian reservations as he had Japanese detention centers during World War II. They were "way stations" that needed disbanding.

Even more dangerous, in Debo's opinion, Myer thought that the federal government should redefine its trust responsibility toward Indian tribes. That relationship, which exempted their land from taxation and entitled them to special services in areas such as health, left them, he thought, mired in poverty and dependence. Thus he took action, despite pleas for caution from groups such as the National Congress of American Indians, a pan-Indian organization formed in 1944 to protect Indian rights and pursue self-determination for Native peoples. After ridding the Bureau of Indian Affairs of holdovers from Collier's administration and gaining greater control over Indian affairs for himself, Myer turned many bureau functions over to other federal agencies or state governments. He also encouraged Indians to move to cities to escape reservation poverty. The stage was now set, Debo feared, for a return to "the old bad days."

Those fears had been realized when House Concurrent Resolution 108 passed unanimously on August 1, 1953. A statement of policy, rather than legislation, it sought to "make the Indians . . . subject to the same laws and entitled to the same privileges and responsibilities as . . . other citizens." It would also "end their status as wards of the United States," while granting them "all the rights and prerogatives pertaining to American citizenship."

To Debo, American Indians had never been wards. Echoing the ideas of Felix Cohen, one of the foremost authorities on Indian law, she saw the concept of wardship as a misunderstanding that had arisen from the Supreme Court decision *Cherokee*

Nation v. *Georgia.* In 1831, Chief Justice John Marshall had
described the relationship between a tribe and the federal government as similar to "a ward to his guardian." Subsequently,
even respected scholars, Debo argued, had used the term "unaware
of its technical meaning."

The relationship between the federal government and Indian
tribes stemmed instead, she maintained, from "contractual agree-
ments." Indian tribes had given up vast holdings in the past, but
in return they expected the United States to honor its commitment to provide protection for their reduced holdings and
deliver the services promised, such as health care and education.
In this sense, "[t]he United States as trustee is obligated to protect
the property, but has no control over the person of the beneficiary." Finally, Angie noted, all Indians had become citizens of
the United States in 1924 and were already entitled to their
"rights and prerogatives."

Congress followed HCR 108 with Public Law 280, which
authorized California, Minnesota, Nebraska, Oregon, and Wisconsin to extend their authority, including civil and criminal law,
over reservations, subject to treaties and statutes. Moreover,
Sections 6 and 7, inserted into the bill by Senator Hugh Butler
of Nebraska, gave all other states unilateral permission to bring
reservations under their jurisdiction. Although President Dwight
David Eisenhower had suggested amending the act by requiring
states to consult with the tribes beforehand, he signed the legislation without that provision.

By 1954 Eisenhower's secretary of the interior, Douglas McKay,
wanted the government entirely out of the business of overseeing Indian affairs. As soon as each tribe was deemed ready—on
the basis of its degree of acculturation and its ability to survive
economically without federal trusteeship—it would strike out on
its own. Its assets, including land or income from land and its
natural resources, could be retained by the tribe or distributed to
its members on a per capita basis. Either way, assets would become
subject to taxation.

To Debo, this recapitulation of the failed policy instituted
under the Dawes Act would have the same tragic consequences.

Despite her grief over losing the most important person in her life, she was determined to fight the new policy of termination with every ounce of her being. In her mid-sixties, she was free from the burden of caretaking. She was also more secure financially, for she had inherited a farm in Okeene, Oklahoma, and the rental income it provided would supplement her social security when she retired. These factors would now allow her to become more involved in activism. Over time, she would emerge as a strong voice for greater justice for her country's Native peoples.

CHAPTER 7

Battling Termination

IN summer 1954 Debo discovered that the federal government planned to terminate its role as trustee on behalf of the Paiutes. Fearful that these four bands, who owned forty-six thousand acres of desert land in Utah, lacked the resources to protect their interests, Debo wrote Secretary of the Interior McKay protesting the move. Unfortunately, neither her objections nor those of others prevented President Eisenhower from signing the Paiute termination bill. When she learned later that the BIA had transferred oversight of Paiute land to a Salt Lake City bank and trust company more than 160 miles from the reservation, she felt almost helpless. Surely there were ways to challenge the new policy.

Given her heightened interest in Indian affairs, Debo was now serving on the board of the Association on American Indian Affairs. This Philadelphia-based organization was the result of earlier mergers of regional American Indian Associations. Beginning in the 1920s groups had formed in various locations to fight issues such as the Bursum Bill, legislation advanced in 1922 that had threatened the land and water rights of Rio Grande Pueblo Indians. In 1946 the regional groups had merged into a national organization, which elected Oliver La Farge as its president.

Early in summer 1955, several months before her mandatory retirement from Oklahoma A & M, Debo conducted fieldwork for the AAIA journal, *Indian Affairs*. Later she shared her findings on the impact of termination on Indians at workshops in Methodist churches in Oklahoma, Kansas, and Texas. Those in attendance heard the arguments she advanced in two articles for *Indian Affairs*. The first had been published that spring, and the second would appear that winter.

In *And Still the Waters Run* Debo had shown that, although some Indians, especially among the mixed-bloods, had assumed leadership positions in the new state of Oklahoma, the full-bloods were often "completely baffled by the new land ownership pattern and an alien system of law and courts." After the "plundering of their property under state law," they withdrew to the hills or out-of-way places, and when restrictions against sale and taxation ended, these impoverished Indians lost much of their remaining land. The little they retained was often subdivided among numerous heirs.

Oklahoma's East-Side Indians now possessed only some 2 million acres of restricted land—of the 40 million they had owned in 1889. Debo reminded her audiences that restrictions, however, were now being removed from their land at an accelerated rate, often as a precondition to permitting Indian owners to receive assistance or old-age benefits. Moreover, an additional 750,000 acres would become unrestricted in another year when the youngest allottees turned fifty. Although Representative Ed Edmondson had introduced legislation to forestall that outcome, the Department of the Interior insisted on a maximum three-year extension in all but the most unusual cases.

If Oklahoma's "East Side" full-bloods still struggled, the situation was even worse in the semiarid "West Side," where the increasing mechanization of large-scale agriculture left Native peoples unable to make a living. In desperation, younger members of the Plains tribes were moving to cities, where, Debo insisted, "they live in poverty and degradation."

To Debo, the policy of termination was wrong in every way. The prevention of further tragedies in Oklahoma required, not the curtailment of older programs, but their extension. Certainly the agricultural loan system and educational programs, including vocational training, should be restored. And rather than encouraging Indians to leave their homelands, Angie suggested that the Bureau of Indian Affairs consult them and cooperate with their tribal organizations to bring industries to Indian communities in Oklahoma and elsewhere. Finally, she urged the BIA to end its "meaningless shifts in personnel. The value of a good Indian

Service employee mounts in geometrical progression with his years of tenure," she asserted. As she concluded each presentation at the workshops, she urged her audiences to write Congress to protest the hardships the new policies were inflicting on Native Americans throughout the country.

When Debo returned to Stillwater late in July 1955 to vacate her office, she looked around the place she had worked for the past eight years. The time she had spent with librarians, "a most wonderful group of people," had been among the happiest years of her life. Still, she looked forward to retirement since it promised more time for research and writing.

Instead, by early fall Angie was again on the lecture tour, speaking to various denominations throughout Oklahoma on the dangers of the new Indian policy. At this point she was worried about its impact on the Menominee of Wisconsin. This Algonquian tribe of almost thirty-three hundred had prospered by managing a rich store of timber on their 234,000 acres of unallotted lands. In 1951 the Indian Claims Commission, formed five years earlier to settle disputes between tribes and the federal government, had awarded them $7.5 million following their successful suit against the BIA for mismanaging their forests. Since many Menominees were poor, tribal leaders began distributing two-thirds, or $5 million, of their settlement to members in 1953, with each person expecting to receive about $1,500. The Senate, however, at the instigation of Arthur V. Watkins of Utah halted the distribution until the Menominees agreed to termination.

Watkins later argued that termination would give the Menominees "full control of their own affairs," along with "all of the attributes of complete American citizenship." Debo, however, saw his policy as an abrogation of the federal government's sacred treaty obligations. In 1854, the Menominees had given up 3 million acres of land for their present holdings with the understanding that the United States would protect their remaining lands and supply other vital assistance. The Menominee Termination Act, signed by President Eisenhower on June 17, 1954, mandated instead that all protection and services would end in 1958.

Debo's fears were well founded. After complying with the Senate's demand and making its initial distribution, the tribe soon discovered that the Department of the Interior had mandated a second distribution of $778 per member. Now without funds, they also found that their changed status would leave them owing taxes and huge bills to bring their utilities and hospital up to state standards. Thus, rather than benefiting them, termination would plunge them into grim poverty. Eventually the ill-fated policy would be reversed in the Menominee Restoration Act of 1973, largely because of the emergence of DRUMS (Determination of Rights and Unity for Menominee Shareholders), ably directed by tribal member Ada Deer. But, in late 1955, these events lay in the future, and Debo, convinced that the new policy would harm the Menominees, was filled with foreboding and dread.

Seeking every avenue to inform the public about the true nature of termination, Debo recommended Dorothy Van de Mark's "The Raid on the Reservations" to John Fischer, editor of *Harper's Magazine*. Its appearance in the March 1956 issue informed Americans that termination was "a cover for recently accelerated legislation to separate the Indians from their lands and resources, an old and dishonorable game."

As Van de Mark explained, the would-be exploiters used "'emancipation' double-talk" to assure Congress and the American people that termination, relocation to the cities, and assimilation into the larger population would eradicate the ills facing Indians. But the real problems for Indian populations were "poverty, ill health, poor education, and economic stagnation"; termination and relocation would only worsen the situation.

Other threats loomed as well. Passage of the proposed Butler-Malone bill, which sought to rescind the Indian Reorganization Act, would force tribes to distribute their lands and holdings to members, many of whom were "inexperienced in modern business procedure." Consequently, more Indians would lose their remaining land. Finally, the present interim assistant director of Indian affairs, Wesley D'Ewart, a former Montana congressman, had championed "giveaway legislation" for western lands in

1953. If the Senate confirmed his appointment, that, along with passage of the Butler-Malone bill and failure to rescind Resolution 108, would complete "the raid on the reservations."

Debo's letter to the editor in the April issue of *Harper's* elaborated further. The reforms presently under assault, although associated with Franklin Delano Roosevelt's New Deal, had actually originated in an earlier period. Even during the more conservative administrations of Calvin Coolidge and Herbert Hoover, scholars and bureaucrats had recognized that forced allotment and assimilationist policies had damaged Native people irreparably. Now, however, those intent upon subjecting Indians to "naked exploitation" had become more hypocritical. Modern-day exploiters used slogans, such as "grant full citizenship," "abolish wardship," and "free the Indians from the reservations." Again, Debo reminded readers that Indians had attained "full" citizenship in 1924 and were not "confined on reservations any more than other citizens [were] confined to homes they happen to own." The "dire poverty" in which some Indians lived would be alleviated through "education and economic opportunity" rather than through "'emancipation' from their last landed refuge."

Both Glenn L. Emmons, BIA commissioner since August 1953, and Wesley D'Ewart responded to Van de Mark. The former dismissed her essay as "tilting at windmills and knocking over straw men," while D'Ewart accused her of "inciting emotions" rather than offering "a thoughtful analysis of Indian problems." After all, the Eisenhower administration had requested $137 million for Native peoples, ten times the amount appropriated a decade earlier.

More important, D'Ewart saw the administration as upholding important American values. The government was "built on the freedom of the individual, the right to develop one's capacities, to manage one's own affairs, to go and come as one chooses, and to own and pass on property to one's children." Americans believe, he added, that "segregation is wrong and that wardship for competent people is repugnant to our way of life."

Van de Mark emerged from this exchange fearful that she would be investigated as a communist, a grave threat during that period. In this cold war era, Senator Joseph McCarthy's investigations into "fellow travelers"—communist sympathizers—had left many writers blacklisted and unable to work as journalists or in the motion picture and television fields. Debo, not easily terrorized and prepared to sue any person who accused her of being a communist, saw Van de Mark's article as a useful way of reaching the larger public, especially since it had appeared in one of the nation's most respected magazines. Fischer agreed that the article was useful and thanked the Oklahoma historian for recommending the essay and for her recent letter to the editor. He also asked her to send on to him "any repercussions" from her region of Oklahoma.

Angie, having heard no comments or discussion, sought to generate her own "repercussions." In a letter to Savoie Lottinville she noted that the "good people" of Marshall were "too busy watching the *$64,000 Question*" on television to read *Harper's*. She therefore urged him to contact Fischer and indicate his reaction to the article, along with any comments he had heard. In closing, she observed that had she lived in the 1830s she would have had to "watch the Indians dying on the westward trek." Unfortunately, what was transpiring now was "just as bad."

At sixty-six, Debo was experiencing some distressing changes. On April 29, 1956, she took communion and taught Sunday school for the last time in the Methodist church she had attended since 1902 and had pastored during World War II. Its dwindling membership had persuaded her to join the larger congregation at the Evangelical and Reformed Church of Marshall. She also watched helplessly as a close friend grew weaker from terminal cancer. Kathleen Garrett, a member of the English department at Oklahoma A & M, was the daughter of Vashti Edmondson Garrett, a 1897 graduate of the Cherokee Female Seminary. Thus Kathleen was an important tie to a part of the state's vanishing cultural past. At the same time, her ability to cope cheerfully with physical disabilities, which stemmed from her childhood bout with polio, inspired all who knew her, including Debo. When Garrett died in late July, Angie drew comfort from her own faith in a hereafter. As she wrote Carolyn Foreman, "I know good and sincere people who are not sure of an after life; but I think they are going to be very happily surprised when they get on the other side of the curtain. I cannot imagine," she added, "a spirit like Kathleen's going out like the flame of a match. Life would have no meaning if that were so."

Whatever her personal losses, the threat to American Indians consumed Debo's energies. When she learned that the army planned to tear up graves and raze the home of Quanah Parker, the noted Comanche chief, to build an artillery field at Fort Sill, Oklahoma, she dashed off a spirited protest. To her immense satisfaction, *Harper's* published the letter in December 1956.

As 1956 ended, Debo looked back on the year with some frustration. Rather than spending her retirement writing books, she had become ever more active in the struggle against what she perceived as new threats to Indian welfare. Still, since she was now in her late sixties, she was less concerned about maintaining her professional standing through publication and more attentive to the ongoing needs of present and future generations of Indians. It was unthinkable, she informed her circle of relatives and friends in her annual Christmas letter, that she would "refuse to apply the findings of my years of research to a desperate contemporary situation. If I ever see a decent Indian policy in effect once more, I will draw a long breath and settle down to my proper work."

Early in 1957 Angie discovered, to her consternation, that Commissioner Emmons had been cited in an article in the November 1956 issue of *The Clubwoman,* the journal of the General Federation of Women's Clubs. He was arguing once more that termination served the Indians' best interests. Moreover, the Eisenhower administration was so concerned about the welfare of American Indians that, after conducting "sound economic surveys," it would introduce "new manufacturing plants" to reservations. These factories, along with the relocation of other Indians to major urban centers, would increase their opportunities for employment and economic advancement.

Wasting no time, Debo wrote the editor of *The Clubwoman,* noting that "not one of these manufacturing plants near the reservation has yet appeared." To the contrary, the commissioner had closed a Cherokee weaving site in Oklahoma, a Sioux garment factory in South Dakota, and Indian canneries in Alaska. Emmons had stood by, moreover, while a Bulova Jewel Bearing plant employing "one hundred desperately poor Indians" in North Dakota had closed its doors.

Debo's last example was a reference to the Rolla, North Dakota, ordnance plant near the Turtle Mountain Chippewa Reservation. Conditions there illuminated the problems arising from the new policy. Senator William Langer of North Dakota had held meetings of the Juvenile Delinquency Subcommittee around the country in centers of Indian population. Since he saw opportunities for industrial employment as important in preventing crime among poorer youth, he wanted the Rolla plant left open. In addition, he was joined by senators from ten other western states who agreed with him that the plant was vital to national interests. As the military's sole producer of jewel bearings, its closure would leave the United States dependent on a foreign supplier. To counter that possibility, Langer and others were sponsoring Senate Bill 809, which would encourage industries to locate near reservations through a combination of loans and grants.

Even though Commissioner Emmons agreed with Senator Langer that reservations needed industries, he was even more determined to extricate the federal government from Indian affairs. In the end, he opposed Langer's bill, thereby assuring its defeat. Debo was incensed. Emmons had been willing to spend $3.5 million in the past year removing Indians to cities, but he was unwilling to allocate federal aid to develop economies on reservations experiencing desperate poverty. In Debo's view, many Indians had left their homelands only to avoid starvation.

The number of Native people living in cities had been increasing since World War II, when new employment opportunities in defense industries had drawn many younger Indians from reservations. But those who were arriving in urban centers in the 1950s were often unprepared for their new lives. Many lacked marketable skills and found themselves unemployed and impoverished. Cut adrift from their families and tribal heritage, they faced a friendless and often prejudiced world and an alien environment.

Unfortunately, the Eisenhower administration's continuing attachment to its present policies only increased the number and severity of these tragedies. The plight of Native people was becoming so severe that concern for them overshadowed all other issues in Debo's life.

But other parts of her life gave Angie immense satisfaction. If she ever questioned her wisdom in retiring to Marshall, the townspeople, proud of her achievements, erased all doubts when they set aside March 28, 1958, as Angie Debo Recognition Day. They invited friends and dignitaries from far and wide. Muriel Wright, the historian who had written the scathing review of *The Rise and Fall of the Choctaw Republic,* sent regrets that she could not be present. Among those who attended, the noted Muscogee-Creek and Pawnee artist, Acee Blue Eagle, expressed gratitude for Debo's struggle on behalf of Native peoples. Angie was also delighted that N. B. Johnson, an Oklahoma supreme court justice, was present. A leading Cherokee, he had served as president of the National Congress of American Indians. That pan-Indian organization had gained additional stature and respect since its founding in 1944 by fighting tenaciously against termination and its threat to Native lands and traditions. Finally, Debo welcomed John Joseph Mathews, whose *Wa'Kon-Tah* in 1932 had brought national attention to the Civilization of the American Indian series of the University of Oklahoma Press. Now he was working on a history of his people, which would appear in 1961 as *The Osages: Children of the Middle Waters.*

On this occasion, C. T. Shades, superintendent of the local schools and master of ceremonies, read congratulatory letters from dignitaries, including President Eisenhower and Oliver La Farge, still president of the AAIA. As the ceremonies concluded, Raymond Bryson noted that Marshall High's first graduating class of 1913, which included Debo, had selected as its motto, "Making through the trackless wilds a trail for others to follow." A plaque bearing that very inscription would now honor Debo in the Marshall High School.

Angie probably reflected on Muriel Wright's absence that evening, for tensions had recently increased between them.

Outwardly they remained cordial, and Debo, never one to harbor animosities, always gave Wright due praise for her accomplishments and her continuing productivity as a scholar. At the same time, however, under Wright's editorship, the *Chronicles of Oklahoma* had published no scholarly reviews of Debo's subsequent works (WPA state guide excepted) since *The Rise and Fall of the Choctaw Republic*. Nonetheless, in 1949, Debo had published an article in the *Chronicles,* presenting evidence that she and other Oklahoma historians, including Wright, had been mistaken about the actual site of the Civil War battle of Round Mountain (or Round Mountains). The engagement, fought on November 19, 1861, between Creeks loyal to the Union under Opothle Yahola and Indians loyal to the Confederacy and the Texas cavalry under Douglas Cooper, was important as the first Civil War battle fought in Indian Territory. The confusion, Debo argued, had arisen because Annie Heloise Abel, who had specialized in the history of the Five Tribes during the Civil War era, had concluded that a map in the National Archives, drawn by Special Indian Agent John T. Cox, identified the correct location. Abel had used that map, which placed the site north of present-day Keystone, near the confluence of the Arkansas and Cimarron rivers, in her 1915 *The American Indian as Slaveholder and Secessionist*.

Joseph B. Thoburn and Muriel Wright, collaborating on a 1916 history of Oklahoma, had accepted Abel's view, as had Debo in *The Road to Disappearance* and *Tulsa: From Creek Town to Oil Capital*. Residents of Yale, Oklahoma, in Payne County, however, had long disagreed. Their local tradition held that fragments of blue china and pieces of stoves, wagon irons, and cooking implements, which they found in a campground near an area known as the Twin Mounds, east of present-day Stillwater, came from the battle. The debris, they conjectured, had been left behind by the pro-Union Creeks, who fled with Opothle Yahola to Kansas.

After studying both the site and Indian archives, Debo interpreted later Creek accounts as congruent with this conclusion. She believed, moreover, that statements by Pawnee Indians, who found similar artifacts after settling the region in 1875, strengthened the case for Payne County. Wright, unswayed by such arguments, maintained that Cox had identified the correct location farther east.

Despite ongoing scholarly debate and her continuing fight against termination, Debo was at peace with herself in a new way. For the first time, she was enjoying relative affluence. During the fall of 1957, she had taught a full schedule of courses, including a history of Oklahoma and a U.S. survey course, when her friend, Professor Berlin B. Chapman, had taken a sabbatical leave from what was no longer Oklahoma A & M but now Oklahoma State University.

With this extra income, Debo wanted to see Russia. To that end, she enrolled in a European seminar for social action through her new church affiliation. Led by the Council for Christian Social Action of the Congregational Church, the group was traveling to East Germany, Poland, and—the high point—the Soviet Union, with stops in Western Europe.

Debo, who had followed events in Russia with intense interest since the Revolution of 1905, had long dreamed of visiting that country. Now was an opportune time. Since Joseph Stalin's death in 1953, the new Soviet leader, Nikita Khrushchev, had inaugurated reforms. Angie hoped that at long last Russian leaders would bring their people into a new and happier era.

As she prepared to travel abroad, Debo had little inkling that this would be the first among many trips that would take her over a large portion of the world. Eventually, she would visit not only Europe but Mexico, portions of Africa, and Alaska as well. These journeys would broaden her perspective on race relations in her own country by placing the problems of the United States in a larger context. She would learn that people around the globe were struggling for freedom and advancement and, at the same time, the right to maintain their traditional way of life. Her travels would also underscore the high moral cost her nation was paying for the entrenched racism that lay at the heart of its "real imperialism."

CHAPTER 8

The Wider World Illuminates
the Homeland

IN early July 1958, Angie was touring England and Europe with
the Council for Christian Social Action. While the group visited
the usual attractions, including the Tower of London, the British
Museum, Westminster Abbey, Stratford-on-Avon, and Warwick
Castle in England and Notre Dame Cathedral, the Invalides, and
the Louvre in France, they took away more than photographs
and postcards from these two countries. They gained a greater
understanding of international problems and the contributions
they could make as Christians in a polarized world. On one hand
were the nations that had recently emerged from colonialism but
still lacked true self-determination and the other groups throughout the world that still struggled for independence. And on the
other hand were nations determined to retain their possessions,
the last vestiges of imperial glory. The dangerous rivalry between
the United States and the Union of Soviet Socialist Republics
exacerbated these divisions.

The tourists also learned that race relations in the United States
weighed heavily on the minds of Europeans. At a tea hosted by
members of Parliament prior to a session of the House of Com-
mons, Angie paid close attention as Llywelyn Williams, M.P.,
responded to a question about England's problematic relations
with its former colony, India. He reminded his American guests
that their country had not yet put its own house in order. Continuing racial segregation at home was undercutting United
States standing in the world.

Days later in Paris when André Fontaine, foreign editor of *Le
Monde,* addressed the group, Debo again listened intently. The
situation in Algeria, where a movement to overthrow colonialism

had recently brought down the Fourth Republic, struck him as similar to that faced in the American South. "Promises were made to Algeria in 1947 to give them rights. Laws were passed but nothing was done."

Suzanne Labin, another French commentator, reinforced those commonalities. She argued that, although French colonialism was more humane than that of the Soviets, it was not enough to be "better than the devil." Her country had made mistakes; "the most objectionable was the disregard of the human dignity of the natives. Disdain for other races is the most deeply rooted of all human errors," Labin observed, "because it is bound to the most highly developed of all human illusions, which is enhancement of one's own self. You know that it is the same old prejudice, my American friends, which feeds segregation in *your* country."

After touring East and West Germany, Angie and the other seminar participants traveled to Poland. In Warsaw, they visited the site of the Jewish ghetto. Only two hundred of the half million Jews who had lived in this section of the city in 1942 were still there at the end of World War II. That fact brought home to Angie and her group the very real dangers inherent in pseudoscientific theories of racial inferiority, such as those that Adolf Hitler's Nazi regime had subscribed to and had imposed on conquered areas of Central and Eastern Europe.

The traveling seminar then flew to Moscow, where they arrived late at night on July 21. When Angie viewed the city by moonlight—the city she had yearned to visit for so long—it struck her as "strange, beautiful, [and] fabulous." Its people seemed "[p]roud, energetic, [and] confident." Debo and her compatriots visited the major sites, taking in the Lenin Mausoleum and the Kremlin before traveling to Leningrad (formerly St. Petersburg), where they stayed at the October Hotel. Later they viewed the artistic treasures in the Hermitage Museum in the Old Winter Palace and toured the October Revolution Museum.

Finding herself in Russia after years of studying the country thrilled Angie. Nothing had prepared her, however, for the "strange contrast between the barbaric splendor of the past—the many-domed churches, the palace treasures of the czars—and its confident forward look." She sensed the Russians' pride when they spoke, in excellent English, of Sputnik, the first satellite to be launched into space. The statement Angie heard most often, however, was "We want peace."

Debo had always hoped that the Russian people would overthrow the forces of tyranny, but, despite Khrushchev's reforms, she felt the weight of a police state around her. Although the Russians were bookworms—constantly reading, even in the Metro stations and on the subways—their libraries held only those volumes the censors approved. Angie refused to step inside these buildings or any "place where people are permitted to read just the things that some dictator wants them to read." Even though visiting Russia marked the realization of a long-standing dream, she was relieved to breathe "free air" again when she arrived in Helsinki, Finland, on August 3.

Home by mid-August, Debo reflected on her tour. Certainly her commitment to free speech had deepened. She was also more convinced than ever that her country's failure to achieve racial justice threatened its standing internationally, and by 1959, she was serving as a member of the Oklahoma Advisory Committee for the Commission on Civil Rights.

Since her retirement, Debo had become active in the Marshall Woman's Club. Given her recent experiences, she encouraged the organization to bring foreign students from nearby Oklahoma State University to town. During the Christmas season of 1959, local families showed students from Argentina, China, Iran, Japan, and Pakistan around their farms and explained the workings of their equipment and their methods of agriculture. The youth reciprocated by appearing at holiday events in their native dress to share their countries' religious traditions and celebrations.

Meanwhile, Marshall continued to shrink as more residents gave up their family farms and moved to cities. Debo's earlier forecasts in *Prairie City* were coming true as the region's farmers were drawn increasingly into the larger world—but with a difference. Youth from abroad were bringing the world itself to Marshall's doorsteps as they formed strong ties with local families.

Angie had enjoyed her European trip so much that two years later, at seventy, she accompanied a similar seminar group to Mexico. This time they were visiting a Roman Catholic country where only a small minority were Protestant. Debo was distressed that even here, where full-blood Indians still remained a large entity—about one-sixth of the population—the more numerous mestizos, or mixed-bloods, often viewed them as inferior. Was there no place where Native peoples were accorded equality and justice?

Debo took copious notes on Mexico's anthropology and history while she attended lectures in the Museum of Anthropology in Mexico City. These sessions covered, among other issues, the status of women, a topic largely ignored in her earlier travels. Since poorer Mexican women were denied educational and occupational opportunities, many saw no alternative to early marriage. Consequently, they often bore numerous children, making their families' ascents from poverty even more difficult.

Although all the lecturers acknowledged that Mexico had made substantial progress in the twentieth century, Debo was concerned about the government's policy of maintaining low wages to attract capital and investments from abroad. She discerned "a latent unrest in Mexico (I hope I'm wrong) if labor doesn't get [its] fair share." She had seen enough to know that, whatever the future held, workers were already suffering "at 15 pesos a day." They, and not the wealthier classes, bore the cost of national development.

Angie, like many in her party, suffered from the nausea and diarrhea commonly known as "Montezuma's revenge." Despite her illness, she was determined to see the countryside. Later, she recalled the "breath-taking beauty of the landscape and architecture, impressive remains of pre-Columbian civilizations, and poverty and backwardness along with dedicated efforts to relieve [both]." When her group arrived at the mission at Cheran, an Indian town numbering about six thousand residents, Debo considered herself amply rewarded. Although hotel accommodations were poor, she gained a true sense of how contemporary Indians lived in Mexico.

Once she had returned home and recuperated from her trip, Angie began working on brief biographies for *Notable American Women*. The commissioning of this compendium signaled the beginning of a change in the history profession. In 1955 the noted Harvard historian, Arthur M. Schlesinger, had observed that females were seldom included in the *Dictionary of American Biography*. The three volumes of *Notable American Women* attempted to correct that oversight. Debo's assignments included the biographies of Milly Francis, a Creek woman awarded a Congressional Medal of Honor; noted Oklahoma clubwoman Roberta Campbell Lawson; and Alice Brown Davis, an activist who functioned briefly as chief of the Florida Seminoles. In addition, Debo summarized the life of Ann Eliza Worcester Robertson, who served as a teacher among the Creeks and translated Scripture into their language. Angie also submitted a brief essay on Cynthia Ann Parker. Captured as a child by the Comanches, Cynthia had given birth to Quanah Parker, the chief whose home Angie had sought to protect from destruction earlier. Although Cynthia Parker was returned to her Texas relatives in adulthood, her heart, Debo noted, remained with the Comanches until her untimely death in her late thirties.

Angie also watched the developing political battle that fall with growing interest. She rejoiced when John F. Kennedy won the presidency in November 1960, in part because she always supported the Democrats, but also because she saw his victory as signaling a change in Indian policy. When the president-elect appointed Stewart Udall secretary of the interior, Debo was elated. The former Arizona congressman was both a conservationist and an advocate of bringing economic development to Indian reservations. By February 1961 a special task force, chaired by W. W. Keeler, principal chief of the Cherokees, was considering changes in Indian policy. Angie, confident that termination would be repudiated, looked forward to spending less time fighting injustice and more time writing history.

In August she began by editing a work she had used in *The Rise and Fall of the Choctaw Republic*. H. B. Cushman, the child of missionary parents who had accompanied the Choctaws to

Indian Territory, later renewed his friendships with former Indian companions while attending Marietta College in Ohio. In 1899 he visited the Choctaws and Chickasaws in their homeland as they faced the breakup of their tribal lands and the end of their autonomy. Moved by that experience, he recorded his reminiscences. He also added to them, Debo recalled years later, "some religious reflections, and so forth, until his book was about twice as big as it ought to be, and had a good bit in it that wasn't of any value." When her friend, book dealer and printer, John Hinkel of Stillwater, obtained the copyright to *History of the Choctaw, Chickasaw and Natchez Indians,* Debo removed the extraneous material and added her introduction and an index for a new edition.

If Angie felt relieved about the possibility of a more benign Indian policy, her involvement in both the Indian Rights Association and the Association on American Indian Affairs alerted her to a new struggle unfolding in Alaska. Following its admittance as the forty-ninth state in 1959, Alaska's Native peoples—Indians, Aleuts, and Eskimos (the latter now usually called Inuits or Innuits)—were in danger of losing their lands as Indians had lost theirs in the lower forty-eight states. In August 1962, La Verne Madigan, executive director of the AAIA and able activist, died after she was thrown from a horse. In shock, Angie wrote in her diary, "God help the Indians and Alaskan natives. Nobody else can." Debo was wrong, for, as it turned out, she soon discovered that she herself could take action. In her 1962 Christmas greeting, she alerted friends and relatives to the problems Alaskan Natives faced. Again she was being drawn into activism.

Keeping abreast of developments, Angie sent information from the AAIA and IRA to friends and neighbors. After touring the British Isles in the summer of 1963, she returned home reinvigorated. She enjoyed a pleasant autumn until November 22. When Ramona O'Neill called that afternoon with news that President Kennedy had been shot, Angie sat immobilized by her radio until word of his death was broadcast. Later that evening she joined her neighbors, the O'Neills, and afterwards wrote in her diary, "It helped a little for us to be together."

On Sunday, November 25, Debo shared her reflections on Kennedy's death with her church congregation. Although she grieved that an assassin's bullet had claimed him in midlife, she found comfort in an insight "that sometimes comes to us when we write." Perhaps, Angie told those gathered in the church, "his youth and charm, plus the shock of his tragic death, [would] create a 'Kennedy legend'—akin to the 'Lincoln legend'—that [would] make his personality and his recorded words a living influence throughout the future of his country and of the world." If so, "his shining presence in the American pantheon might turn the course of history more than the deeds he could have accomplished had he lived."

In the nine years since her mother's death, Debo had completed no major work. But her release from the demands of caretaking and employment had given her the chance to travel widely. That, in turn, had broadened her vision by deepening her understanding of the interrelationship of her country's treatment of people of color and its moral authority in the larger world. Her new insights only reinforced her conviction that her nation's greatest problem stemmed from the lack of justice and equality accorded minorities.

Angie's interest in the larger world continued unabated. One fall day in 1964 she and the Marshall Woman's Club welcomed Oklahoma State University students from Sudan, India, Nicaragua, and Thailand to their town. Under her direction, friends and neighbors presented a slide show of "cattle drives, the race for homes, our early sod houses and schools, etc.," while others added "family reminiscences." The students were taken to the nearby Chisholm Trail and shown "the site of the first crossroads store, the mark of a dugout home in a creek bank," and other sights. At noon that day they all shared a chuck wagon meal at a roadside park. There one little boy discovered "an Indian knife of beautifully chipped flint." Happily, Debo's neighbors recognized this artifact as signifying their "real beginnings."

Summer 1965 found Angie substituting as teacher of creative writing for her friend, author Terry Allen, at the Institute of American Indian Arts in Santa Fe. The three-year-old school offered Native youth of secondary school age (often orphans or Indians from broken or unstable homes) courses that ranged from painting and sculpture to music, drama, and writing. Before turning the class over to Debo, Allen had encouraged her students to plan their future by instructing them to write their auto-biographies "from the time you were born until you are thirty years old." The quality of those papers left Angie astounded and reinforced her appreciation for Indian creativity and artistic expression. Later, when New Mexico State University selected eighteen winners from a statewide writing conference for youth, six were chosen from Allen's writing classes. (Two years later the University of Oklahoma Press would publish *Miracle Hill*, the work of Emerson Blackhorse Mitchell, a Navajo student who had learned English at the Santa Fe Institute.)

In 1966 Debo enjoyed another memorable summer when she realized a long-sought dream. Her friendship with Philip Ngegwa, a young Oklahoma State University student from Kenya, had heightened her interest in that region of the world. At seventy-six, as indomitable as ever, she toured central Africa with the American Committee on Africa. The group arrived at Kinshasa (formerly Leopoldville), the capital of the Democratic Republic of the Congo, early on the morning of July 30. Although tired, Debo attended the scheduled lectures and afterwards reflected on the struggles tearing the former Belgian possession apart. After achieving independence in 1959, tribal conflicts had erupted, exacerbated by cold war rivalries and the continuing impact of Belgian mining interests in the province of Katanga. "I haven't much hopes for that populous conglomeration of disunited tribes," Debo concluded. "If they ever make a nation it will be after much time and travail." She blamed much of the trouble on "the cruel oppression by wicked old King Leopold" and later the country's development under Belgian rule that never prepared the people for independence.

As Debo's group waited to board their aircraft for Entebbe, Uganda, "soldiers armed to the teeth took a plane preceding ours." Jolted, Angie realized she was traveling in an area of danger-ous volatility. She was relieved when the group reached their destination early Sunday morning, July 31. In the next few days they visited Murchison Falls and traveled the Nile by motor launch to a safari lodge. At night Debo heard the hippopotamuses grunting in the river and the roar of elephants. During the day, she and her group observed crocodiles, monkeys, and exotic birds.

On August 3, after a hot, crowded bus ride, the tour arrived at Fort Portal after nightfall. The next day Angie was sick with a "bad cold & diarrhea," as guides drove them over the Rwenzori Mountains to see the rain forest. Proudly, she noted in her diary that she had crossed the equator. Two days later, upon arrival at the Grand Hotel in Kampala, she was desperately ill. A nineteen-year-old woman, Betty Nakedde, a nursing student employed that summer in her family's hotel shop, cared for Debo until she was out of danger. Immensely grateful, Angie spent an evening with the young woman, listening to her life story. When the tour departed for Kenya and Tanzania, Debo expressed the hope that one day they would meet again.

The high point of the African trip for Angie was her journey to Luxor, Egypt, a source of fascination since her Chicago days when world-renowned Egyptologist James Henry Breasted had lectured on campus. Moreover, she wanted a stone from the Valley of the Kings for the O'Neills, since she could afford this side trip only because they had paid for the additional cost. Despite her recent illness she braved the heat, which reached 112 degrees, as guides took her and a smaller party to the pyramids. She returned home with two stones, one from the front of Tutankhamen's tomb and the other from the area before Seti's.

Although Angie arrived back in Marshall still sick, the trip had been worthwhile. She had made a valued friend in Betty Nakedde, and she now understood more fully the struggles facing the newly independent African states. On the whole, her travels through the new central African nations had left her exasperated. "They need capital, but they haven't enough exports to acquire it; they can't export more until their industry and agriculture is modernized; they can't modernize until they have more skilled labor and management; they can't develop more s. l. and m. until they have more schools," she informed friends. "But, they can't establish more schools until they have a larger tax base; they can't have a l.t.b. until they have more capital to start new industries; and so on over the same circle. It reminds me," she added, "of the sentence we used to translate in our high school Latin. 'All things had to be done by Caesar at once.'" Still, she was optimistic. Seeing their governments as "democratic," and the people as "industrious and capable," Angie predicted that they would triumph.

In her greetings for Christmas 1966, Debo focused on the "meaning" of the season, and expressed the wish that the United States would cease "dropping bombs and extend that meaning to Viet Nam!" The war in Southeast Asia struck her as an ever more troubling tragedy. A faithful Democrat, she blamed her party's setbacks in the midterm elections on frustration over the conflict. "People don't know what is the matter so they just strike out at all constructive movements," she observed.

She also feared that Americans were turning away from civil liberties. When Everett Dirksen, senator from Illinois, introduced a constitutional amendment to permit prayer in the public schools, Debo became incensed. She wrote Oklahoma senator Fred Harris, noting that as a devout Christian who attended church, taught Sunday school, and believed in the efficacy of prayer and Bible reading, she had "no desire to force my private religious practices on those who have equal freedom to their own beliefs." In her view, "it would be a calamity to weaken our constitutional guarantees."

The summer of 1967 found Angie in Norman, teaching a National Defense Institute course on Indians of the United States. Spurred on by Sputnik and competition with the Soviet Union, Congress had passed the 1958 National Defense Education Act to strengthen math and science education in the United States. Soon other subjects qualified for funding. Debo's students at the summer institute taught Indian children at Indian Bureau, church, and public schools. In an effort to bolster their understanding of their pupils, the institute at the University of Oklahoma offered them coordinated courses in American Indian history and anthropology.

Although her relationship with Muriel Wright remained tense, Debo chose Wright's *Guide to the Indian Tribes of Oklahoma* as the major textbook for the course, since it covered a number of tribes. The course, The United States and Its Original Inhabitants: An Indian Interpretation, was entirely Angie's, however, and her syllabus informed students that the class would be taught "*from the Indian point of view.* This will apply to the geographical setting," Debo noted, "for example, Lewis and Clark did not *go out* from St. Louis and encounter Indians, but the Indians saw the explorers *coming up* the Missouri River to them. The same," she added, "will apply to intangibles; events and policies will not be traced from above, but from the inside looking out. We will be interested in the Indians' reaction to people and events and the effect on the Indians."

Her students' enthusiasm and conscientiousness turned the course into an exhilarating experience. When the institute ended, Debo wondered how some of them were able to afford the trip home, since she was certain they were penniless after buying every book she recommended. Several, moreover, asked for copies of her notes, a request Angie had to refuse since no one could read them, save herself.

Still their requests set her thinking. Although Wright's work was an excellent summary, it dealt only with Oklahoma Indians, and much had happened to Native peoples since its publication in 1951. When Debo asked Ed Shaw, Lottinville's successor, if the University of Oklahoma Press was interested in a survey of Indians in the United States, his enthusiastic yes settled the matter. She would write that book.

After a trip to New Mexico to refresh her memory on the background of the Pueblo Indians and their relations with the nomadic Indians and the invaders from New Spain, Angie returned home. Now better informed about the Indians of the Southwest, she settled down to sustained writing. By December 1967, she was at her desk from eight until noon daily except for Sundays.

Despite her progress, Angie wrote Edward Dale and his wife Rosalie that Christmas that she still had "a long way to go." But her doctor had recently declared her "*a Perfect Human Being*," so she expected to complete her book. Only one problem concerned her: the "crashing of bombs in Viet Nam, with the resulting paralysis of domestic progress and the decline of our moral prestige throughout the world." Debo saw Lyndon Johnson as misled by his generals. They thought "that the way to make a country into a happy democracy is to flatten it, and when that doesn't work, escalate the process." Regrettably, the president knew no Indian history. "The best hardware of the time didn't help much when the Seminoles hid out in the Everglades or the Apaches in the mountains," she observed. "I hope—and pray—that next year we may have a presidential candidate of one party or the other who would reverse this policy."

As Angie faced her seventy-eighth birthday, she saw her work, a study of America's "real imperialism," as more timely than ever. Originally she had wanted to examine her country's treatment of its Native peoples to throw light on continuing problems at home as Americans assumed the mantle of world leadership after World War II. But Savoie Lottinville, as director of the University of Oklahoma Press, had told her that such a book would not sell. He had suggested instead that she write a history of the Indians of North America. Debo had responded that, if she could narrow the subject to Indians of the United States, she might tackle such a work one day. Slowly over time, the events of her life and national and international developments had brought her to the point that completing that work was now the foremost goal of her life.

Debo knew that her country needed the insight that came from examining its past as the first step toward righting old wrongs. Equally important, the history of Indian-white relations demonstrated the futility of using military power to change the values and culture of another people.

Certain that her projected book was essential to her fellow Americans, Angie Debo, still energetic and hearty, was hard at work. From her home in Marshall, Oklahoma, she was writing an overview of the history of Indian-white relations in the United States. And to the best of her abilities, she was telling that story *from the Indian point of view.*

CHAPTER 9

A "Scholar-Warrior"

ON January 31, 1968, North Vietnamese regulars and South Vietnamese guerrillas, the Vietcong, launched an offensive against the United States and South Vietnamese forces. Coming without warning on Tet, the beginning of the Vietnamese New Year celebration, it stunned Americans. Television viewers saw the Vietcong briefly occupy the United States embassy in Saigon. Although the offensive failed militarily, the determination behind it left many supporters of the war shaken. Increasing numbers of Americans, characterizing themselves as "doves," swelled the ranks of the antiwar movement. Angie, viewing the war as tragic and misguided, held Lyndon Johnson responsible for its continuation.

She tried to concentrate entirely on writing, but without Lina to screen calls, the telephone often interrupted her. Exasperated, she placed an ad in a local newspaper, stating that were she employed in a store or bank, all would "understand that I couldn't stop and visit with them. It [is] the same with writing a book." She asked her friends not to call her before noon.

As winter wore on, Debo watched the presidential campaign of the senator from Minnesota, Eugene McCarthy, with mounting interest. She rejoiced when the antiwar advocate drew almost as many votes as the president in the March New Hampshire primary. When Senator Robert Kennedy of New York, the brother of the slain president, entered the race pledging to end the war as well, Angie was elated. Since she viewed him as a crusader against poverty and discrimination, she saw her country as enjoying "two great candidates for the price of one."

On Sunday, March 31, Angie and her close friend, Gerry Schaefer, listened to President Johnson's televised address. After promising to deescalate the war, he announced that he would not seek reelection. Angie, like most Americans, was shocked. Few imagined that this vibrant man, who loved power and had proved adept at winning congressional approval of social programs in his earlier years as chief executive, would step down. The nation's continuing involvement in the Vietnam War had destroyed his presidency.

On April 5, one week before Good Friday, Angie saw flags flying at half-mast; Martin Luther King, Jr., had been assassinated a day earlier. "Lincoln, Kennedy, King—even Christ—at this time," she lamented in her diary. Two months later to the day, she turned on the morning television news to discover that Robert Kennedy had been shot in Los Angeles while addressing a crowd following his victory in the California primary. Despondent, she made little progress on her book that day or the next.

Given these events and her long-standing interest in civil liberties, Debo became increasingly active in the American Civil Liberties Union. She had followed the organization since it had assisted the family of an Indian girl killed by police in a Chicago slum. Later, when filling out a questionnaire in her mail, Debo discovered that her views "with one exception" (which she never disclosed), coincided with those of the association. Since no Oklahoma affiliate existed, she became "a solitary member." After Hugh O'Neill announced that he had filled out a similar questionnaire with the same results, Debo and O'Neill—and others from Stillwater, Tulsa, and Norman—joined Frank O. Holmes, the pastor of the First Unitarian Church in Oklahoma City, to form the Oklahoma Civil Liberties Union.

Debo was disappointed when the Democratic Party rejected the peace plank at the national convention in Chicago. On election day she voted for Hubert Humphrey, but when Richard Nixon, the Republican candidate, won in a closely contested race, she accepted his victory with equanimity. He showed "more balance" and his new "seriousness" meant, she thought, that he had overcome his earlier tendency to abandon scruples for political gain.

In 1969, shortly after the Gordian Press reissued *Prairie City,* Marshall residents hosted their first "Prairie City Days" celebration to honor the work and their hometown. After a tour of the original schoolhouse, crossroads store, and church sites, residents and visitors attended a photographic exhibit. Finally, Debo, wearing an 1890s dress and shawl and her grandmother's hat, rode in a mule-drawn covered wagon at the head of the grand parade. After residents crowned her Queen of Prairie City, she returned home joyous but too exhausted to attend the evening street dance.

As Debo finished her newest book, now entitled *A History of the Indians of the United States,* she dedicated it to the O'Neills, "who read and understand." On July 20, she celebrated by watching Apollo 11, the first manned flight to the moon, lift off on television. The sight of Neil Armstrong taking his first step on the lunar surface moved her "beyond words." Like many of her compatriots, Debo felt renewed hope for her country, still torn apart by the Vietnam War and the recent assassinations.

In her forthcoming work Debo had included a chapter on the problems faced by Alaska's indigenous people. Entitled "The White Man Gets a New Chance," it urged Americans to help the state's Native peoples avoid the shameful loss of land that the Indians had sustained in the lower forty-eight states.

With the book's publication assured, Angie joined a tour to see the forty-ninth state. By August 1969 she was gazing at Mount McKinley, "wild life, tundra—the works." When her group arrived in Barrow, the northernmost settlement in the United States, Debo "looked across the frozen Arctic towards the North Pole." There and at other settlements, such as Kotzebue, she interviewed Alaska's Native peoples, seeking to understand the difficulties they were experiencing as they struggled to maintain their traditional way of life, based as it was on hunting. On the whole, however, the excursion disappointed her. The information the guides dispensed, she said, "lack[ed] depth." It was her last tour.

When the AAIA described the plight of Alaska Natives in its 1969 newsletters, Debo summarized the information in her Christmas circular. She directed her correspondents to write their representatives, senators, and President Nixon, asking them to support HR Bill 14212 or Senate Bill 3041. Letters to senators were to go out immediately, but others could wait until after the holidays.

The roots of the Alaskan problem went deep. The indigenous people had historically bequeathed their land "by word of mouth and our continued possession." In purchasing Alaska from Russia in 1867, the United States had acquired the right to govern and tax, but it had taken no steps to protect the rights of Native peoples. Injustices were exacerbated when defense installations were built and developers moved in after World War II. Still there was hope. "Because the terrain and climate of Alaska does not invite the settlement and agricultural pattern of the lower forty-eight states," Debo explained, "ninety percent of the land was still in the public domain."

Nonetheless, the 1884 territorial act and the 1958 statehood act, while acknowledging the property rights of Alaska's Native peoples, had allowed Congress to determine their title. At the same time, statehood permitted Alaska to claim 102,550,000 acres from the public domain. Suddenly, Angie explained, "the state and various individuals began pulling the land out from under the natives." In 1969, following the discovery of oil in Prudhoe Bay, companies had given the state more than $900 million in bonuses for oil leases on the North Slope. More would come.

Worse, confusion reigned in the Department of the Interior, which oversaw the Bureau of Indian Affairs. Although the BIA tried to help the Native peoples of Alaska retain their land, another agency under Interior, the Bureau of Land Management, was awarding lands to the state and various hunting and recreational groups. Developers at the New York World's Fair in 1964, for example, had been permitted to sell "wilderness estates" carved out of an Indian village. The BLM rescinded its consent later, but only after a clerk discovered a cloud on the title from an Indian claim filed in 1917.

Stewart Udall, as secretary of the interior, had frozen all sales of land selected by the state in 1966. Since his order would expire late in 1970, Alaska's Native peoples were seeking title to 40 million acres, "the minimum necessary to sustain them." Debo viewed their request as reasonable since, as 20 percent of the population, they were asking for 10 percent of the land, much of it "barren tundra." In July, however, the Senate passed legislation awarding them only 10 million acres, or one-fourth of the land they had requested. If signed into law, the bill would force Alaskan Natives to face starvation or welfare, "a sad end to a sturdy and self-supporting people."

Complicating the matter, Debo noted, stories about Alaska received little attention nationally. Unless citizens persuaded Congress to act, the State would capitulate to developers, and "the Alaska natives would follow the old, sad pattern of Indian history in the 'Lower 48.'"

The response Debo received surpassed her expectations. Some of her friends were teachers or professors who asked their students to write their representatives and senators on behalf of Alaska's Native peoples. Others copied her letters, sending them to acquaintances and relatives and starting a chain reaction. Still others were clergy who reiterated her message from the pulpit or reproduced her information in church newsletters.

Raymond Bryson, a recipient of Debo's Christmas mailing, was a member of the Board for Homeland Ministries of the United Church of Christ, the successor to the Evangelical and Reformed Church. He suggested that she contact Rev. John R. Moyer, the board's secretary for special programs, and Tilford Dudley, a regional director of the church's Council for Social Action. Bryson also sent an article Debo had written for the *United Church Herald* to Oklahoma's congressional delegation.

Shortly afterward, Bryson found himself seated beside La Donna Harris, the wife of Oklahoma's senator Fred Harris. As they conversed, he explained his friend's campaign. Harris, a member of the Comanche tribe, suggested that Debo testify before Congress. Early in September 1970, the historian, whose *Indians of the United States* was due out in October, appeared in Washington. Testifying for the AAIA, she provided expert witness on behalf of Alaska's indigenous people.

In her testimony Debo warned against repeating the old pattern seen in the lower forty-eight states, where American Indians had suffered such massive losses of land that even compensation left them without an economic base. After taking their land, the government had usually overseen their remaining holdings rather than allowing them to manage their assets collectively. Over time, their property had been further divided "into individual shares," which only led to greater "impoverishment." Finally had come "termination," the policy by which the federal government absolved itself of any further responsibility, leaving Native people vulnerable to further exploitation and poverty.

Although she hoped that Alaska would be different, Debo told Congress, "the bill passed by the Senate is an exact recapitulation of these three and a half centuries of exploitation [and] blundering." Since the state's indigenous people often relied on hunting caribou for their subsistence, and it took "a lot of tundra to feed a caribou," she insisted that one-fifth of the state's population was surely entitled to 40 million acres, or one-tenth of the land. The Senate bill, which reduced their share to 10 million, would not sustain them. To those who argued that Alaska's Native peoples should turn to industry, Debo noted that one day they might; presently such opportunities were nonexistent.

Worse yet, the Senate bill also called for creating a commission composed primarily of non-Natives to oversee the land, a return to the very paternalism she decried. The communally owned property of the indigenous peoples would be "divided into individual shares subject to sale." Facing hunger and destitution, they would sell their land as tribes had done in the lower forty-eight states. After all, she reminded her listeners, "how long would our collective property—national, state, local—remain intact if any citizen could claim his share and dispose of it?" Rather than repeat the same old mistakes, policymakers should, for once, "do it right." The next Congress must devise better legislation.

When Walter Hickel, secretary of the interior and former governor of Alaska, resigned that fall after criticizing Nixon's response to student antiwar demonstrations, Debo was elated. She had always viewed Hickel as "no friend of the natives' land needs." She was correct; by November, the House of Representatives was working on a new bill.

Throughout this period Angie kept in touch with her growing network, giving them vital information on the developing bill and sending them the names of committee members from both houses. She also suggested arguments they could use in their own letters, including those they wrote Nixon. Debo now saw the president as a sincere friend of the Indian. In a speech delivered on July 8, 1970, he had expressly repudiated termination by invoking principles similar to those Debo had advanced earlier. The federal government, Nixon stated, bore responsibilities to Indian tribes based on "solemn obligations" and "specific commitments." Moreover, when termination had been tried, the results had devastated the tribes involved and inspired widespread fear among others. The new path Nixon promoted would encourage Indian self-determination, based not on "*whether* the Federal government has a responsibility to Indians" but rather on "*how* that responsibility can best be fulfilled."

Despite the president's commitment to Indian self-determination and the support he gave the Taos Pueblos of New Mexico as they sought to regain Blue Lake, a place sacred to their religious traditions, Debo was increasingly disenchanted with Nixon. Given his failure to extricate the United States from Vietnam, not even support for a wiser Indian policy redeemed him in her eyes.

As the Vietnam War dragged on, Angie expressed her frustration by becoming a more dedicated activist. If she could not change what she saw as the president's misguided foreign policy regarding Southeast Asia, she would work for greater justice at home. Earlier in her career, she had seen the historian's role as that of working "to discover the truth and publish it. Present it to the electorate, present it to the people." As a historian herself her role "was ended when I did that," she had once thought. But now she understood that scholarship alone was insufficient. Like "the farmer or [the] dentist or anybody else," the historian was morally obligated to fight injustice.

Fortunately, Debo's newest book brought her royalty check from the University of Oklahoma Press in 1971 to more than $8,500, the largest she had ever received—and one that she needed as she incurred heavy copying and mailing expenses. As she later recalled, she bought sheets of stamps as if they were "wallpaper" to keep her growing circle of correspondents informed about the Alaskan Native claims issue. Although Angie never mentioned her telephone costs, her many long-distance calls must also have sent her bills phone soaring.

Debo found other ways to work for her cause as well. Asked to speak to groups, she always discussed the Alaskan situation, noting, "No matter what subject I was supposed to speak on, that is what I spoke on." After her speeches, she left information packets for those interested in assisting her crusade and collected their names and addresses. Soon her activist network totaled 265 persons.

More important, many of Angie's friends duplicated her efforts. James Ralph Scales, formerly president of Oklahoma Baptist University and later dean of the College of Arts and Sciences at Oklahoma State University, was now president of Wake Forest University in North Carolina. He contacted every member of Congress and both senators from his state. As he noted in a letter to the O'Neills after Angie's death, "I am sure that Senators Sam Ervin and Everett Jordan thought that a college administrator from North Carolina had developed a curious enthusiasm for Eskimos, but I did as I was told."

In addition, Angie relayed strategy, some from sources she never identified and some of her own devising. Observing that Senator Henry Jackson of Washington, a member of the Subcommittee on Indian Affairs, intended to run for president, she advised her correspondents to write him about the Alaskan Natives, although they were to use their own words in order to avoid any semblance of form letters.

Debo's networking bore fruit. On March 31, 1971, she learned that Representative Lloyd Meeds, also from Washington, had introduced a new bill that would give Alaskan Natives 40 million acres. On April 6, President Nixon proposed his own bill, which included the same acreage. Immediately, the eighty-one-year-old woman set about composing, copying, and mailing letters to her entire network. Afterwards she fell into bed, exhausted from her labors.

The congressional subcommittee drafted its new bill shortly before recess that year. One teenager, a member of Debo's network, was overjoyed. "I was so happy when I received your letter . . . so excited and thrilled to hear that the bill was finally reaching the House floor that I immediately set out to write an announcement for school," the girl wrote Debo. With her principal's consent, she summarized her involvement over the public address system and asked her fellow students to write Congress. Although many fellow students appeared apathetic, she later discovered that a number had visited the principal's office, seeking more information about Alaska's Native peoples and requesting their representative's address.

The House passed the Alaska Native Claims Settlement Act on October 20, 1971. The Senate followed with its own bill on November 1. Debo now mobilized her network once again, asking members to contact conference committee members from both the House and the Senate to make certain that the reconciliation process took away none of the allocated 40 million acres from the final draft.

This was a real danger. Among those opposing the more generous settlement was the Bureau of Land Management, which was distributing acreage for homesteading and oil drilling. Other groups, especially lobbyists for oil companies, believing that "the greatest oil field in North America [was] located on Indian land," had been urging a smaller settlement all along.

On December 14, 1971, Angie learned that the bill giving Alaska's Native peoples title in fee simple to 40 million acres had passed both houses. In addition, it awarded them $962 million for ceding their claims to other land. Of this amount, $500 million would come from a 2 percent royalty from minerals extracted from lands belonging to the state and the federal government. Twelve corporations, based on the ethnic character of the people in various regions, would be established to administer and oversee future developments without oversight from the BIA.

Angie and her circle of correspondents received a joyous Christmas gift when President Nixon signed the ANCSA on December 18, 1971. Oil companies and developers, impatient to see the issues resolved, had acquiesced to the demands of Natives and friends. "But," as Angie reflected years later, "there would have been . . . no settlement, if good citizens had slept while the usual process of dispossessing the original Americans had been allowed to take its course."

Debo also felt encouraged by other signs of progress, especially the changing attitudes of her friends and neighbors in Marshall. She was pleased when they gave a shower to a young interracial couple, a local man who had married a woman from Uganda whom he had met while serving in the Peace Corps. When the couple's son was born, Angie recorded her hope that he would "grow up in an increasingly integrated society."

Spring 1972 brought good news; Princeton University Press was reprinting *And Still the Waters Run*. It would carry the subtitle *The Betrayal of the Five Civilized Tribes* and would include additional illustrations and a new introduction. Debo was overjoyed. "This is my most important book," she wrote the press. "If you were to put all the others on the opposite side of the scale, it would overbalance them." She was correct. To the present, it remains a pioneering work that describes in meticulous detail the economic, political, and social impact of assimilationist policies on five different peoples who had developed their own cultures and had lost far more than a vast amount of their land and its resources. They had sustained as well a terrible assault on their spiritual heritage, and the losses for many were beyond recounting.

Debo was riding a crest. Recent events had heightened the public's interest in works on Native peoples, and the civil rights movement of the 1960s had called attention to the injustice African Americans suffered from segregation and discriminatory policies that limited their opportunities for advancement. In many southern states they had been denied the ballot. The Civil Rights Act of 1964 and the Voting Rights Act passed a year later now rendered such practices illegal.

American Indians, who also endured discrimination, wanted not only their rights as citizens but the right to retain their cultural heritage and their self-determination as different peoples.

In that light, Titles II through VII of the Civil Rights Act of 1968 spelled out the constitutional rights of Indians under both federal and tribal government. The act also stipulated that states could not exert jurisdiction over Indian lands without tribal consent, a reversal of Public Law 280 passed in 1953.

Still, the differing demands of Native peoples left many non-Indians confused. Those who had supported civil rights from the standpoint of ending segregation, in law and practice, often had difficulty understanding the demands of a minority that defended its right to remain different while simultaneously calling for its full rights as citizens. In this context many turned to scholars capable of explaining American Indian history in terms the lay public could comprehend.

Debo was among those capable of delineating the history of Indian-white relations with ease and clarity. She understood that many tribal people preferred self-determination, whereas others sought to achieve varying degrees of acculturation or even assimilation. In her view, such matters were best left to the Indians themselves to decide. She paid little attention, however, to the demands of militant groups such as the American Indian Movement. Within a few months, AIM, led by youthful Indians from cities such as Minneapolis and Chicago, would conduct the Trail of Broken Treaties. That march on Washington, D.C., which would culminate in a takeover of the BIA building in November 1972, would strike Angie as counterproductive for people who, constituting less than 1 percent of the population, were a very small minority in American society. In her view, Indians would achieve progress more rapidly through education and legislation than through disruptive activities that threatened to antagonize the general public.

When it came to Oklahoma Indians, the focal point of her life, Debo had become more hopeful about their future. In her introduction to the 1972 reprint of *And Still the Waters Run*, she recapitulated many of the points made in her 1951 *Five Civilized Tribes of Oklahoma*. Simultaneously, she summarized the more recent developments that inspired her new optimism: Congress had restored the revolving loan fund, although with agriculture becoming increasingly large-scale, Indians now used the fund primarily for small business ventures. The earlier educational acts passed in the 1940s and 1950s were still in place. And more recently the Office of Economic Opportunity created during the Johnson administration had supported cooperative initiatives launched by the University of Oklahoma to bring Indian and non-Indian leaders together to solve community problems.

Debo saw that, although poverty still existed among Oklahoma's full-bloods, their problems were finally being addressed. Even though she no longer conducted fieldwork to determine the effectiveness of programs, she believed that new programs and opportunities were producing "a generation of Five Tribes full-bloods drawing strength and security from their past but equipped to face the present." Perhaps at last, "with an enlightened Federal policy, a dedicated Area Office, and a growing public awareness . . . the lost fullbloods are being saved."

On May 29, 1972, Angie learned that Edward Dale had died. Throughout the day she grieved inwardly as she recalled the last time she had seen him. Two years earlier, she and Gerry Schaefer had stopped by her mentor's residence in Norman after leaving the index for *Indians of the United States* at the University of Oklahoma Press. Dale, in his early nineties but dressed in a dapper shirt and bow tie, had been overjoyed to see his guests. As the two women were taking leave after their brief visit, he had begged them to spend the night with him and Rosalie. Unfortunately, the harvest season had required that Gerry return home to prepare meals for workers in the field. As they left, Angie had told her friend that, in all likelihood, she had seen her beloved teacher for the last time.

After attending Dale's funeral in Norman, Angie felt a pervasive and unshakable sadness as thoughts of him floated in and out of her consciousness. She acknowledged in her diary that he had been "a strong influence" on her life and her writing.

Shortly afterward, Debo began work on a biography of Geronimo, the Chiricahua leader. She had begun researching the life of the Apache warrior soon after her mother's death in 1954. Initially she had hoped to publish an article on him for *American*

Heritage, then put out by the Association for State and Local History.

As a child Angie had imagined the Apache as a bloodthirsty warrior wearing a necklace of scalps. At one point she had even given a particularly "cross-grained" turkey his name. Later, as a student of American Indians, she had noted that ethnologist Frederick W. Hodge dismissed him as "only a medicine man," unimportant to most of his people and famous simply because the press publicized his exploits.

Debo thought the real story might be more complicated. Her friend and fellow librarian Ruth Hammond, the daughter of the Fort Sill chaplain who had served during Geronimo's imprisonment at the post, remembered him as "a kind old man." Hammond also recalled his shrewdness, for he had supplemented his income by selling bows and arrows and charging extra for those he autographed.

In the 1950s, Debo had interviewed members of the Chiricahua band at Apache, Oklahoma, including Jason Betzinez, Geronimo's second cousin, who was then working on his memoirs. During his childhood, Betzinez and his family had fled with the warrior from the San Carlos Agency in 1882. Although Jason remembered Geronimo as a man with faults, the warrior had been "open with his roistering"—more honest than other leaders— and, above all, brave. "In times of danger," Betzinez recalled, "he was the man to be relied upon."

Debo also talked with Benedict Jozhe, another of Geronimo's relatives. His mother, Geronimo's close friend, had found the old warrior lying on the ground and partly submerged in icy water one freezing February morning in 1909. Geronimo had evidently fallen from his horse following an evening of heavy drinking. Six days later he died of pneumonia.

The information Debo uncovered contradicted the common stories. Geronimo had not been a fearful marauder, wearing human scalps and commanding thousands of warriors. Indeed, the Apaches, fearing dead bodies, had seldom practiced scalping, and the number of his followers had been small. The more Angie learned, the more convinced she became that historically the warrior had been maligned. Increasingly she saw him as a stalwart leader searching for freedom for his fugitive band.

By the time Debo finished her article, *American Heritage* had changed. Largely through the efforts of Oliver Jensen and others formerly associated with *Life* magazine it had been transformed into a more substantial publication that sought a wider circulation. The well-known author Bruce Catton was now editor-in-chief. When he received Angie's article, he dismissed it as a factual summary of no interest to "a casual reader." Infuriated, Debo responded that the former editor of the magazine had commissioned the work. Although Catton sent her a check for two hundred dollars, *American Heritage* never published her article. Disappointed, she filed it away, consoling herself that one day she might return to the subject. She knew that her interviews with the Apaches had uncovered invaluable information, and as the years passed she realized that her insights would die with her if she failed to tell Geronimo's story.

In 1960 Jack D. Forbes's *Apache, Navaho, and Spaniard* had convinced Debo that the arrival of the conquerors from New Spain in the late sixteenth century had disrupted the former trading relationship between the nomadic Athabascan peoples and the settled Pueblo Indians. In the end, Spanish policies of divide and conquer and implacable hostility toward the Athabascan bands that became known as the Apaches had forced these Indians to become raiders. Debo gained further insights when Dan L. Thrapp's *Al Seiber, Chief of Apache Scouts* appeared in 1964, followed three years later by his *Conquest of Apacheria*. Both works provided valuable information on Indian-white relations during the period when Geronimo was viewed as a criminal.

Throughout these years Debo also corresponded with Eve Ball, teacher and writer from Ruidoso, New Mexico, and a friend of the Apaches who lived on the nearby Mescalero Reservation. Like Debo, Ball saw these Indians as unfairly vilified by scholars. In 1970 she published *In the Days of Victorio,* the memoirs of Warm Springs Apache James Kaywaykla, who had spent his childhood with another fugitive band under the leadership of the able and wily Chief Victorio.

Debo drew on all these works. She was also indebted to the scholarly contributions of anthropologist Morris Opler, the foremost ethnologist on the Apache way of life. Finally, Gillette Griswold, director of the U.S. Army Artillery and Missile Center Museum at Fort Sill, compiled important records for her on the Apaches who had lived at Fort Sill during a part of their captivity.

By 1972 Debo was determined to present Geronimo as a slandered figure deserving of respect. His followers regarded him as a man of power who, at one point, they recalled, had held off the daylight for several hours to prevent their capture by pursuing troops under Lt. Col. George A. Forsyth. "I saw this myself," one Apache assured Opler.

This was to be her first biography, and Debo used different methods as she approached her task. She examined Geronimo's "individual experiences, his motivations, his personal life and character." She sought clues to his personality in his relations with his family, followers, and leaders, both Apache and outsiders. Above all, she wanted to bring the medicine man and his band to life "as actual human beings with their distinctive characteristics." For Debo, Geronimo's characteristics included his "energy, his determination, and his sturdy independence." Driven by a "strong economic sense," he cared for his family and his band through hunting and raiding. Later, in captivity, he exploited his notoriety by selling souvenirs and banking funds he earned as a "Wild West exhibit." Ingenious and pragmatic in his thinking, he was a formidable enemy, "ruthless in competition, stern and unbending in his judgments, [and] unrelenting in his hatreds." But his love for his children, his loyalty to his friends, and his deep attachment to his homeland, "the unchanging sentiment of his life," softened his character for Debo and won her respect.

From Angie's perspective, the enmity between Geronimo and Euro-American leaders had arisen because, coming from different cultures, they "never arrived at the same definition of truth." United States authorities and military leaders saw Geronimo as "a liar whose word could never be trusted; but if one [could] follow his reasoning," Debo argued, bringing to bear the insights of ethnologists who understood that different cultures often assign different meanings to behavior, he was "a man of essential integrity." He was deeply spiritual, and when he made a promise "with oath and ceremony—mere poetic trimmings to the white man—he kept his pledge." In her view, "A lesser man could not have written his name so boldly on the history of the Southwest."

Whether Geronimo had, in fact, left as strong an imprint on the Southwest as Debo claimed, the personal qualities that attracted her to him are apparent. In addition to the traits she and the warrior shared—energy, determination, and independence, for instance—Geronimo presented Debo with a case study of one of her favorite topics. Again and again she was drawn to the subject of how people who had lost their homelands made a new and more circumscribed life for themselves in an alien environment. Beyond that theme, however, Angie had accepted the challenge of writing about a leader of southwestern people rather than confining herself to the study of a member of one of the Five Tribes of Oklahoma. For a woman in her eighties, her new work represented a daring departure.

Estimating Geronimo's date of birth as about 1823 and finding little information on his childhood, Angie narrated a probable account of his early years as a member of the Bedonkohes (subsumed under the Chiricahuas by Euro-Americans) on the basis of Betzinez's memoirs and Opler's writings. When it came to the historical record regarding the ongoing conflicts that affected Geronimo's life, Debo found the information more complete. After raiding Mexicans killed his mother, his first wife, and their three children, he became their implacable foe. But U.S. attempts to curb Apache raiding south of the border, after the Treaty of Guadalupe Hidalgo in 1848, soon brought him into conflict with Anglo authorities as well. The influx of Euro-American miners into Apache country led to further raiding and warfare.

Irrespective of enmity or friendship, Debo noted, the United States wanted Apache land. By 1875, bands of White Mountain, Coyotero, and Chiricahuas, many of them hostile to one another, were concentrated in a desolate hellhole know as the San Carlos Reservation. Escaping from that situation, Geronimo and his followers became renegades. Captured by trickery and returned to

San Carlos, Geronimo escaped again and again. His fourth and last surrender occurred in September 1886, after General Nelson Miles persuaded the warrior to give himself up by promising him that his people would be reunited in captivity and eventually on a separate reservation. Instead, the warrior and his followers soon found themselves imprisoned at Forts Pickens and Marion in Florida. After further exile at Vernon Barracks in Alabama, they were sent to Fort Sill, Oklahoma, in 1894.

During captivity, weakened by depression and unable to adjust to a humid environment so different from their southwestern home in the mountains, many Apaches succumbed to disease, especially tuberculosis. Throughout his long life, Geronimo implored federal authorities to allow his people to return to their homeland, but to no avail. Despite his sorrow, Debo pointed out, he advised his followers to accept Washington's decrees.

During his last years, Geronimo's world centered on his family, especially his children Robert and Eva Geronimo, who attended the Chilocco Indian School in northern Oklahoma. As he was dying from pneumonia, he struggled to keep breathing long enough to see them one more time. Unfortunately, the authorities at Fort Sill notified them by letter rather than telephone. When his children were not on the evening train on February 16, 1909, Geronimo surrendered to death and breathed his last at 6:15 the following morning.

Completion of Geronimo's biography took longer than Debo expected, but Ramona O'Neill's willingness to type the manuscript expedited its completion. The young neighbor was so conscientious that she once interrupted Angie while she was sitting under a hair dryer at the local beauty shop to point out that Debo had used the same word three times in one paragraph. That needed changing, Ramona insisted. Appreciative of the young woman's work, Angie thanked her in the preface for "perceptive understanding that amounted to collaboration."

Despite her writing schedule, Debo still contributed to church and community activities. One Sunday in November 1972, when she filled in for the minister, she chose for the text of her sermon "the unholy power of what Eisenhower called the 'military industrial complex.'" Afterwards she sensed that many in the congregation disapproved of her topic, although her close friend Raymond Bryson assured her he liked it. Whatever they may have thought of her sermon, Angie was certain that her fellow parishioners needed to be informed of "such issues."

When Richard Nixon won reelection in November 1972, Debo was dejected. The continuing war in Vietnam and "corruption in govt., surveillance of citizens, denial of fundamental civil liberties" weighed heavily on her mind. She remained so disgusted that on Thanksgiving Day, when she awoke to heavy frost and ice on the backyard birdbath, she decided against celebrating the day. Instead, she laundered clothes and started chapter eight of her biography of Geronimo.

On January 23, 1973, Nixon announced that the United States had signed an agreement with North Vietnam, and a cease-fire would begin four days later. Angie saw peace as four years too late. If only, she wrote in her diary, the United States "had left them alone in 1954, had pulled out when things began to fall apart instead of escalating . . . we would have saved many thousand lives and got the same terms."

Debo's downcast spirits brightened a week later when smiling first and second graders greeted her exuberantly at a local elementary school. Waving hand-drawn greeting cards, they pointed to a cake, decorated in celebration of her eighty-third birthday.

Advancing age brought increasing health problems. In September, she learned from her ophthamologist that she had developed glaucoma. Many of her friends now feared for her safety when she drove her twenty-year-old car to night meetings of organizations like the ACLU. Debo, however, refused to think of buying a new automobile since hers was still serviceable. ACLU board members finally convinced her to ride with them to Stillwater. Determined to finish her book on Geronimo, she admonished them to send only their safest drivers to chauffeur her. Her good friend and fellow board member, Gloria Valencia-Weber, recalled that those who did chauffeur her found it a memorable experience. Angie "freely talked about everything from garden crops to the current crop of politicians."

During these years, Debo served as a resource person for the ACLU. Earlier she had argued that Vietnam War protesters had a First Amendment right to protest their government's policies. Given her strong convictions and her knowledge of the Bill of Rights, the Oklahoma ACLU scheduled her for public debates on free speech issues on public radio and in other forums. As Valencia-Weber remembers, "It was really a pleasure" to have Debo represent the organization. Many assumed that someone named Angie would be "a scruffy, long-haired, bearded-hippie type." Instead, "in walked this wonderful woman with a grand-motherly appearance, incredible knowledge, superb credentials, and a sense of humor. Her adversaries simply did not know how to deal with such a knowledgeable and dignified hell-raiser."

Still, Angie often disagreed with fellow ACLU board members. When several on the board expressed concern about public response to their actions, she stated bluntly that "any desire on the part of the American Civil Liberties Union to be universally loved in Oklahoma is neither laudable nor possible, so 'let's get on with the work.'"

By fall 1973, many Americans suspected that President Nixon had overseen the coverup of a burglary in the Democratic National Headquarters at the Washington, D.C., Watergate Hotel. The burglary itself had been illegally funded through the Committee to Re-elect the President in 1972, a group directed by White House staffers. The public also discovered from a Senate Watergate Committee hearing that Nixon had ordered the taping of all White House conversations. When Archibald Cox, the special prosecu-tor charged with investigating Watergate, took the president to court in October 1973 to force the release of the tapes, Nixon demanded his dismissal. When both Attorney General Elliott Richardson and Deputy Attorney General William Ruckelshaus resigned rather than carry out the order, the press termed the event the "Saturday night massacre." In that light, the national board of the ACLU called on the state boards to submit a resolution urging Nixon to resign. Debo, seeing such action as political and, there-fore, out of place, vehemently opposed it. To her dismay, the majority of the Oklahoma ACLU board voted its approval.

As Angie continued writing, she also began using the network established for passage of the ANCSA to help the Havasupais of Arizona. For centuries they had lived south of the Grand Canyon, planting their crops each summer in a nearby canyon. Late in the nineteenth century, ranchers' herds had begun encroaching on their farmlands. A few years later, the Forest Service, claiming jurisdiction over their fields, drove the Havasupais away. Agents justified their action by characterizing these Indians as "wild and unappreciable." Debo noted that the Forest Service had made that statement "about a people to whom every feature of the landscape had a deeply religious meaning and who had safe-guarded the ecology of the region for twelve centuries!" Further-more, one agent who intervened on their behalf—arguing that they were "the most industrious Indians I have ever known, being good farmers and horticulturalists"—lost his position.

By 1973, the Havasupais were confined to an area of about 518 acres on the floor of the Grand Canyon, or a total of less than one square mile for 435 people. Their location was "unfit for human habitation," Debo asserted, "except during the summer season." Moreover, they lacked adequate firewood for fuel and were forced to send their children to a boarding school three hundred miles away. Although the National Park Service allowed them to graze livestock on its land, any housing they erected was demolished.

When they learned of the Indians' plight, Arizona Senator Barry Goldwater and Representative Morris Udall submitted bills in both houses to enlarge the Grand Canyon National Park while giving the Havasupais additional land in the upland region. Both the Department of Agriculture, in which the Forest Service was located, and the Department of the Interior, which housed the National Park Service, objected. Debo was certain that neither the purported desire of the Park Service to open another park in the upland region nor the Forest Service's concern about conserving natural resources represented the issue here. Instead "greedy bureaucracies" were determined to guard their expanding interests.

The Sierra Club of Arizona, understanding the problems the Indians faced, tried to help the Havasupais, but the executive director of the national organization campaigned against them. With Agriculture, Interior, and the national Sierra Club opposed, the bill that finally passed the Senate omitted the Havasupais' grant. In early 1974, when the House passed a similar bill, their fate seemed hopeless.

Angie alerted her network. Once more she sent out letters asking her correspondents to write and telegraph their representatives and senators and encourage relatives and friends to do likewise. Since other groups, as well as Goldwater and Udall, had maintained their efforts on behalf of the Havasupais, the House finally restored the Havasupai grant, and the Senate acquiesced.

Still Debo's work was not done. In mid-December the Havasupais prepared to return to their winter quarters on the plateau. As Angie finished duplicating almost three hundred letters to send to her correspondents, telling them of the success of their project, she waited for President Gerald Ford to sign the bill. (Nixon, facing charges of obstructing justice, using federal agencies to violate constitutional rights, and defying Congress, had resigned the previous August.) Unfortunately, Ford's advisers convinced him to pocket-veto the bill. On Thursday, two days before the president's inaction could destroy the legislation, Debo again took action.

As soon as long-distance telephone rates went down that evening, she began calling members of her network. She instructed them to telegraph the president and then call friends and neighbors to set off a chain reaction. Ford signed the bill. Debo acknowledged that many others had assisted the Havasupais as well as her group. Nonetheless, she believed that "the telegrams swung the balance."

During fall 1975, Angie appeared on educational television stations for the ACLU as part of a series on the Bill of Rights. Among the topics covered were the Supreme Court's decisions prohibiting prayer in the public schools, which she ardently endorsed. Other questions dealt with the first ten amendments to the Constitution, particularly the First Amendment, which protected freedom of speech.

Despite the services Debo rendered the ACLU, the rift between her and some board members had become a chasm by the following spring. When the Oklahoma board decided to raise money through bingo games, Angie resigned, convinced that such activity encouraged gambling. If her fellow board members believed in their cause, she maintained in her diary, they should finance it out of dues, rather than encouraging people to participate in activities she considered immoral. Once Angie made up her mind about matters she considered right or wrong, no arguments or entreaties could dissuade her. In such instances, she was inflexible and immovable.

Meanwhile, her attention had now turned to the Pima Indians of central Arizona. Because of the rapidly growing population in the region, especially around Phoenix and Tucson, their supply of groundwater had diminished. Moreover, the amount awarded them by Ford's secretary of the interior, Rogers Morton, was insufficient to meet their needs. Once more, Debo instructed her network to contact Senator Henry Jackson and urge him, as chair of the Senate Committee on Interior and Insular Affairs, to convene hearings as quickly as possible. As a result of the efforts of many, Jackson opened the hearings, and the Department of the Interior gave further consideration before issuing the final decision on water allocation for the Pimas. In 1976, in "To Establish Justice," an article she wrote for the *Western Historical Quarterly,* Angie asked for additional volunteers for her network.

During all of her previous annual physical examinations, Angie had invariably heard that she was, as she herself reported, a "perfect human being." But in October of 1976 she learned instead that she had a lump in her abdomen, a possibly malignant growth. As she prepared for surgery, she wrote letters and took care of "many details." The eve of her hospitalization she spent with Hugh and Ramona, her "beloved O'Neills." Five days later, as Angie awaited surgery for colon cancer, she recorded her thoughts in her diary. "I am surrounded by love, room filled with flowers, friends calling and there is the love of God of which I am confident. And I am grateful for 86 years of life. So no matter what tomorrow's outcome is I am the gainer. I can't lose."

By late October, Debo was recuperating at a friend's home in Stillwater, confident that she would recover completely. Still weak, she took comfort in her many visitors and cards, noting, "I have a mountain of gratitude a mile high." Three days later she was home and, by early November, was strong enough to vote for Jimmy Carter in the presidential election.

By the time she composed her Christmas greeting in early December, she had made a remarkable recuperation. Beside her was a copy of *Geronimo: The Man, His Time, His Place,* "a beautiful book with its 68 illustrations." And, what's more, in reading it over, Angie found she actually liked it. That was fortunate, for it was the last book she would write.

Although her circle of activists had done much for the Eskimos, Indians, and Aleuts of Alaska and the Havasupais of Arizona, the Pimas of Arizona still needed help in maintaining their water rights. "If there are others of you who would like to enlist," she wrote her friends and fellow activists in her Christmas note, "just drop me a card and I will add your names to my file. I shall be sending out a new letter early in January in time for the convening of the next Congress."

Angie did not know, as she rejoiced in her recovery, that the years ahead would bring illness and pain more serious than any she had known before. At the same time, they would bring greater honor and wider acclaim than she had received during her entire lifetime.

CHAPTER 10

Days of Pain and Triumph

WHEN subsequent checkups revealed no sign of cancer, Debo made light of her illness. Having lost part of her colon, she informed friends that she now owned a semicolon. Her sense of well-being increased when enthusiastic reviews of *Geronimo* arrived. In spring 1978 the work received the Wrangler Award from the Western Heritage Association of the National Cowboy Hall of Fame.

During the last week of April, Debo traveled to Canyon, Texas. There, West Texas State University (formerly West Texas State Teachers College), the school she had left in the mid-1930s, honored her with a reception at the Panhandle-Plains Museum. The high point in the ceremony came when Phil Langen, Canyon's mayor, presented her with a proclamation declaring April 26, 1978, Angie Debo Day.

Although the town remained small, the museum had expanded into one of the best in Texas and indeed the Southwest. The statue of a cowboy in the museum brought back many memories. Fred Scott, the owner of her boardinghouse in the 1920s and the man whose reminiscences had revived her interest in western history, had served as the statue's model. In Canyon she lectured to a class on Indian history and spoke on writing at the Methodist Student Center. Afterwards she addressed the Friends of the Library at their annual dinner. For one who had left West Texas in 1934 "in grief," the homecoming signified the healing of old and painful wounds.

Shortly after she returned home, Debo experienced painful spasms in her back. "Nothing serious I guess but it had me scared," she confided to her diary. When the young woman who cleaned her house arrived, Angie rested rather than working alongside her as usual. The next morning her condition was worse, and as she walked from the kitchen to the dining room, a sharp pain sent her reeling. She fell, struck her head on a hard object, and bled profusely. As a result of the fall, Angie learned that she had osteoporosis—fragile bones. To rebuild their density, her physician began treating her with an experimental drug developed at the Mayo Clinic in Rochester, Minnesota.

Ever the optimist, Angie convinced herself that her back was improving. In the past her illnesses and infirmities always seemed to show little or no improvement until some "sudden change" brought renewed health. On the basis of past experience, Angie was convinced that her afflictions would soon end. But, even as the back pain subsided, she experienced other problems. She could no longer read for long periods without suffering severe eyestrain.

Early in the summer of 1978, after receiving an honorary doctorate at Wake Forest University through the efforts of its president, her friend James Scales, Angie learned that the ACLU had awarded its first Angie Debo Civil Liberties Volunteer Award to Maygene Giari. The Bartlesville woman, a former Shanghai correspondent for Time-Life, was active in the ACLU and the League of Women Voters, among other groups, and had campaigned for prison reform, a cause important to Debo. These two honors—the one from Wake Forest and the presentation of an award named for her—lifted Angie's spirits, especially since she admired the first recipient of the ACLU award.

Despite her growing infirmities, Debo left for New Orleans in October 1978 to receive the biennial award for *Geronimo* from the Southwestern Library Association. After officers of the organization showed her around the city, she met Eudora Welty at a reception. The well-known southern writer from Jackson, Mississippi, was receiving a similar honor from the Southeastern Library Association for her fiction. When Welty read from her book during the ceremony, Angie realized the extent of her hearing loss; she heard nothing of the speech. Still she enjoyed the celebration afterwards at "one of those Jazz Brunches typical of New Orleans."

In her Christmas letter to friends that year, Angie explained with humor that, like Oliver Wendell Holmes's "Wonderful One-Hoss Shay," she and her typewriter had broken down. Although "the pieces are in process of being reassembled," her "git-up and-go / Has got up and went." Still, she said, she had "no reason to complain. I am thankful for eighty-eight years . . . of active life. And even the journey down the mountain may be interesting in a new and different way."

In the new year, Debo received the Award of Merit from the American Association for State and Local History. In April, shortly after summoning the necessary strength to ride in the Prairie City Days parade in Marshall, she learned to her consternation that her prescription drug for osteoporosis had been recalled as too risky. Faced with mounting pain and fatigue, she reluctantly wrote to the members of her network for Indian reform that they would have to continue without her leadership.

Angie could not attend the fiftieth anniversary celebration held by the University of Oklahoma Press in September. She painfully typed a letter to Ed Shaw, then director of the press, expressing her appreciation for the contribution the press had made to her career. "It has made the difference between a dissertation manuscript gathering dust in some remote corner of the library and a fairly long shelf of published books plus uncounted articles," she noted. "I cannot judge how important these published works are to society in general, but to me they represent the creative use of the only life I have on this planet." At the same time, she was grateful to all the directors of the press—Joseph Brandt, Savoie Lottinville, and Shaw—and wondered if she was the only writer who had published under all three. "Sometimes," she added, thinking of their combined impact on American Indian history, "I play with a half-formed conviction that Savoie invented the word 'ethno-history' and that I invented [that] kind of writing."

When Debo turned ninety, her church congregation celebrated her birthday at Margaret's Cafe in Marshall with many of her friends from Bartlesville, Stillwater, and other surrounding towns in attendance. "It was a cold, dark day but a happy one for me," Angie wrote in her diary. In April, still weak and again in

pain, Debo confined her activities in the Prairie City Days celebration to riding at the head of the parade in a model T belonging to Marshall resident Stanley Hitt.

Several months later, after she barely missed colliding with
another car, Debo regretfully sold her old Chevrolet. And she
began using a walker to move about her house. No longer able
to play the reed organ Lina had bought her in the early 1900s,
she gave that cherished possession to a cousin in Kansas City.

Through her continuing friendship with Gloria Valencia-
Weber, now director of Minority Programs in the Psychology
Department, at Oklahoma State University, Debo was introduced to Glenna Matthews. A history professor at the university,
Matthews had earned her doctorate at Stanford University,
where she had studied under the noted scholar, Carl Degler. His
*At Odds: Women and the Family from the Revolution to the
Present* (1980) represented a synthesis of scholarship in the field
of women's history to that point. In his view, American women
had achieved greater leisure and autonomy within the home
largely because of industrialization and falling birth rates. At the
same time, Degler pointed out, rising educational levels had left
increasing numbers of them aware of their subordination in a
patriarchal society. Thus, women were torn between their sense
of responsibility to their homes and their desire to challenge the
pervasive "separate sphere" ideology that prevented their full
participation in the public arena. This was true, especially in politics
and in the higher-paying and more prestigious male-dominated
professions.

As one of Degler's students, Matthews was teaching women's
history at OSU, which gave her much in common with Debo.
Although Angie had never investigated women's history as a
separate category, by examining the history of western expansion and settlement from the Indian point of view, she had helped
to challenge old paradigms. In similar fashion, scholars investigating the history of women were looking at familiar subjects,
such as the American Revolution or the Populist movement,
from the standpoint of their impact on females. Consequently, in
both fields new perspectives were bringing fresh insights and

interpretations. Events, issues, and movements, once seen as long settled, were now yielding new interpretations.

Thus common ground already existed between the ninety-year-old woman and the scholar a half century or so her junior. Matthews was enthralled when Debo talked about her life and the problems she had encountered as a female historian tackling a controversial subject. Feminist scholars, who had concluded that the "personal is political," knew, as historian William Chafe later wrote, that "freedom and autonomy did not exist as external objects or goals to be achieved but had to begin at the very core of one's life—in the family, at home, with lovers and partners, in friendships as well as business and professional relationships." Angie Debo had lived her life according to her most cherished values by pursuing scholarship and writing, irrespective of poverty and setbacks. As an activist she had worked tirelessly for justice. It mattered little that she had never joined the feminist movement in a formal sense. In truth, she had liberated herself.

On May 29, 1981, Angie met with Matthews and Valencia-Weber for her first oral history interview. Shortly after, she began sharing with them her correspondence and diaries and answering questions about various issues and incidents in her past. Although taxing for her, these sessions provided a welcome diversion. On many days the only entries in her diaries were the words, "Pain! Pain! Pain." In addition, these meetings also gave her another way to contribute to history, and Debo struggled to answer their questions as truthfully as possible. When Matthews and Valencia-Weber obtained a grant from the Oklahoma Humanities Committee (presently the Oklahoma Humanities Council), Aletha Rogers, a highly skilled technician, began taping the oral history interviews. During these sessions, Angie reflected on her life and the choices she had made. Despite setbacks and difficulties, she harbored no regrets: "All of my experience was a series of rewards, the pleasure of using whatever gifts I had creatively." Nor did she regret not having married: "I lost, but I would have lost something that actually meant more to me if I had chosen differently."

When asked which historian had influenced her the most, Debo never hesitated; it was Professor Dale. Asked about other historians, such as Walter Prescott Webb, the Texas historian whose *The Great Plains* (1931) had interpreted the West as a place in which the geography of aridity was dominant, Debo acknowledged that she had assigned his work to her classes. Yet Webb had never really influenced her. "If there is any similarity [in our work]," she said, "it's probably a similarity of our own experiences." Nor had Grant and Carolyn Foreman, despite a close friendship, affected her work—except in their "integrity and their contributions to knowledge." Certainly she had never emulated their style, since, in her view, neither one was a polished writer.

In response to further questions, Debo noted that she had never followed the common practice among scholars of sending her work around to other authorities for advance reading. Later Matthews and Valencia-Weber noted in an article for the Organization of American Historians newsletter that her failure to do so had exacted a price, although they offered no specific assessment.

On that point, they were correct, but Debo never welcomed criticism. Although in 1935 she had accepted harsh comments in stoic fashion from Muriel Wright regarding *The Rise and Fall of the Choctaw Republic,* the work in question was already in print and Wright's judgment was rendered after the fact. When it came to the actual process of producing a manuscript, Debo wrote to please herself, a fact that had been true even when she was completing her dissertation. That desire to please herself, rather than any other critic, was the source of her strength. At the same time, her unwillingness to seek input from other scholars had cut her off from ideas and approaches that could have expanded her thinking and improved her work. (With more scholarly exchange, she might have integrated into her histories of American Indians the theories of acculturation developed initially in the 1930s and '40s by anthropologists Robert Redfield, Ralph Linton, and Melville J. Herskovits, among others. Those ideas might, in turn, have sharpened her analysis of the differing responses of Native peoples when they came into sustained contact with Euro-Americans determined to destroy their autonomous cultures and assimilate them by force.)

Debo also noted in the interviews that she had not attended many scholarly meetings since, throughout much of her life, she had lacked the funds to make those trips. She had, however, attended conferences of the Indian Rights Association and the Association on American Indian Affairs. Those meetings and ongoing contact with other members of these organizations had kept her well informed about the impact of governmental policy on the well-being of various tribes. That impact, never far from her consciousness, had been conveyed in her work. In the end, she had written history not simply for the pleasure of uncovering the story behind events but also to gain support for more humane and just Indian policies.

On the occasion of the third interview, in December 1981, Debo discussed the events leading up to the cancellation of her contract with the University of Oklahoma Press after it had scheduled a publication date for her work on the termination of the Five Tribes. At one point, she decided to tell her interviewers the name of the person, who, in her view, was responsible for advising the University of Oklahoma Press against publishing *And Still the Waters Run.* When Joseph Brandt had turned her manuscript over to President Bizzell, she explained, those around him had submitted it to Edward Everett Dale. Dr. Dale had "expressed great appreciation for the good research but he said, 'Now so and so is doing this and this for the University; we shouldn't publish that.' And so," Angie continued, Oklahoma decided not to publish the book, "which I think was the right thing." Unfortunately, in this statement, this woman who had always strenuously sought truth conveyed her mistaken belief to others. Moreover, it is sad to think that she never knew that it was not Dale but his protegé, Morris Wardell, who had written the unsigned reader's report that led to the cancellation of her contract.

In addition to meeting with Matthews and Valencia-Weber, Angie assisted young scholars during these days. She offered advice and encouragement to Michael Green, a professor at Dartmouth whose work on the Creeks had won her admiration. To her delight, he visited her in July 1981. Debo also remained close to Carter Blue Clark, a history professor at California State University at Long Beach. The son of her good friend from WPA days—J. Stanley Clark—and Lois Carter Clark, a woman of Creek ancestry who was active in Indian affairs in the Episcopal Church, Blue Clark was researching the topic of "the Supreme Court's post–Civil War assault on Indian legal rights." By examining the context and events surrounding the 1903 Supreme Court decision, *Lone Wolf* v. *Hitchcock*, he sought to explain the nadir of tribal sovereignty in the United States. In that decision, the Supreme Court had upheld the right of Congress to change unilaterally the terms of a treaty. Debo, Clark maintained, had provided "the inspiration for this project."

During these years Angie also read and critiqued Danney Goble's dissertation on Oklahoma progressivism and Kenny Brown's on Senator Robert L. Owen. She was especially pleased when her old friend James Scales, now retired from Wake Forest, and Goble dedicated their book on Oklahoma politics to her.

Although Angie no longer coordinated her activist network, she stayed abreast of Indian affairs. In summer 1982, she learned that President Ronald Reagan had vetoed a bill that would have allocated "a small measure of justice" to the Papagos (Tohono O'Odham) of southern Arizona. Earlier, Congress, by a wide majority in the House and unanimously in the Senate, had agreed on a settlement with the Papago Tribal Council that assured them access to groundwater from the Central Arizona Project. Reagan, in his veto message, maintained, however, that the federal government had never "been a party to the negotiation."

In this, Reagan was wrong. Members of the staffs of Arizona Senators Barry Goldwater and Dennis DeConcini had indeed been involved, along with representatives from the BIA and the Bureau of Reclamation. But because the federal government agreed to assume nearly all costs involved in supplying the tribe with groundwater, it was, in the president's view, a "federal bailout." Two days after the veto, still distressed, Debo confided to her diary that the legislation would have returned their water rights to "these thrifty Indians who built irrigating ditches and lived in abundance long before Columbus."

The Supreme Court had ruled in *Winters* v. *United States* (1908) that Indians were entitled to the water they needed to irrigate arable land on their reservations even if non-Indians claimed it by prior appropriation. Otherwise, the limited supply would be gone, leaving Native peoples unable to farm, the occupation Congress had intended for them from the beginning. In 1976 the Supreme Court, in *Cappaert* v. *United States,* had brought groundwater under the Winters Doctrine as well.

Despite the Supreme Court's decisions, delegations from western states tenaciously contested these victories in Congress. Thus many tribal leaders and supporters of Indians sought compromises through negotiation rather than striving to expand Indian rights under *Winters.* In that light, it was not surprising that the Papago Tribal Council in 1981 traded their rights under the Winters Doctrine for congressionally backed guarantees of a dependable supply of high-quality groundwater.

Now Reagan's veto overturned that agreement. "I spent what strength I have today planning ways to help [the Papagos]," Debo wrote in her diary on August 8. "I worked on that since 1979 and won—all but the veto." Later that day, Angie's fears were alleviated when a member of the AAIA called to assure her that the organization would never desert the Papagos.

Over the next few weeks, the City of Tucson, anxious to solidify its bond rating, joined with mining and farming interests and the state of Arizona to share the cost of providing the Papagos with groundwater. When Representative Morris Udall attached the Papago agreement as a rider to another reclamation bill favored by the Reagan administration, the vetoed legislation took on new life. On October 12, 1982, President Reagan signed the Southern Arizona Water Rights Settlement Act into law. Among its provisions, the act guaranteed Papago water rights and allotted them funds for irrigation works.

Debo's decision to let others right the world's wrongs was reversed that fall when she read in a newsmagazine that Arizona, Geronimo's birthplace, wanted to reinter his remains at Fort Bowie. Angie suspected that the state really desired a new tourist attraction, since she saw no evidence that Geronimo's descendants or members of his band had been consulted. To set "history straight," she voiced her objections to Sr. Martha Mary McGaw, who later recounted Debo's campaign to assure fair treatment for the Apache leader in *The Sooner Catholic.*

When McGaw asked Debo why she spoke out on behalf of minorities, the aged historian harked back to her childhood. A teacher she recalled only as Miss Gleason from her school days in Welcome, Kansas, had encouraged her to read one McGuffey Reader after another, Debo stated, even though she was moving well beyond her classmates. When Miss Gleason failed to pass the child of a prominent member of the school board, he charged her with favoring Catholic over Protestant children and demanded that her contract not be renewed. Angie and her parents attended the hearing and after the meeting, she remembered walking home "backwards down the road," protesting to her parents: "That wasn't true what he said about Miss Gleason that she was only good to Catholic children. She kissed me when I read for her, and I'm not a Catholic." On that day, Angie decided, "there would never be any bigotry . . . in my life."

In spring 1983 Debo learned that, through Glenna Matthews's efforts, Barbara Abrash, a New York City film producer, had heard the portion of her oral history tapes that had been played on public radio. Abrash was captivated by Debo's story, and before long her coproducer, Martha Sandlin, arrived in Marshall to film Debo's participation in the April Prairie City Days celebration. Sandlin came highly recommended; *A Lady Named Baybie,* her 1980 documentary on a blind singer on New York City streets, had won high praise and awards. Learning that Sandlin was originally from Holdenville, a town southeast of Norman, Debo greeted her by noting, "Well, you're an Oklahoman, so you might understand." Later, Angie's participation in the Prairie City Days parade gave Sandlin excellent footage.

Through the efforts of historian Anne Morgan, Debo was also awarded the University of Oklahoma's Distinguished Service Award. Seven years earlier, she had received the Henry G. Bennett Distinguished Service Award from Oklahoma State University, but this new distinction, coming from her alma mater, had its own special meaning. Since she was too frail to attend commencement when the award would customarily have been given, President William Banowsky and his staff presented it to Angie in Marshall's Catholic Parish Hall on May 18, a day she described as beautiful and bright.

As the oral history interviews continued, Valencia-Weber, Matthews, and Rogers assured Angie that whenever she felt overwhelmed, they would stop the session. Although Debo tired easily, the ongoing contact with creative and committed individuals buoyed her spirits. Still, there were times when the women's relative youthfulness underscored the losses she had sustained in aging. Once, when Valencia-Weber and Rogers arrived wearing new spring outfits, Angie admitted, "I wish I could wear pretty clothes like you girls do." She had only one dressy garment, she noted, since she was "so bent over the others won't go on."

As the interviews continued, Debo discussed her failing health. She was not discouraged, she maintained, for during the past few years of "being feeble and helpless, I have learned how good people are." Friends and neighbors helped her maintain her home. After Margaret's Cafe sent her the noon meal, Angie napped and early in the evening warmed leftovers for supper. Each day Hugh and Ramona O'Neill checked on her, monitoring her needs and wants, taking care of emergencies, and making certain she had a fresh flower in her living-room vase.

In mid-August 1983, when Debo learned that Gloria Valencia-Weber would soon be entering Harvard Law School, she felt a keen sense of loss. The two shared, in addition to a strong commitment to maintaining civil liberties, a host of memories extending back over the years. Very likely Angie knew that her example and friendship had encouraged the younger woman to embark on the rigorous endeavor of becoming a lawyer.

Despite such losses, Debo counted her blessings when she discovered shortly before Christmas that the University of Oklahoma Press planned to reissue *Oklahoma: Foot-loose and Fancy-free* in time for the 1989 centennial celebration of the opening of Oklahoma Territory. Days later she learned to her great joy that the press would also publish *And Still the Waters Run* under its colophon. Painstakingly, she made corrections in both works.

Shortly after she turned ninety-four, Angie learned that Matthews and Valencia-Weber had received a $38,500 grant from the Oklahoma Humanities Committee for a film about her writing career. More money would be required, but this was a start. In her diary Angie wondered if anyone would find it "interesting," but she reminded herself that those involved were "putting much skill into it."

In April 1984, Oklahoma newspapers reported that the New York City–based Institute for Research in History, along with Oklahoma State University, the Oklahoma Humanities Committee, and individual and corporate donors had raised $84,000 for the project. They had made sizable progress toward the $130,000 needed to produce the first film ever made on the life of a woman historian.

As her infirmities increased and the pain of osteoporosis intensified, Debo drew enough strength from the comfort of her surroundings to continue the interviews. She loved the five-room bungalow her brother had built and found solace in the familiarity of its furnishings, such as the oak dining-room table he had made, which she covered with Lina's lace tablecloth. And Angie still heated her meals on the stove her mother had bought in the late 1920s.

She also derived reassurance from Goldilocks, her yellow rosebush. When a neighbor had given it to her years before from a stock brought by early settlers, she had planted it only to be polite since she saw it as "old-fashioned." Now, however, she valued it more highly "than I do the ones that come from nurseries because I've learned to appreciate things that are hardy. It's not ever-blooming, but it doesn't fade and I don't know of any nursery yellow rose that doesn't fade." Every year it blossomed for six weeks in the spring, the limit for Oklahoma roses, given the summer heat.

When Hugh O'Neill told her later that her American Beauty and her other roses on the front porch trellis were also doing well, she was appreciative. She was now confined to the house and could not otherwise have known of their loveliness. Despite her deteriorating vision, though, Angie could still make out the lilac bush from her kitchen window. As "a descendant of the lilac that was on the pioneer homesteader's farm when we came here ten years after this land was opened," it carried her back to her childhood. Nearby was a trumpet vine, which attracted hummingbirds a foot or so from her window.

In 1984 Representatives Robert Henry of Shawnee and Penny Williams of Tulsa introduced a bill in the Oklahoma legislature, selecting Debo as the first woman whose portrait would be hung in the capitol rotunda. Charles Wilson, from Miami, Oklahoma, best known for his paintings of the state's Indians and his *Roots of Oklahoma* murals in the capitol building, was the commissioned artist.

Throughout the summer, Angie, clad in her favorite jacket, a gift from Carolyn Foreman, mustered the strength to pose for her portrait. When she discovered that Wilson thought Kate Barnard more deserving of the honor she—Debo—was receiving, she was pleased. "Our Good Angel, Kate" remained her heroine.

As the day for her "hanging" drew closer, Wilson began coming on Sundays as well as weekdays. If Angie had earlier been tired, she was now exhausted. Still, honors kept coming, and one old wrong was righted. In October, Angie received another distinction when she was selected for the Oklahoma Women's Hall of Fame. The same month, a new edition of the 1941 state study, *The WPA Guide to 1930s Oklahoma,* arrived in her mailbox. Through Anne Morgan's efforts, Debo's original chapter, entitled "Red People," which had been deleted earlier and which emphasized Oklahoma history from the standpoint of imperialism and conquest, was now in its rightful place.

Angie also heard from Joseph Brandt. Her old friend congratulated her on her recent honors and the articles about her in Oklahoma newspapers. He was especially pleased that the paperback edition of *And Still the Waters Run* now appeared in the University of Oklahoma Press catalog. Angie was so moved by his letter that, despite her frailty, she responded. She owed him, she wrote, her "entire writing career, no less." Simplifying the complexities of her life from the vantage point of advanced age, she noted that she had entered a Ph.D. program only to write a dissertation since women were denied teaching positions. She had not known that commercial publishers cared little for books on Indians. In her opinion, if Brandt had not established the Civilization of the American Indian Series, no one would have published her dissertation. Moreover, the excellent volumes that appeared in this series, such as *Wah'Kon-Tah,* had awakened interest in the field so that her book on the Choctaws received "national—perhaps world recognition. . . . Anyhow," she continued, "the reviews encouraged me to resign a precarious position and launch into a more precarious writing career. . . . You never knew that," she added, "but it was the turning point for me. Except for you my *Choctaw Republic* would be a manuscript on a dusty shelf somewhere, and none of my other books would have been written."

Ending her letter, which had taken her several days to write, Debo noted that Sallye Brandt would likely have a hard time deciphering it for her husband. "I have never met you Sallye," Angie added, "but I love you." The letter was mailed on November 5, 1984. Joseph Brandt never received it. Four days earlier he had gone upstairs to lie down after complaining of chest pains. When Sallye Brandt checked on him shortly afterwards, she found him dead of a heart attack.

On Monday, April 8, 1985, Angie Debo's picture was hung in the capitol rotunda in a ceremony at Oklahoma City. Representative Robert Henry functioned as master of ceremonies and Governor George Nigh issued a proclamation. James Scales gave the keynote address, praising Debo as scholar and activist. Afterward, Wilson unveiled the portrait and a reception followed. That night a happy Angie wrote in her diary, "The ceremony of dedicating and unveiling the portrait was a beautiful occasion and [I] am more grateful than I can say to the people who planned it and made it possible for me to participate (feebly). I am too tired to write more."

When Angie turned ninety-six in January 1986, the town of Marshall turned out again to honor her birthday. As a reporter noted, "If Debo has succumbed to age at all, it is in the timing of her life. Her activities, even a birthday, are timed to fit what friends call 'the window' in her days—an hour in the morning and in the afternoon, when she is at her witty best." As the crowd pressed around her, Debo took it in stride. "I have another 10 minutes; I could hold you spellbound with my eloquence," she joked, adding, "If I had any." Still, as the party ended, someone asked her what she had learned from her long life. After a brief hesitation, Angie replied, "All that any of us really have is our life. And if we waste that, we waste everything."

Throughout the years since she had traveled to Africa, Angie had corresponded with her friend, Betty Nakedde, now Betty Mubiru since her marriage. Mubiru had borne three children—Grace, Jimmy, and Allan in 1970, 1974, and 1976, respectively. After the soldiers of Ugandan dictator Idi Amin had murdered her husband, father, and brother, she had taken her children to Kenya, where the family had lived in refugee camps for six years. In 1986, when she brought her family back to Tororo in her native land, the skeletons of murdered victims still hung in trees and bushes. Debo, treasuring their friendship and grateful for Mubiru's care after she had fallen ill in Africa in 1966, wrote her faithfully to bolster her morale. She also set aside funds in her estate to educate Mubiru's children.

Over the Thanksgiving weekend of 1986, Gloria Valencia-Weber visited Debo. She had finished her Harvard law degree and would soon become a law clerk in the office of Judge Lee R. West, U.S. District Court for western Oklahoma. Angie was proud of her success, for the younger women in her life were, in a very real sense, her surrogate daughters. Almost unconsciously, she brought to her relationship with them much of the same tender care and pride in their achievements that her own mother had once given to her.

By January, Debo felt well enough to write in her diary, "Bright, beautiful day. But cold, no snow melting. I am working on a final revision of my Creek history. Slow work, slow mind in the 97th year. But I have much for which to be thankful—the beauty of sky and sunshine, the goodness of people, the sight (in one eye) to read."

On February 11, 1987, Angie received a letter from Brenda Brandt telling her that her mother Sallye had died of colon cancer on January 15. That day and the next thoughts of Joseph Brandt constantly flowed through her mind as she recalled that her last letter had never reached him. "I still grieve about that," she admitted.

Debo's physical world now centered on her couch, where she sat during the day with her afghan, books, paper, pens, pencils, and a telephone nearby. On March 7, she struggled to make further corrections in *The Road to Disappearance*. Michael Green's careful scholarship in *The Politics of Indian Removal: Creek Government and Society in Crisis* (1982) had alerted her to inaccuracies in her account of the fraudulent "treaty" of Indian Springs.

Later that month the sight of daffodils from her north window, a sign that spring was arriving, lifted her spirits—as it had in years past. In April, although Angie no longer rode in the Prairie City Days parade, she provided information to friends and neighbors about early settlers in the region. And she began giving away many of her treasured items to those she loved, deriving pleasure from knowing that they would enjoy the objects she would never use again. In that spirit she gave Ramona, most assuredly a surrogate daughter, Lina's set of china.

On July 3, 1987, Debo wrote for the last time in her diary, "Lovely day—not too hot. Nothing in particular happened." As the year wore on, Angie and her friends looked forward to the screening of the film on her life. That fall the historian learned that she would receive the Award for Scholarly Distinction, a recognition of lifetime achievement from the American Historical Association.

Since Debo could not attend the annual association meeting in Washington in late December, Glenna Matthews agreed to accept it on her behalf. Matthews at this point was teaching at the University of California at Irvine. Though she had recently broken her foot in an accident, she sensed that if she failed to visit Angie during the Christmas break, she would never see her again. After flying to Tulsa, she rented a car, and despite the cast on her foot and the falling snow, drove to Marshall one Saturday morning early in December.

When the two saw each other again, their talk ranged easily as it always had over many topics. At one point Angie thanked Glenna for the film about her life since, as a result, her books would gain a wider audience. Aware that Debo's waning strength limited visits to an hour, Matthews rose to leave. The two women held hands as Glenna told Angie that she loved her. "I love you oceans" was Debo's reply. As Matthews left, tears welled in her eyes, and she wept as she drove back to Tulsa. She knew that they had said good-bye for the last time.

In January 1988, Governor Henry Bellmon arrived at the Bryson home in Marshall to present Debo with the American Historical Association Award that Matthews had earlier accepted on her behalf. Those present laughed heartily when Debo told the governor, a winner of the ACLU Angie Debo award, that he was the only Republican who had ever received her vote.

On Saturday, February 20, 1988, a day that Gloria Valencia-Weber had set aside to show Debo the film based on her life, Angie was admitted to St. Mary's Hospital in Enid, Oklahoma. The next day she died. She never saw "Indians, Outlaws and Angie Debo."

Debo's funeral was held in St. Paul's United Church of Christ in Marshall on Wednesday afternoon, February 24. That day state flags flew at half-mast. As Raymond Bryson recalls, those close to her were not mourning her death but celebrating her life. Gloria Valencia-Weber delivered Angie's eulogy, praising Debo as one who had contributed as a member of her community, a historian of Oklahoma, a pioneering scholar of American Indians, a human rights advocate, an activist on behalf of equality, and a guardian of civil liberties. George Tiger, representing the Creek Nation, reflected on Debo's dream that one day the world's races would "walk hand in hand. Her vision has come true," he added. "She has gone to her appointed place where there is no Trail of Tears and no color lines."

Afterwards a long cavalcade of cars accompanied Debo's casket to Marshall's North Cemetery where she was buried in her family's plot. Raymond Bryson chose a simple stone to mark her grave site, not far from the home she had occupied for many years. Responding to a suggestion from Hugh and Ramona O'Neill, he selected an inscription that exemplified Debo's approach to her profession. "Historian, discover the truth and publish it."

CHAPTER II

Assessments

ANGIE Debo's oral history interviews, given between 1981 and 1985, have proved a reliable source concerning the facts of her life. Available evidence almost always confirms her statements. As her close friend and fellow historian, Glenna Matthews, described her, she was "the soul of integrity," a woman who was scrupulously honest.

But although Debo may have consciously sought to "discover the truth and publish it," she was also human. In at least one instance she arrived at a wrong conclusion. Lacking sufficient and conclusive evidence, she identified her beloved mentor, Edward Everett Dale, as the author of the report that led to the cancellation of her publishing contract with the University of Oklahoma Press for *And Still the Waters Run*. Unfortunately this statement, which appears in "Indians, Outlaws and Angie Debo," maligns her teacher. For those who argue that Dale undoubtedly influenced the unsigned report that Morris Wardell wrote (the two were extremely close), that possibility invites speculation but yields no final answer.

In another area—her commitment to reform—Debo's record is truly impressive. Coming of age in the Progressive Era, when the state of Oklahoma was born, she grew up valuing social justice. The strong impact reformer Kate Barnard made on her during her adolescence reinforced this tendency, as did the year she spent at the University of Chicago where she attended a class on psychology of religion and visited places such as Hull House. In midlife she returned, as if directed by an internal compass, to many of the issues Barnard had written about earlier, such as the fate of Indian orphans assigned to unscrupulous and exploitive guardians.

Disappointed that cogently presented and thoroughly documented historical evidence failed to bring about reform, Debo decided more was needed to right the wrongs she uncovered. Armed with facts, theoretical understanding, and unflagging commitment, she created a network capable of affecting legislation despite her limited means and declining health and strength.

If these were the broad outlines of Debo's character, what was she like as a person others knew as a friend or a neighbor? The true Angie Debo was complicated, possessed of both strengths and frailties. Among her strengths, Debo nurtured throughout her life a wry sense of humor and a resiliency derived in part from her family's commitment to the Oklahoma spirit. Hardships, like the "starving times" in areas newly opened to pioneers, were predictable and would pass in time. More important was the way one responded to such vissisitudes. From her mother, Lina Debo, Angie learned to avoid dramatizing tragedies. From her father, Edward Debo, she learned to meet disappointments, such as selling land where oil was later discovered, with as much good cheer as possible. For the most part, especially as she grew older, Debo lived up to these precepts and examples.

The historian displayed other traits that stood her in good stead. She wasted little emotional energy on animosities. Despite her problems with L. F. Sheffy, chair of the history department at West Texas State Teachers College, and her ongoing disagreements with the Oklahoma scholar Muriel Wright, Debo feuded with neither one.

If humor, resiliency, and forbearance provided the tonics that eased Debo through adversity, at her core she harked back to a long-standing tradition in Protestantism. She harbored a bedrock faith in a personal covenant between the individual and her God. If she used her innate gifts and talents creatively, she was certain that Providence would guide and bless her efforts.

Still, while personally devout, Debo never proselytized or sought to impose her beliefs on others. In part, this arose from her dedication to preserving freedom of speech, for, next to her religious faith, she valued most highly the constitutional separation of church and state in America. An early member of the

Oklahoma chapter of the American Civil Liberties Union, she steadfastly opposed any violation of First Amendment rights that guaranteed freedom of speech and expression of thought.

Debo also believed in tolerance and toleration. From her home in Marshall, Oklahoma, she looked forward to an increasingly integrated society in which children of all hues would be completely accepted by American society. She opposed discrimination on any basis whatsoever.

Evidence from her personal conduct and habits reveals her sense of stewardship for the goods of the earth and its resources. She used grants frugally, often returning unused funds to agencies even when they were her only source of income. Throughout her life, she kept her wants to a minimum. Her consumption patterns remind one of the folk adage, "Use it up, wear it out, make it do, or do without." Having little interest in material possessions, Debo relied on the pleasures of nature. She loved flowers and songbirds and, until glaucoma and cataracts took their toll, sunsets and the star-filled sky at night. Her deteriorating vision represented her greatest physical loss in old age.

Miss Angie, as the Marshall community knew her, treasured her friends and neighbors. Residents of her town remember that however busy she was or, later, however infirm, she showed genuine concern for their illnesses and losses. And if their luck changed for the better, she rejoiced in their good fortune. Hugh O'Neill, who lived several doors from her, recalls that when he was recovering from a serious illness, Debo fashioned him an "elixir" of crumpled balls inside a jar. Each day, as he unwrapped one, he discovered one of her favorite sayings inside. Although he cannot remember them exactly, they were not the usual nostrums. Rather, they were statements such as Mark Twain's "I am a great & sublime fool. But then I am God's fool, & all His works must be contemplated with respect." Since Debo loved the Book of Proverbs, she probably included some of her favorite passages from that part of the Bible as well. Her neighbor never forgot the gift that sustained his spirits during a painful time.

Although Angie Debo lived with a sense of stewardship for earthly goods and cared deeply for others, she also exhibited a healthy self-regard. She believed firmly in her right to leisure. After she taught her Sunday school class, she treated Sunday as a day of rest, not only for religious reasons but because, she insisted, she owed herself that minimum amount of relaxation.

After her mother died and she had retired as curator of maps at Oklahoma State University, Debo became a world traveler. Although she cooked on her mother's late 1920s stove and typed on a table instead of a desk, she satisfied her deepest longings by touring not only Europe but the country that fascinated her most—Russia. Later, in her seventies, she journeyed through Mexico, Africa, and Alaska. Sometimes she fell ill during her trips, but she learned as much as possible from her tours, taking in the sights and enjoying herself, whatever her discomfort or pain. For Miss Angie, every adventure was to be deeply savored, including that dip in the road on the highway between Marshall and Stillwater.

In her last decade, even knowing she faced death, Debo retained her indomitable spirit. No matter what, she saw herself as a winner. Pain and helplessness had taught her the generosity of friends and neighbors, something she could have learned, she believed, in no other way.

In addition to these admirable qualities, Angie also displayed imperfections and traits that elicited hostility from some people. As Gloria Valencia-Weber noted in her eulogy, Debo's was a formidable personality. She was "a strong, dominating person, extremely independent, who tried to live as independently as possible until the very end." Such traits undoubtedly antagonized some, especially those who expected women to remain deferential and subservient.

Hugh O'Neill remembers that Miss Angie was so precise about performing tasks that she reminded him of an old adage from the army: "There was the right way, the wrong way, and the army (Angie) way." Debo "was a person of quite remarkable intelligence and she was used to doing about everything in a businesslike and logical manner." This aspect of her character at times "led to a tendency for her to believe that the way she did something was just about the *only* proper way to do it." Certainly the staff she supervised for the Oklahoma Federal Writers' Project knew this characteristic firsthand. While serving as administrative head in Oklahoma City, Debo saw the lack of writing skills among her workers as the source of her frustration—that and the time she spent attending meetings and conferences. Although these factors added to her burdens, giving her staff explicit directions as if they were children in a classroom undoubtedly generated antagonism in some and frustration in others. Thankfully, whatever the economic cost to her personally, Debo remained only a brief time in bureaucratic positions for which she lacked the required temperament.

Debo's tendency to believe that her way of doing things was the right way was also evident in her writing. As an author it was both a source of difficulty and, at the same time, her greatest strength. Even when she was working on her dissertation, she took exception to Professor Dale's initial criticisms and wrote the thesis her way. Later, faced with negative reports from the University of Oklahoma Press regarding the manuscript that became *Oklahoma: Foot-loose and Fancy-free,* she threatened to take it to another publisher rather than revise it to meet her readers' criticisms. Eventually, she made some changes, but, in areas such as race relations and the characterization of religious practices she remained adamant. If she could not speak her mind on those issues, the manuscript would not be published.

On the whole, Debo was an unusual individual, embodying traits that she ascribed in her writings to her hometown and state. In *Prairie City* she celebrated "the free-masonry" of shared hardships and small triumphs that accompanied early pioneering in Oklahoma. With the railroad's arrival, commercialized activities and speculation disrupted that world, and by the 1920s much of the earlier cohesiveness was gone.

The appeal, nonetheless, remained. Throughout her life, community ties remained uppermost in Debo's value system. She demonstrated this attachment by retiring to Marshall rather than remaining in the larger university town of Stillwater. From her hometown, she wrote, engaged in activism, and worked to bring OSU students from all over the world to her neighbors' celebrations. She became in the process an increasingly central figure in the life of her town. For that reason and because she was the former lay pastor of the Methodist Church and the historian who had immortalized the town in *Prairie City*, Marshall's residents, in turn, gave Miss Angie extraordinary care during her old age and infirmity.

But although Debo valued community, she was also an incorrigible maverick, not unlike the typical Oklahomans she described in *Oklahoma: Foot-loose and Fancy-free*. That individualism, she noted in her manuscript proposal, "makes every Oklahoman stand alone."

Overall, these seemingly contradictory aspects of Debo's personality—her commitment to community and her strong individualism—help to explain her strengths and her professional success. On one hand, she was grounded securely in Marshall, emotionally and socially. On the other, her maverick qualities made her a "lone wolf," as Oklahoma historian Arrell Gibson described her, capable of striking out in new directions and becoming a pioneer in western and American Indian history.

With respect to her contribution to the field of history, Debo's work is significant for two reasons. First, she served as a bridge between the older school of western historians, heavily influenced by Frederick Jackson Turner and his frontier thesis, and the more recent New Western Historians, who view Euro-American movement into the trans-Mississippi West through a darker lens. Second, as Debo herself grasped in her later years, her work on American Indians, which brought to bear the insights of ethnologists and the results of her own fieldwork, was a forerunner of ethnohistory. In chronicling Indian-white relations, she told the story, as fully as possible, from the Indian point of view, bringing Native peoples rather than Euro-Americans to the foreground. Thus Debo anticipated elements of the New Indian History, which represents the cutting edge of the field at the end of the twentieth century. Because of her impact on these two fields—western American history and American Indian history—her life and work illuminate ways in which history as a discipline changes over time.

198 ANGIE DEBO

As scholar Patricia Limerick explains, New Western Historians take issue with Turner's frontier thesis in distinct ways. They see the West as a place—"the trans-Mississippi region in the broadest terms, or the region west of the hundredth meridian." As they note, in "The Significance of the Frontier in American History" Turner argued that each time another wave of pioneers entered a region farther west, their society reverted to a more primitive stage. Thus, as pioneers rebuilt their former institutions, they created more indigenously American communities on each successive frontier. (In *The Significance of Sections in American History* (1932), Turner stated that sections, or settled regions, were as important as the frontier in determining American history. New Western Historians, however, still object to his view of the West as a moving frontier or process. The West, they insist, should be studied as a specific place.)

Debo, applying Turner's ideas, saw the movement of pioneers into Oklahoma as the culmination of the frontier process he described. Since the people moving into her state were the end product of nine generations of successive frontiers, they were the most indigenously American of all, and the whole panorama of United States history was telescoped in Oklahoma's recent past. Moreover, many of the original pioneers were still living while she researched and wrote her books. Although her own family had arrived a decade after the first great land rush of 1889, they too came from ancestors who had participated in this process on various frontiers over time.

Despite Debo's application of Turnerian ideas, she superseded Turner in an important way. As Richard Hofstadter noted in *The Progressive Historians: Turner, Beard, Parrington* (1968), Turner gave little thought to the sufferings of American Indians displaced by non-Indian settlers. Despite his interest in the common people rather than the elite, as a scholar he "lacked a strong feeling for the tragedy of history."

Debo, by contrast, confronted historical tragedy head on, never hesitating to judge past morality, especially when it was shrouded in hypocrisy. Her concern for those who stood on the other side of Turner's frontier ties her to the New Western

Historians who see the "settling" of the West as conquest and its subsequent history as Limerick's "legacy of conquest."

The West as a place where people of various races, nationalities, and cultural and social classes converged, often on the basis of inequality and injustice, is another theme advanced by the New Western Historians. That idea is implicit in all of Debo's works on American Indians. Her presentation of the fate of Native peoples bears close similarity to the assessment Richard White offers in *"It's Your Misfortune and None of My Own": A New History of the American West* (1991). In this reinterpretation of the West as a region, he describes a place where successive groups of invaders often exploited land and resources for their own benefit, irrespective of the cost to earlier inhabitants.

The New Western Historians also disagree with Turner's view that 1890—the year that the superintendent of the census had identified as signaling the end of the frontier—represented a turning point not only in the region's history but in United States history as well. With the frontier gone, as Turner explained, "a new field of opportunity, a gate of escape from the bondage of the past" also vanished and, with it, American exceptionalism. The New Western Historians disagree, arguing instead that continuity, or the "unbroken past of the American West," explains the region's history. In Limerick's words, "the conquest of Western America shapes the present as dramatically—and sometimes as perilously—as the old mines shape the mountainsides."

Certainly Debo's works traced developments after 1890, the year of the so-called closing of the frontier. Moreover, she saw the earlier events as having a continuing influence down to the present day. In *And Still the Waters Run,* she wrote that by studying the aftermath of the termination of the government of the Five Tribes, the dispersal of their lands in allotments, and the sale of their "excess" lands, she was uncovering a period that historians of the westward movement had usually neglected. The subject was important to her. For "the reaction of this process upon the ideals and standards of successive frontier communities is a factor in the formation of the American character that should no longer be disregarded by students of social institutions."

Another important attribute among New Western Historians, according to Limerick, is their constant reevaluation of the definitions of "progress" and "improvement." On that basis, Debo deserves charter membership in this group, for she began analyzing the cost of "progress" as a graduate student working on her doctorate with Professor Dale. By the time she finished her dissertation, she saw that, from the Indian point of view, "progress" had cost the Choctaws their autonomy. In *And Still the Waters Run,* she found that "progress" had brought vast numbers of the full-bloods of the Five Tribes from self-sufficiency to dire poverty.

Debo saw that progress also exacted a heavy price from non-Indians. In *Oklahoma: Foot-loose and Fancy-free,* she anticipated, at least fleetingly, the insights of later New Western Historians like Donald Worster who stress environmental issues. She noted, for example, the wasteful farming methods that accompanied the opening of new regions to settlement and development. "To establish a family on the land, to build a new society—this was the American ideal. And," Debo added, "slashing the timber, destroying the grass, mining the soil—this was noble, too; this was a part of the process." Because of "the bad practices inaugurated at Jamestown and repeated on successive frontiers," much of Oklahoma's irreplaceable top soil was irretrievably lost. Even worse was the "pioneer psychology" behind the practices.

Finally, Limerick reminds readers that the New Western Historians eschew "the conventional, never-very-convincing claim of an omniscient, neutral objectivity" and instead "admit that it is OK for scholars to care about their subjects, both in the past and the present, and to put that concern on record." Although Debo asserted that she never lost faith in her ability to remain objective, despite claims that the scholar "slants his findings according to his own bias," she sometimes found, she stated, "all the truth on one side of an issue." In that statement, she eschewed "neutral objectivity" and emerged as an advocate "at the bar of history" for Native peoples or, in the words of Cherokee scholar Rayna Green, "a scholar-warrior." When Debo's scholarly writings exposing injustice failed to affect policy, her commitment to bringing about change and righting old wrongs led her into impassioned activism.

As Debo's regionalist writings tie together themes from the Old and New Western History, so too her writings in American Indian history form a bridge between the "Old" and "New" Indian History. Scholars as varied as David Nichols, Reginald Horsman, Terry Wilson, Donald Parman, Catherine Price, and David Rich Lewis note that Frederick Jackson Turner saw Indians as part of the wilderness, a barrier to be removed. Functioning as "a common danger," Native peoples unified Euro-Americans moving westward. Beyond that, they were of little importance.

In part, Turner was responding to the currents of his time. Following passage of the Dawes Act in 1887, many Americans assumed that Indians were becoming assimilated into the dominant culture. As Native peoples became settled Christian farmers, owning individual plots of land, they would solve the "Indian problem" in simple fashion; they would cease to be Indians.

During the early decades of the twentieth century, historians who considered Indians at all usually dealt with them in the context of Indian-white relations. Since their knowledge was based on the writings of explorers, missionaries, traders, soldiers, and agents—as reflected in memoirs or governmental, military, and church reports—scholars were interpreting Indian life on the basis of ethnocentric and biased sources. As ethnohistorian Calvin Martin notes, under these circumstances, the historian often approached the American Indian "with only the barest understanding of who his subject was in his own cultural and social sphere; for him, the Indian was an incompletely developed Western European or American, as the case may be, and on this faulty premise he built a seriously flawed literature." Moreover, because of "ignorance of the ethnographic literature and general ethnological theory," Martin continues, the historian remained "at the mercy of his sources, most of them European-American, to be sure, but more importantly, most of them unaware of the subtle and unique features of Indian life."

By contrast, as early as the mid-1930s, Angie Debo was already moving toward an early form of ethnohistory. Unlike the vast majority of her contemporaries, she was incorporating ethnology—

in her case that of anthropologist John Swanton—into her work on the Choctaws.

The practitioners of the older Indian history also viewed Euro-Americans as the actors and Indians the reactors. At the same time, Indian versions of events, based on oral tradition, were dismissed as "legend" or "myth" and thus excluded as evidence from historical accounts. Although Debo narrated accounts of the impact of Euro-American policies on Indian peoples, she sought from the beginning to tell her stories from the Indian point of view. Moreover, she was interested in the effect of these policies, as she explained in *The Road to Disappearance,* "upon the internal life of the tribe," or, in this instance, how it affected the Creeks as a nation or as an autonomous and self-directed entity. Finally, even though she never conducted fieldwork in the sense of living for a time with Native peoples as a participant-observer, she moved beyond archival holdings. She interviewed Indians in their homes and communities and made extensive use of their oral tradition. At an early stage in her career as a historian, she also learned to evaluate government and military documents carefully and cautiously. Her research on the Five Tribes taught her to scrutinize the reports of the Dawes Commission with a critical eye, since these documents often contained biased and deliberately misleading information. Later, while researching the history of the Creek Nation, she discovered that Indian oral tradition should not be summarily dismissed as legend and myth. Rather, it should be evaluated in terms of its congruence with other facts. The documentary evidence in Grant Foreman's *Indian Removal,* for example, corroborated Creek oral tradition, passed from one generation to another for a century.

Debo was ahead of her time in yet another way. As late as 1971, in an article in the *Pacific Historical Review,* Robert Berkofer, Jr., called for a "new Indian history." It would embrace as its "central theme" a recognition of "the remarkable persistence of cultural and personality traits and ethnic identity in Indian societies in the face of white conquests and efforts at elimination or assimilation. By concentrating on this latter theme," Berkofer noted, the historian would render "Indian-

Indian relations as important as white-Indian ones have been previously." To tell that story, scholars would be required to enlarge their view of Indians as people, while simultaneously they would have to extend their studies to include the "time before white contact and beyond the reservation of yesterday to the urban ghetto and national Indian organizations of today."

Debo had been moving toward Berkofer's central theme for decades. Even though, as a marketing tool, she entitled her work on the Creeks *The Road to Disappearance,* she stressed throughout that study the persistence of the Creek spirit. By ending with an excerpt from Chief Pleasant Porter's moving 1900 peroration to the Creek Council, she told her readers that the Creeks, who had contributed so much to the making of Oklahoma and the nation, would never disappear. Porter said it best in describing Creek relations with other Americans when he declared, "We have made ourselves an indestructible element in their national history."

Debo returned to Porter's address in *Indians of the United States* when she emphasized the American Indian's "remarkable record of survival, [and] the preservation of his distinctive identity, through centuries of encroachment by a more numerous and aggressive race." This persistence, she observed, proved "baffling to well-meaning 'civilizers' determined to throw him into the melting pot." And although one reviewer criticized her for not including information on the archaeological evidence from the precontact period, she carried her narrative forward to the time she was writing in the late 1960s. She found that tribal leaders welcomed change, "know[ing] that all people everywhere are experiencing changes." At the same time, however, they faced the future sustained by an ongoing commitment to "spiritual values which have been a part of our lives through all the days that we have known." In the Indians' ongoing ability to sustain their spiritual values across time and space, the careful reader finds the thread of a consistent theme throughout Debo's writings. From her first tribal history of the Choctaws until her last work, a biography of Geronimo, Debo's Indians remain actors, rather than reactors, and, most of all, agents, no matter how predominant the power of whites. Her Indians are never reduced to mere foils in the Euro-American epic of conquest.

Scholars who followed Debo have built on her insights and findings to move beyond her and, in some instances to revise her conclusions. That is predictable and desirable in any field that is flourishing in terms of scholarship. Nonetheless, Debo's works have continuing relevance. If she, like other scholars of the 1930s and beyond, accepted John Swanton's views on the formlessness of Choctaw culture, an idea that the careful scholarship of Patricia Galloway and Clara Sue Kidwell has overturned, Debo recognized earlier than most historians the necessity of applying ethnological insights to the writing of American Indian history. Even though her language, with its use of terms such as "primitive" and "savage," was at times ethnocentric by today's standards, her painstaking research and unflinching courage in the face of unsavory and disturbing factual evidence rendered her an eloquent and true friend of Native peoples everywhere.

Finally, although Debo omitted important religious revivals, such as the one led by the Seneca prophet Handsome Lake, in *Indians of the United States*, she still performed one historical function in unparalled fashion. Even when she still thought in terms of "guid[ing] a subject people into citizenship and cultural assimilation," she had understood, as early as 1944, that her country's treatment of its indigenous people represented its "real imperialism." She knew that, before the United States could assume its role as a moral leader in global affairs, it had to scrutinize its own behavior in terms of its treatment of minorities and live up to its oldest commitments. Describing in 1949 the impoverished and neglected condition of the forgotten full-bloods of the Five Tribes of Oklahoma, she warned her readers: "More than the welfare of a few thousand Indians is at stake. It is a matter of national good faith."

By 1970 Debo had reversed herself and no longer called for "guid[ing] a subject people into citizenship and cultural assimilation." Instead she favored a policy she had first enunciated in 1954 during the dark days of termination. The policy she proposed would

ASSESSMENTS 205

protect the Indians' land (including timber, minerals, waters, all natural resources) and give them a chance by revolving credit to develop it; provide them with vocational and educational training equal to that of other citizens; assist Indians who *choose* to leave their own neighborhoods in *voluntary* relocation; encourage instead of thwarting tribal organization, and recognize the Indians' need for their own social groupings; resist the temptation to direct Indians' private lives; consult Indians freely in formulating policies and reject any that are not approved by the tribes involved.

Debo was convinced that, if her compatriots honored their commitment to their country's indigenous people, some American Indians would remain on their tribal lands and others would enter the larger society. "This," Angie argued, "is as far as we need to go with them. Whether or not it would result eventually in complete amalgamation—the disappearance of Indians as Indians—is immaterial. Give them a chance to live now, and the future will depend on natural evolution."

With the publication of her 1976 biography of Geronimo, a work that evaluated the Chiricahua leader in the context of his moral universe rather than judging him by the standards of the Euro-American world, Debo had traveled a long distance in her journey as a scholar. She had laid the foundation for continual growth by keeping abreast of her field, well into her old age despite intense physical pain and failing eyesight. Thus she remains an example for present and future generations of scholars who labor in the vineyards of history. Getting her facts straight, even when that meant acknowledging her errors, remained her foremost concern.

One person knew this aspect of her character very well. John Drayton, who in 1998 became the fifth director of the University of Oklahoma Press, recalls that when he was editor-in-chief in the early 1980s, he would sometimes answer his telephone and hear a high-pitched voice on the other end. It was Angie Debo telling him that she wanted to make corrections in one or another of her works. To the very end she remained not merely willing but eager to revise herself in light of new scholarship and findings.

That characteristic is the very essence of the discipline of history, for its writing is always an unfinished task.

Historians today are examining the legacy of conquest. Angie Debo, as a female scholar, explored that region on her own terrain, out on her own frontier.

Epilogue

AS Angie Debo's will mandated, the bulk of her estate, including the proceeds from the sale of her bungalow on the corner of Market Street and Oklahoma Avenue in Marshall, were used to help Betty Mubiru of Tororo, Uganda, educate her three children—Grace, Jim, and Allan—through the secondary-school level. Grace, following in her mother's footsteps, became a nurse but unfortunately died of a brief but virulent illness in November 1996. That same year, Jim began his postsecondary studies in marketing and business while Allan completed high school. Betty suffered a stroke after her daughter's death, but, strong and resilient, she made a remarkable recovery. With the education of the Mubiru children largely completed, remaining funds of the Debo estate now go to the Division of World Missions of the Board of Global Ministries, where they are used primarily to help African women and girls gain an education.

Debo's papers, including diaries, correspondence, photographs, awards, and original manuscripts, were donated to the Special Collections Division of the Edmon Low Library at Oklahoma State University at Stillwater. The office of the late President Henry Bennett is now the Angie Debo Room.

In 1991 Edith Gaylord Harper, founder of the Ethics in Journalism Foundation, gave the Edmon Low library $55,000 to microfilm Debo's papers and publish a guide to the collection. Harper also financed the presentation of a lecture on the fiftieth anniversary of the publication of Debo's *Prairie City,* an event that occurred on January 30, 1995, Debo's 105th birthday. Kenny Brown, professor of history at the University of Central Oklahoma and a scholar whose work on Robert L. Owen profited from Debo's criticisms, was chosen to deliver the key-note address. He noted that in the mid-1940s, sociologists such as Otis Durant Duncan and William Foote Whyte had character-ized *Prairie City* as lacking sophistication. From the perspective of the recent past, however, Debo's insights about establishing and maintaining a small town were timely and incisive. A half century earlier, she had understood that, although access to transportation and employment opportunities generated growth, informed community action, strong civic organizations, and good educational facilities remained essential for survival.

Edith Harper's generosity assumed another form. Through a $100,000 endowment to the University of Oklahoma Press, she established the Angie Debo Award. The $5,000 prize is given to the author of the best book about the American Southwest submitted as an original manuscript to the university Press. Richard L. Nostrand was the first recipient in 1996 for *The Hispano Homeland,* published four years earlier. This work is a sophisti-cated analysis through historical geography of the way that Hispanos (people of Spanish and mixed ancestry, including the nomad Indians of the Southwest) created and preserved their sense of Spanish ethnicity. In the process, Norstrand points out, they "shaped and reshaped a Homeland." Thus, as Debo late in life detailed the Indians' remarkable persistence despite repeated assaults on their culture, this work uncovers the sources of "the only surviving Spanish colonial subculture" in the United States. By preserving "a strong sense of place, rooted in village life" and through the continuing "cultural impress" of artifacts, landscape, celebrations, and customs, the Hispanos have maintained their ethnicity, as Nostrand writes, in part as a response to Anglo atti-tudes and the influx of Mexican Americans into the Southwest. They have done so even though they no longer dominate their homeland.

The Debo Award perpetuates the Oklahoma historian's ideals of scholarship, but in addition, Angie Debo had an indelible impact on others whose ongoing contributions and activism pay lasting homage to her memory. Gloria Valencia-Weber, as director of the Indian Law Certificate Program at the University of New

Mexico's School of Law in Albuquerque, keeps Debo's spirit alive. In a course in Native American Rights, a class she teaches as a professor of Native American law, she "combines legal and historical materials," since, as she maintains, "the greater scholarly universe deepens appreciation of American Indian law." Debo's *Indians of the United States* serves as the starting point for her students.

In describing her course, Valencia-Weber argues that tribal sovereignty and its contested meaning remain central to the struggle of Native peoples. Frequently they turn to historians or anthropologists to provide the background, context, and meanings behind treaties and laws. Scholars often disagree on facts and interpretations, and opposing sides usually select different authorities to support their clients' interests and views. In *Harjo v. Kleppe* (1976), however, a case students examine in Valencia-Weber's class, Debo's *And Still the Waters Run* and *The Road to Disappearance* were accepted as the "pre-eminent works in the field" by both the plaintiffs and the defendants. This unusual development testifies to the historian's unquestioned reputation for scholarly integrity. The case, which was heard in the U.S. District Court of the District of Columbia, revolved around the authority and status of the Creek National Council. Allen Harjo, the plaintiff, argued that the Creeks' 1867 constitution had invested "the lawmaking power of that Nation" and control over financial affairs in the Creek Council, a "coordinate branch" of tribal government. He and three other traditionalists charged that when Claude Cox, the principal chief, and Thomas S. Kleppe, secretary of the interior under President Gerald R. Ford, had dispensed tribal funds without the council's approval, they had transformed the office of principal chief into the "sole embodiment" of the Creek Nation.

The central question was whether the "tribal government of the Creek Nation has survived statutory dismemberment." The answer lay in careful historical analysis. Judge William Bryant, in writing the final decision, noted that the 1898 Curtis Act, which forced the Creeks to accept allotment, stipulated that their government would end on March 4, 1906. Until then, while "territorial sovereignty of the Creek Nation had been seriously eroded," it retained its governmental authority in "matters of tribal organization and management, including control of tribal funds." Since the problems accompanying allotment and termination persisted longer than expected, Congress passed the Five Tribes Act on April 26, 1906. Although Section 6 authorized the president to replace any principal chief who impeded the process of allotment and termination with someone more compliant, Section 28 provided for the continuation of tribal government.

In 1971, Allen Harjo, a traditionalist, lost the election for principal chief to Claude Cox and lost again four years later, this time by a narrower margin. At this point Harjo and his supporters challenged Cox, charging him and the secretary of the interior with usurping power that belonged to the Creek National Council under the 1867 constitution. Cox responded by calling for the submission of a new constitution to the BIA.

Harjo v. *Kleppe* laid one matter to rest. Judge Bryant, on the basis of historical evidence derived largely from Debo's works and subsequent court cases, involving numerous statutes and treaties, ruled in favor of the traditionalists. Since the tribal government had never really been terminated, the 1867 constitution was still in force, and the Creek National Council remained a coordinate branch of the Creek Nation.

Another individual whose teaching and scholarship continue to be influenced by Debo is Carter Blue Clark. While serving as vice president at Oklahoma City University in 1994, he fulfilled his ambition to publish the study Debo had inspired him to undertake years earlier—Lone Wolf v. Hitchcock: *Treaty Rights and Indian Law at the End of the Nineteenth Century.* The decision in *Lone Wolf* v. *Hitchcock,* rendered in 1903, represented the point at which Indian sovereignty suffered its greatest blow. When members of the Southern Plains tribes on the Kiowa-Comanche Reservation objected to the sale of a large tract of "surplus land" in 1892, Congress not only upheld the agreement in 1900 but unilaterally modified it on the basis of its "plenary power." Three years later, the U.S. Supreme Court ruled that Congress, given its "[p]lenary authority over the tribal relations of the Indians," could unilaterally "abrogate the provisions of an Indian treaty" and that such an action was not subject to judicial review.

By 1980 Supreme Court Justice Harry Blackmun, in *United States* v. *Sioux Nation,* a case involving a similar question of congressional abrogation of a treaty, characterized *Lone Wolf* as "discredited." But even if *United States* v. *Sioux Nation* seems to herald greater justice and a move away from congressional invocation of "plenary power," Professor Clark warns against premature optimism. As late as 1978 the Supreme Court had ruled in *Santa Clara Pueblo* v. *Martinez* that whereas tribes had sovereign rights, "Congress has plenary authority to limit, modify, or eliminate the powers of local self-government which the tribes otherwise possess." That same year, the Court stated even more bluntly in *United States* v. *Wheeler* that tribes retained sovereignty "only at the sufferance of Congress." Clearly, the threat to American Indian sovereignty continues. But as a scholar proud of his Creek heritage and an individual influenced by Debo, Carter Blue Clark maintains his struggle for justice for American Indians.

In yet another instance, a western writer who never met Debo expressed his "appreciation" for her in the *New York Review of Books* in October 1997. It was his way, he stated, "of paying a little interest on a long-accruing debt." Larry McMurtry, author of the Pulitzer Prize–winning *Lonesome Dove,* among other well-known novels and works, had first encountered the Oklahoma writer in 1950, when at age fourteen, he had found a copy of *The Road to Disappearance.* Although forty years passed before he was "able to understand the whole," simply knowing it was written by a woman in Oklahoma, a place "set aside for the unruly," proved inspirational. Over time, as he read her "sinewy sentences," he concluded "that it might be possible to organize one's life around literature—not write it, I didn't aspire to that, but just read it and, in some way, live with it." If that idea seems commonplace to many, McMurtry noted his upbringing. "I could look off the porch of our ranch house, straight up the length of the Great Plains, all the way into Canada, but the only evidence I had that there were such things as writers in all that stretch of land was this book I had found in a parking lot, by a woman from Oklahoma." Young McMurtry saw that this woman had "somehow ordered her life around books and study. Having that fact to contemplate," he noted, "was, in context, an inestimable gift."

Later, McMurtry read her other works and expressed his admiration for *The Rise and Fall of the Choctaw Republic* and *And Still the Waters Run,* both of which, like *The Road to Disappearance,* dealt with "dispossession." But it is his comments on *Geronimo* that are the most striking. The "real singularity" of this work, he asserts, correctly assessing Debo's greatest strength, "is that she manages—while remaining faithful to the history— to tell much of this celebrated story from the Apache, rather than the white, point of view."

Although Debo's search to establish justice lives on in her continuing influence on the lives of others, one reform that she championed has achieved ambiguous results. The 1971 Alaska Native Claims Settlement Act is viewed today as problematic in its outcome. Since the federal government had never assumed trusteeship for lands owned by Alaskan Natives (except for seven territorial reservations later ruled invalid), the ANCSA dictated that the state's Natives would manage their resources through village corporations under the oversight of twelve regional corporations. (A thirteenth regional corporation, located in Seattle, exists for Alaskan Natives who reside outside the state.) These corporations, in turn, own the land.

In 1983 Canadian jurist Thomas Berger discovered in his investigation for the Alaska Native Review Commission, a group supported by the Innuit Circumpolar Conference and the World Council of Indigenous People, that many Native leaders and elders were fearful of impending loss. If the corporations failed to prosper—a definite possibility, given the cyclical price for oil, minerals, and timber—their people could lose more than income from these assets. They could lose their land, the mainstay of a way of life that others frequently characterize as subsistence. To them, however, subsistence means not bare, minimal existence but rather the maintenance of an ancient spiritual relationship in which the land, waters, and animals supply the people's basic needs and wants. More important, their way of life keeps their ancestors' traditions alive in the present.

Unfortunately, other forces are at work in the forty-ninth state. Although Title 8 of the Alaska National Interest Lands Conservation Act (1980) held the state responsible for overseeing the management of wildlife and fish on federal lands so that indigenous peoples could maintain their way of life, the Alaska Supreme Court in 1989 ruled otherwise. Responding to the challenge of sportsmen's groups and others, it held in *McDowell* v. *Collingsworth* that Title 8 of the ANILCA violated the equal protection clause of the state constitution. When the state failed to bring its law into conformity with federal law, the U.S. Fish and Wildlife Service assumed responsibility for overseeing hunting and fishing on Alaska's public lands, beginning July 1, 1990. Bitterness and acrimony increased between state and federal authorities, and as anthropologist Thomas Thornton notes, by the late 1990s, "the prospects for realizing a stable, long-term solution in the near future seem dim."

When all the divisions and conflicting viewpoints are included, no simple solution emerges for the people of Alaska. Nevertheless one fact remains. Those who supported the 1971 ANCSA won for the state's indigenous peoples far greater resources than they would otherwise have gained in that era. Moreover, amendments to the act in 1988 gave Native people greater flexibility in restructuring their corporations, allowing them to restrict sales of land or shares and bringing the generation born after 1971 under the terms of the settlement.

The continuing controversies and unresolved issues surrounding the ANCSA would distress Debo if she were alive today. Still, she would know that, whatever the limitations of the 1971 act, the Native people would have won only 10 million acres of land if she and others had not fought valiantly on their behalf. Now, as a result of the act, they own through their corporations 44 million acres. (Four million acres have been added to the original 40 million awarded in 1971.) Because of Debo's involvement in this issue and others affecting Native peoples and because of her scholarship, many American Indians revere her memory.

In 1994 the Cherokees decorated Debo's grave in honor of her efforts to preserve their nation during her lifetime. She joined illustrious company. Other graves they venerated included those of Tennessean William Bate, the only United States senator to oppose the 1898 Curtis Act, and of Supreme Court Justices Smith Thompson and Joseph Story, members of the Marshall Court who argued persuasively in the 1830s in defense of Cherokee sovereignty. Finally, the resting places of Samuel Worcester, Elizur Butler, and Evan Jones, missionaries who were imprisoned for challenging Georgia laws that violated Cherokee sovereignty, were also honored.

The ceremonies honoring Debo took place on Saturday, May 28, 1994. Wilma Mankiller, the first female principal chief of the Cherokees, laid a wreath on Debo's grave in Marshall's North Cemetery. Afterwards, Charlie Soap, her husband, performed a benediction in Cherokee, and the pilot who had transported them to the site prayed in English. As Mankiller explained, "Angie Debo had an incredible influence on the history of the country and the state. This is a way for us to remember her and pay her our respects."

Oklahomans of all races honor their most famous woman historian in other ways. On April 2, 1995, at Edmond, Oklahoma, a town fifteen miles north of Oklahoma City, local dignitaries, members of the school district, and Miss Angie's friends and neighbors dedicated the Angie Debo Elementary School. Edmond, as Kenny Brown notes, boasts among its residents the country music singer Garth Brooks, and its renowned Oak Tree Country Club occasionally hosts the PGA Open golf tournament. If these characteristics seem at odds with the values and lifestyle of the Marshall woman, further reflection reveals that her example, as the daughter of pioneers who became a well-known writer, is inspirational to the children of Oklahoma. Certainly no memorial would have pleased her more.

Finally, many of Miss Angie's closest friends still keep her memory alive. Glenna Matthews insists that Debo gave her the courage to strike out in new directions. Matthews followed her seminal study, *"Just a Housewife": The Rise and Fall of*

Domesticity in America (1987), with her prize-winning *The Rise of Public Woman: Woman's Power and Woman's Place in the United States, 1630-1970,* published in 1992. The next year, she coauthored, along with Linda Witt and Karen M. Paget, *Running as a Woman,* a historical analysis of the problems female candidates face when they seek political office. Matthews remains a productive scholar; she is currently examining the lives of wage-earning women in Silicon Valley, among other projects.

Connie Cronley, who corresponded with Debo and visited her often during her last years, recalls her as one who encouraged women authors. Angie shared with Cronley her own disappointments and setbacks and advised her, as a freelance writer, never to give up her work, whatever her discouragements. Recently Cronley left a demanding position as general manager of the Tulsa Ballet Theatre and returned to writing after a hiatus of several years. As the 1990s come to an end, she has concluded several freelance writing projects with foundations and other groups and more are forthcoming. Like her mentor, Cronley is determined to live her life according to her own values and principles, whatever the outcome.

In Marshall and the surrounding area, residents still remember their most famous citizen. Gerry Schaefer, now retired from schoolteaching, often visits classrooms in area schools to tell the children about Debo's love of nature and her sense of humor. Several doors from Angie's old house, Hugh and Ramona O'Neill treasure her rocking chair, the "Sunday" mustache cup that Lina Debo gave her husband, Edward, and the china that once graced the Debos' dining-room table. The two stones Angie brought back from Luxor remain on their living-room shelves. At their back entrance, dressed stones from Beattie, Kansas, serve as doorstops. Angie had gathered them from the wheat field that covers the site where her family had lived when she was born.

Although Main Street of Debo's hometown reveals empty facades where businesses formerly flourished, the town lives on. Of all the places Debo drew on for *Prairie City,* a work now part of the curriculum for Oklahoma schoolchildren, Marshall provided the greatest inspiration.

The drive west from Stillwater on State Highway 51, turning off on Highway 74 to Marshall, has been renamed the Angie Debo Memorial Highway. It is beautiful in any season but especially in the autumn when the wheat fields are greening. The farmers here in the region north of the Canadian River plant winter wheat, a descendant of the Turkey Red wheat, which the Russian-Germans brought to America in the nineteenth century. The shoots appear in the autumn, then mature under the snow that blankets the plains and prairies.

Sometimes in late May, but usually in early June, the harvest season begins in Logan County, Oklahoma. With each passing decade, midwestern agricultural schools, such as the one at Oklahoma State University at Stillwater, experiment with winter wheat, crossing it with new strains and producing hardier hybrids. These efforts have produced a crop more resistant to disease, pests, and fungus.

Debo, who tilled the fields of western and American Indian history, lies buried not far from these wheat fields, her grave site lying in the northeastern section of the cemetery. There, Hugh O'Neill notes, it is "protected from the cold northwest winds so common in the winter here."

Like the wheat, her academic fields have had their periods of dormancy, their winter seasons when they lay covered with snow. Recently, they have surprised the scholarly world by bringing forth a harvest of surprising vitality and abundance. The appearance of the New Western History has attracted wide attention. Even those who disagree vehemently with its conclusions acknowledge that this new strain, originating from earlier seeds and hybrids, has generated impassioned debate and controversy. That, in turn, has brought new insights and given rise to even more debates.

For American Indians, the ethnohistorian, the product of the cross-fertilization of anthropology, history, archaeology, linguistics, and political science, is determined to tell the Indian story from the Native point of view and from the period before contact to the present day. Moreover, the ethnohistorian pays as much attention to Indian-Indian relations as to Indian-white and understands that Native peoples have always borrowed from other cultures, while remaining Indians. The result is the emergence of the New Indian History, which allows indigenous peoples to reclaim their past. With that understanding, they can fight more effectively for self-determination and for the right to maintain themselves as a people. In the process they contribute to the constant revitalization of the United States, a country made strong by its inclusion of diverse peoples and cultures.

Today Angie Debo's earthly remains are at peace not far from the farmlands that beckoned to her as a nine-year-old girl on November 8, 1899. Two and a quarter miles away, at her former home, Goldilocks, the hardy yellow rose, sheds its last petals as the combines move into the wheat fields to harvest the crop.

Bibliographic Essay

ANGIE Debo's diaries and personal papers are located in the Angie Debo Manuscript Collection in the Edmon Low Library at Oklahoma State University in Stillwater. This microfilmed collection contains childhood and adult diaries, correspondence, speeches, papers, manuscripts, travel notes, and business and tax records. It also includes earlier drafts of *And Still the Waters Run* and the typescript copies of the oral history interviews conducted by Glenna Matthews, Gloria Valencia-Weber, and Aletha Rogers between October 23, 1981, and June 8, 1985. See also "Angie Debo, 1890–1988: An autobiographical sketch, eulogy and bibliography," which lists all of Debo's works and includes the insightful eulogy Gloria Valencia-Weber delivered at Debo's funeral. Finally, the office once occupied by President Henry Bennett now houses furniture, photographs, awards, and memorabilia from Debo's Marshall home.

Oral history interviews provided additional insights. I conducted them with Glenna Matthews of Berkeley, California, on April 15, 1994, at Atlanta, Georgia; with Carter Blue Clark of Oklahoma City on May 18, 1994; and with Raymond Bryson and Hugh and Ramona O'Neill, all of Marshall, Oklahoma, on May 21, 1994. On October 21, 1994, I interviewed Gloria Valencia-Weber in Albuquerque, New Mexico; Geraldine Schaefer of Marshall, Oklahoma, on December 3, 1995; and Connie Cronley of Tulsa, Oklahoma, on August 13, 1996. Anne Morgan of Norman, Oklahoma, and Rennard Strickland, then living in Oklahoma City, Oklahoma, shared their memories of Debo on June 25, 1996. I also conducted telephone interviews with the late Berlin B. Chapman, professor emeritus of Oklahoma State

220

University, on November 21, 1994; with Ruth Lowes, who taught with Debo at West Texas State Teachers College, on July 1, 1996; and with Frederick W. Rathjen on that same date. Martha Sandlin and Barbara Abrash, coproducers of "Indians, Outlaws and Angie Debo," gave telephone interviews on June 2, 1996, and July 26, 1996, respectively. Guy Logsdon of Tulsa, Oklahoma, shared his memories of Angie Debo as a fellow librarian on February 3, 1997. I also spoke with LeRoy H. Fischer, professor emeritus of Oklahoma State University, by telephone on February 26, 1999. Both the late B. B. Chapman and Ms. Lowes rated Debo's teaching abilities as "excellent." Finally, I have corresponded intermittently, since December 1994, with Betty Mubiru of Tororo, Uganda, a beneficiary of Debo's estate. In October 1996, she sent me an audiotape of a biographical sketch of her life and her memories of meeting Debo. Edward A. DeClerck, attorney for Debo's estate, provided information regarding Debo's bequest to Mubiru.

The Western History Collection of the University of Oklahoma contains Debo correspondence in the Angie Debo Collection; the Edward Everett Dale Collection (which includes all his correspondence, lecture notes, seminar papers from Harvard, and departmental material); the University of Oklahoma Press Collection; the Joseph A. Brandt Collection; and the Savoie Lottinville Collection. The Princeton University Press files relating to Joseph Brandt and the publication of *And Still the Waters Run* have been deposited in the Brandt Collection as well. Researchers interested in the controversy surrounding *And Still the Waters Run* should examine carefully the summer 1937 correspondence in the William Bizzell Papers. Finally, Jimmie Hicks, historian and student of Dale, disagreed vehemently with "Indians, Outlaws and Angie Debo." His essay, "A Critique of the PBS Television Program, 'Indians, Outlaws and Angie Debo,' *The American Experience,* #103," is located in the Jimmie Hicks Collection in the Western History Collection at the University of Oklahoma.

The Oklahoma State Historical Society in Oklahoma City houses the Grant and Carolyn Foreman Manuscript Collection, which contains Debo correspondence. See also the *Marshall Tribune* and the *Kingfisher (Oklahoma) Free Press* and county histories such as *The Logan County History, 1889–1977, Volume 1: The Families* and *The Logan County History, Volume II: The County and Its Communities* (Guthrie, Okla.: History Committee, Logan County Extension Homemakers Council, 1980).

The Cornette Library at West Texas A & M (formerly West Texas State Teachers College and West Texas State University) at Canyon, Texas, has several files on Angie Debo and houses the correspondence of L. F. Sheffy, for many years the chair of the history department at that school. In addition, the Panhandle-Plains Historical Museum Research Center contains oral history interviews and tapes with residents of the Canyon area, including Fred Scott, owner of the boardinghouse where Debo resided, and Ima Barlow and Olin Hinkle, both retired professors, who were interviewed by A. K. Nott. *The West Texas State Teachers College Quarterly*, Bulletin Nos. 39 through 73 (Catalogs 1924–25 through 1934–35) contain insights into Debo's Canyon years. Finally, Frederick W. Rathjen provides an excellent overview of the region in *The Texas Panhandle Frontier* (Austin: University of Texas Press, 1973). Peter Petersen, professor of history at West Texas A & M, provided information for Barbara Abrash and Martha Sandlin when they were making "Indians, Outlaws and Angie Debo." With his permission and that of Barbara Abrash, I made use of their correspondence and benefited greatly from their incisive insights.

Angie Debo also corresponded with Sr. Mary Mark Orr and Dollie Wamsley, regarding local history in Kansas. Those letters are located in the Special Collections Department, DePaul Library, Saint Mary College, Leavenworth, Kansas.

Michael Harrison, director of the Michael and Margaret B. Harrison Western Research Center at the University of California, Davis, in Fair Oaks, participated in Debo's activist network. He graciously allowed me to copy the extensive correspondence between them.

Debo's own voluminous writings provide an overview of her scholarly development. See "The Historical Background of the

American Policy of Isolation," *Smith College Studies in History* 9 (April-July 1924): 71–165, coauthored with James Fred Rippy. A comparison of Debo's Ph.D. dissertation, "History of the Choctaw Nation from the End of the Civil War to the Close of the Tribal Period," University of Oklahoma, 1933, with *The Rise and Fall of the Choctaw Republic,* volume 6 in the Civilization of the American Indian Series (Norman: University of Oklahoma Press, 1934), shows Debo's willingness to add ethnological insights once she no longer faced a dissertation committee. *And Still the Waters Run* (Princeton, N.J.: Princeton University Press, 1940) was followed by *The Road to Disappearance: A History of the Creek Indians,* volume 22 in the Civilization of the American Indian Series (Norman: University of Oklahoma Press, 1941). *Tulsa: From Creek Town to Oil Capital* (Norman: University of Oklahoma Press, 1943) and *Prairie City: The Story of an American Community* (New York: Knopf, 1944) demonstrate Debo's continuing indebtedness to Turnerian ideas and Edward Everett Dale. *Oklahoma: Foot-loose and Fancy-free* (Norman: University of Oklahoma Press, 1949; reprint, 1987) remains a useful introduction to the state. Debo's *The Five Civilized Tribes; Report on Social and Economic Conditions* (Philadelphia: Indian Rights Association, 1951) explores the Five Tribes after passage of the 1936 Oklahoma Indian Welfare Act. *A History of the Indians of the United States* (Norman: University of Oklahoma Press, 1970) is often reprinted three decades after its publication. Finally, the *Times (London) Literary Supplement* characterized Debo's *Geronimo: The Man, His Time, His Place* (Norman: University of Oklahoma Press, 1976) as a revisionist work in 1992, sixteen years after its publication.

Debo's edited works include, with John M. Oskison, *Oklahoma: A Guide to the Sooner State,* American Guide Series, compiled by Workers of the Writers' Program of the Work Projects Administration in the State of Oklahoma (Norman: University of Oklahoma Press, 1941). See also *The Cowman's Southwest: Being the Reminiscences of Oliver Nelson, Freighter, Camp Cook, Cowboy, Frontiersman in Kansas, Indian Territory, Texas, and Oklahoma, 1878–1893,* volume 4 of *The Western Frontiersman* (Glendale, Calif.: A. H. Clark, 1953), and Horatio B. Cushman, *History of the Choctaw, Chickasaw, and Natchez Indians* (Stillwater, Okla.: Redlands Press, 1962).

Aside from "Indians, Outlaws and Angie Debo," no biography of Debo has existed before this work. Important articles include Suzanne Schrems and Cynthia Wolff, "Politics and Libel: Angie Debo and the Publication of *And Still the Waters Run*," *Western Historical Quarterly* 22 (May 1991): 184–203; and Glenna Matthews and Gloria Valencia-Weber, "Against Great Odds: The Life of Angie Debo," *OAH Newsletter* 13 (May 1985): 8–11. Kenneth McIntosh places Debo in historiographical context in his essay "Geronimo's Friend: Angie Debo and the New History," *Chronicles of Oklahoma* 66 (summer 1988): 164–77. Sister Martha Mary McGaw illuminates Debo's childhood in "Geronoimo Doesn't Have a Better Friend than Angie," *Sooner Catholic,* September 23, 1984. Finally, Geraldine Schaefer of Marshall, Oklahoma, has privately printed a small pamphlet, "Memories of Miss Angie," which highlights Debo's sense of humor and love of nature. See also Albert L. Hurtado's comments on Debo as an activist scholar in "Public History and the Native American," *Montana The Magazine of Western History* 40 (spring 1990): 58–69.

In interpreting the life of any woman in twentieth-century America, the insights of women's history are important. I am indebted to Gerda Lerner, *The Creation of Feminist Consciousness: From the Middle Ages to Eighteen-seventy* (New York: Oxford University Press, 1993), for establishing the importance of women's history. In developing a context for Debo's life, I have relied on insights from William Chafe, *The Paradox of Change: American Women in the 20th Century* (New York: Oxford University Press, 1991); James R. McGovern, "The American Woman's Pre-World War I Freedom in Manners and Morals," *Journal of American History* 55 (September 1968): 315–33; and Nancy Cott, *The Grounding of Modern Feminism* (New Haven, Conn.: Yale University Press, 1987). For understanding women in higher education at Chicago University, see Marion Talbot, *More Than Lore: Reminiscences of Marion Talbot* (Chicago: University of Chicago Press, 1936), and Ellen Fitzpatrick, *Endless Crusade: Women Social Scientists and Progressive Reform* (New

York: Oxford University Press, 1990). See also *Women and Higher Education in American History*, eds. John Mack Faragher and Florence Howe (New York: Norton, 1988), and *Lone Voyagers: Academic Women in Coeducational Institutions, 1870–1937*, ed. Geraldine Joncich Clifford (New York: Feminist Press, 1989). Earlier attitudes toward women holding doctorates in history appear in William B. Hesseltine and Louis Kaplan, "Women Doctors of Philosophy in History," *Journal of Higher Education* 14 (May 1943): 254–59. See also Judith P. Zinsser, *History and Feminism: A Glass Half Full* (New York: Twayne, 1993), and Bonnie Smith, *The Gender of History: Men, Women, and Historical Practice* (Cambridge, Mass.: Harvard University Press, 1998). For the impact of the second-wave women's movement on Debo, I have drawn on insights from William H. Chafe's "The Personal and the Political: Two Case Studies," in *U.S. History as Women's History: New Feminist Essays*, eds. Linda K. Kerber, Alice Kessler-Harris, and Kathryn Kish Sklar (Chapel Hill: University of North Carolina Press, 1995). I am indebted to Peggy Pascoe for her insight into western women as "intercultural brokers." See "Western Women at the Cultural Crossroads," in *Trails toward a New Western History*, eds. Patricia Nelson Limerick, Clyde A. Milner II, and Charles E. Rankin (Lawrence: University Press of Kansas, 1991): 40–58. Linda Reese provided invaluable information in *Women of Oklahoma, 1890–1920* (Norman: University of Oklahoma Press, 1997). Elliott West's classic study, *Growing Up with the Country: Childhood on the Far Western Frontier* (Albuquerque: University of New Mexico Press, 1989), is unexcelled in terms of childhood, family life, and society on the plains and the prairies.

One of the most useful works on regionalism is Richard Lowitt's insightful "Regionalism at the University of Oklahoma," *Chronicles of Oklahoma* 73 (summer 1995): 150–71. See also Robert L. Dorman's *Revolt of the Provinces: The Regionalist Movement in America, 1920–1945* (Chapel Hill: University of North Carolina Press, 1993), which places Debo and her writing in the larger context of southern and western writing in the years between World War I and World War II. Mary Ann Slater shares brief but telling insights into Debo in "The Oklahoma Writers' Project: 1935–1942" (master's thesis, Oklahoma State University, 1985).

Works helpful in interpreting Oklahoma include *Oklahoma: New Views of the Forty-Sixth State,* eds. Anne Hodges Morgan and H. Wayne Morgan (Norman: University of Oklahoma Press, 1982). In that volume, Anne Morgan's "Oklahoma in Literature," 175–303, and Rennard Strickland's "Oklahoma's Story: Recording the History of the Forty-sixth State," 175–263, were especially illuminating. Also valuable is *The Culture of Oklahoma,* eds. Howard F. Stein and Robert F. Hill (Norman: University of Oklahoma Press, 1993). In that volume, see Gary L. Thompson, "Green on Red: Oklahoma Landscapes," 3–28; Howard R. Lamar, "The Creation of Oklahoma: New Meanings for the Oklahoma Land Run," 29–47; and Pat Bellmon, "The Passing of Grit," 186–97. Danney Goble, *Progressive Oklahoma: The Making of a New Kind of State* (Norman: University of Oklahoma Press, 1980), remains important for Oklahoma's political history. *"An Oklahoma I Had Never Seen Before",* ed. David D. Joyce (Norman: University of Oklahoma, 1994), is a thought-provoking set of essays. Finally, Rennard Strickland provides insights into Indian views in *The Indians in Oklahoma* (Norman: University of Oklahoma Press, 1980).

Among those who influenced Debo, Edward Everett Dale played a crucial role. See Edward Everett Dale, *The West Wind Blows: The Autobiography of Edward Everett Dale,* ed. Arrell M. Gibson (Oklahoma City: Oklahoma Historical Society, 1984), and *Frontier Historian: The Life and Work of Edward Everett Dale,* ed. Arrell Gibson (Norman: University of Oklahoma Press, 1975). Also consult David J. Murrah, "Edward Everett Dale," in *Historians of the American Frontier,* ed. John Wunder (New York: Greenwood Press, 1986), 229–39. Wunder's edited work also includes an appraisal by Michael Green of another of Debo's influences; see "Grant Foreman," 262–78. See as well J. Stanley Clark's evocative "Grant Foreman" in *Chronicles of Oklahoma* 31 (autumn 1953): 226–46.

Useful essays on the founding and early days of the University of Oklahoma Press are John Joseph Mathews, "Scholarship Comes to Life: The University of Oklahoma Press," *Saturday Review of Literature* 25 (May 16, 1942): 20–21; Arrell M. Gibson, "A History of the University of Oklahoma Press," *Journal of the West* 7 (October 1988): 553–61; and Steven Crum, "Bizzell and Brandt: Pioneers in Indian Studies," *Chronicles of Oklahoma* 66 (summer 1988): 178–91. Finally, Joseph Brandt, first director of the University of Oklahoma Press, gave his views in "A Former President Speaks," *Sooner Magazine,* August 1950, 10–11.

In approaching the "Old Western History" as opposed to the "New Western History," Frederick Jackson Turner's "The Significance of the Frontier in American History," *Frontier and Section: Selected Essays of Frederick Jackson Turner* (Englewood Cliffs, N.J.: Prentice-Hall, 1961), is the starting point. Recent works on Turner include Wilbur R. Jacobs, *On Turner's Trail: 100 Years of Writing Western History* (Lawrence: University Press of Kansas, 1994), and Allan G. Bogue's magisterial *Frederick Jackson Turner: Strange Roads Going Down* (Norman: University of Oklahoma Press, 1998). History underwent profound changes in the late nineteenth and early twentieth centuries. See Peter Novick, *That Noble Dream: The "Objectivity Question" and the American Historical Profession* (New York: Cambridge University Press, 1988). Fred Bailey chronicles the life of one of Debo's Chicago professors in *William Edward Dodd: The South's Yeoman Scholar* (Charlottesville: University Press of Virginia, 1997).

Scholars took issue with Turner long before the official rise of the New Western Historians, as Richard W. Etulain's edited work, *Writing Western History: Essays on Major Western Historians* (Albuquerque: University of New Mexico Press, 1991), demonstrates. See also Gerald D. Nash's *Creating the West: Historical Interpretations, 1890–1990* (Albuquerque: University of New Mexico Press, 1991), an invaluable introduction to earlier and more recent developments in the historiography of the West.

Patricia Nelson Limerick's *The Legacy of Conquest: The Unbroken Past of the American West* (New York: Norton, 1987) brought the New Western History before the general public. See also Limerick, "What on Earth Is the New Western History?" *Montana The Magazine of Western History* 40 (summer 1990): 61–64.

Richard White's *"It's Your Misfortune and None of My Own": A New History of the American West* (Norman: University of Oklahoma Press, 1991) surveys the West without invoking Turner's frontier thesis. Another New Western Historian, Donald Worster, noted the environmental cost of Euro-American expansion in *Dust Bowl: The Southern Plains in the 1930s* (New York: Oxford University Press, 1979). By contrast, William Cronon, "Revisiting the Vanishing Frontier: The Legacy of Frederick Jackson Turner," *Western Historical Quarterly* 18 (April 1987): 157–76, sees the Turnerian narrative as irreplaceable. See also William Cronon, George Miles, and Jay Gitlin, "Becoming West: Towards a New Meaning for Western History" in *Under an Open Sky: Rethinking America's Western Past,* eds. William Cronon, George Miles, and Jay Gitlin (New York: Norton, 1992), 3–27, which argues for a continuing search for new interpretations of the West.

The novelist Larry McMurtry observed in "How the West Was Won or Lost," *New Republic,* October 1990, 32–38, that many historians had been critical of the process of Euro-American movement across the continent, and he included Debo's Indian trilogy as important critiques in "the old history." McMurtry continued his examination of Debo in "Broken Promises," a thoughtful essay on her Indian works in *New York Review of Books,* October 23, 1997, 14–17. Important earlier criticisms of Turner, which helped pave the way for the New Indian History, include Richard Hofstadter's critique in *The Progressive Historians: Turner, Beard, Parrington* (New York: Knopf, 1968) and David Nichols, "'Civilization over Savage': Frederick Jackson Turner and the Indian," *South Dakota History* 2 (fall 1972): 383–405. Finally, two collections of essays explore the arguments among New Western Historians and others. See Gene M. Gressley, ed., *Old West/New West* (Waveland, Wyo.: High Plains, 1994), and Forrest G. Robinson, ed., *The New Western History: The Territory Ahead* (Tucson: University of Arizona Press, 1998).

Paul Prucha provides a detailed but lucidly written overview of Indian-white relations and the concepts and motivations that inspired governmental policy in *The Great Father: The United States Government and the American Indians,* 2 vols. (Lincoln: University of Nebraska Press, 1984). Historiographical essays that proved helpful in describing directions in the writing of American Indian history include Reginald Horsman, "Recent Trends and New Directions in Native American History," in *The American West: New Perspectives, New Dimensions,* ed. Jerome O. Steffen (Norman: University of Oklahoma Press, 1979); Robert C. Carriker, "The American Indian from the Civil War to the Present," in *Historians and the American West,* ed. Michael P. Malone (Lincoln: University of Nebraska Press, 1983), 177–208; Terry Wilson, *Teaching American Indian History* (Washington, D. C.: American Historical Association, 1993); Donald L. Parman and Catherine Price, "A 'Work in Progress': The Emergence of Indian History as a Professional Field," *Western Historical Quarterly* 20 (May 1989): 184–96; David Rich Lewis, "Still Native: The Significance of Native Americans in the History of the Twentieth-Century American West," in *A New Significance: Re-envisioning the History of the American West,* ed. Clyde A. Milner II (New York: Oxford University Press, 1996), 213–40. See also R. David Edmunds's centennial essay, "Native Americans, New Voices: American Indian History, 1895–1995," *American Historical Review* 100 (June 1995): 717–22, and William T. Hagan's "A New Indian History," in *Rethinking American Indian History,* ed. Donald L. Fixico (Albuquerque: University of New Mexico Press, 1997), 43–70.

For understanding the fuller historical context that informed the debate about Indian-white relations, Robert Berkofer's *White Man's Indian: Images of the American Indian from Columbus to the Present* (New York: Knopf, 1978) remains unsurpassed, as does Brian Dippie's *The Vanishing Americans: White Attitudes and U.S Indian Policy* (Middleton, Conn.: Wesleyan University Press, 1982). Robert Bieder's *Science Encounters the Indian, 1820–1880: The Early Years of American Ethnology* (Norman: University of Oklahoma Press, 1986) is invaluable for nineteenth-century attitudes.

For the bridge between the nineteenth and early twentieth centuries, see A. L. Kroeber, "The Work of John R. Swanton," in *Essays in Historical Anthropology of North America: Published in Honor of John R. Swanton* (Washington, D.C.: Smithsonian Institution, 1940). A good summary of the impact of accultur-

ation theory on ethnological studies, a development that Debo
did not incorporate into her works, is found in the Social Science
Research Council Seminar (1953) on Acculturation, "Accultur-
ation: An Exploratory Formulation," *American Anthropologists*
56 (1954): 973–1002. No one explores Indian policy, expecially
in terms of the Dawes Act of 1887, without consulting Paul
Francis Prucha, *American Indian Policy in Crisis: Christian
Reforms and the Indian, 1865–1900* (Norman: University of
Oklahoma Press, 1976), and Frederick Hoxie, *A Final Promise:
The Campaign to Assimilate the Indians, 1880–1920* (Lincoln:
University of Nebraska Press, 1984). An essay that offers conclusions different from those of Debo regarding the Five Tribes'
acceptance of allotment is W. David Baird, "Are the Five Tribes
of Oklahoma 'Real' Indians?" *Western Historical Quarterly* 21
(February 1990): 5–18. Baird, however, verified Debo's findings
that Allen Wright had accepted a kickback in *Peter Pitchlynn: Chief
of the Choctaws* (Norman: University of Oklahoma Press, 1972).

Changes in Indian policy began in the 1920s, as Randolph
Downes noted in "A Crusade for Indian Reform,1922–1934,
"*Mississippi Valley Historical Review* 32 (1945–46): 331–54. That
movement gained momentum from Charles Meriam, *The
Problem of Indian Administration* (Baltimore: Johns Hopkins
Press, 1928). For overviews of the Indian New Deal, see Ken-
neth R. Philp, *John Collier's Crusade for Indian Reform,
1920–1954* (Tucson: University of Arizona Press, 1977); Graham
D. Taylor, *The New Deal and American Indian Tribalism: The
Administration of the Indian Reorganization Ace, 1934–45*
(Lincoln: University of Nebraska Press, 1980); and Lawrence
Kelly, *The Assault on Assimilation: John Collier and the Origins of
Indian Policy Reform* (Albuquerque: University of New Mexico
Press, 1983). For information on D'Arcy McNickle, see Dorothy
R. Parker, *Singing an Indian Song: A Biography of D'Arcy
McNickle* (Lincoln: University of Nebraska Press, 1992). Peter
W. Wright offers good background on the passage of the
Oklahoma Indian Welfare Act in "John Collier and the Oklahoma
Indian Welfare Act of 1936," *Chronicles of Oklahoma* 50 (autumn
1972): 347–71.

Alison R. Bernstein covers Indian history during World War II in *American Indians and World War II: Toward A New Era in Indian Affairs* (Norman: University of Oklahoma Press, 1991). For the emergence of termination as a fully expressed policy, see Kenneth R. Philp, "Dillon S. Myer and the Advent of Termination: 1950–1953," *Western Historical Quarterly* 19 (January 1988): 37–59. Philip, in *Termination Revisited: American Indians on the Trail to Self-Determination, 1933–1953* (Lincoln: University of Nebraska Press, 1999), notes that some Native peoples, especially the sheepherding Navajos, welcomed termination as a chance to reverse John Collier's policies inaugurated during the 1930s. Debo responded to the 1950s threat to Oklahoma Indians in "Termination and the Oklahoma Indians," *The American Indian* 7 (spring 1955): 17–23, and "What Oklahoma Indians Need," *The American Indian* 7 (winter 1956): 13–16. Her views echo those of Felix S. Cohen, general counsel for the Association on American Indian Affairs. See Felix Cohen, "Indian Wardship: The Twilight of a Myth," *The American Indian* 6 (summer 1953): 8–14. Also valuable are Donald L. Fixico, *Termination and Relocation: Federal Indian Policy, 1945–1960* (Albuquerque: University of New Mexico Press, 1986), and Larry Burt, *Tribalism in Crisis: Federal Indian Policy, 1953–1961* (Albuquerque: University of New Mexico Press, 1982). See also Burt's "Factories on Reservations: The Industrial Development Programs of Commissioner Glenn Emmons, 1953–1960," *Arizona and the West* 19 (winter 1977): 317–32. For information on the Menominee, see Nicholas C. Peroff, *Menominee Drums: Tribal Termination and Restoration, 1954–1974* (Norman: University of Oklahoma Press, 1982). Robert A. Hecht provides useful insight into the formation of the Association on American Indian Affairs in *Oliver La Farge and the American Indian: A Biography* (Metuchen, N.J.: Scarecrow Press, 1991).

As an activist, Debo saw the 1971 Alaska Native Claims Settlement Act as according the indigenous people of that state a greater degree of justice. See Angie Debo, "To Establish Justice," *Western Historical Quarterly* 7 (October 1976): 405–11. Debo's statement to Congress is found in *Congressional Record–Senate,*

92d Congress, 1st Session, March 23, 1971, 7408–9. By the mid-1980s, Thomas R. Berger saw the act as a failure in *Village Journey: The Report of the Alaska Native Review Commission* (New York: Hill and Wang, 1985). Ramona Ellen Skinner's *Alaska Native Policy in the Twentieth Century* (New York: Garland, 1997) finds both benefits and problems. See also Thomas Thornton, "Subsistence: The Politics of a Cultural Dilemma," in *Alaska Public Policy Issues: Background and Perspectives,* ed. Clive Thomas (Juneau, Alaska: Denali Press, 1999), 205–19.

Debo was also an activist on behalf of Indian water rights. For background on Indians and this important resource, see Lloyd Burton, *American Indian Water Rights and the Limits of Law* (Lawrence: University Press of Kansas, 1991). No one should overlook Norris Hundley Jr., "The Winters' Decision and Indian Water Rights: A Mystery Reexamined," *Western Historical Quarterly* 13 (January 1982): 17–42, and his earlier "The Dark and Bloody Ground of Indian Water Rights: Confusion Elevated to Principle," *Western Historical Quarterly* 9 (October 1978): 455–82. Senator Barry Goldwater fought for Havasupais water rights. See Peter Iverson, *Barry Goldwater: Native Arizonan,* volume 15 in *Oklahoma Western Biographies* (Norman: University of Oklahoma Press, 1997). For Debo's impact on the *Harjo* v. *Kleppe* ruling, see United States District Court for the District of Columbia, *Allen Harjo, et al.* v. *Thomas S. Kleppe,* et al., *Opinion and Order,* Civil Action No. 74-189, filed September 2, 1976, Angie Debo Papers, Edmon Low Library, Oklahoma State University, Stillwater. Also see Tom Holm, "The Crisis in Tribal Government," in *American Indian Policy in the Twentieth Century,* ed. Vine Deloria, Jr. (Norman: University of Oklahoma Press, 1985), 135–54. For information on the origin of the term "scholar-warrior," which was coined by the Cherokee scholar Rayna Green, see Gloria Valencia-Weber, "Law School Training of American Indians as Legal-Warriors," *American Indian Law Review* 20, no. 1 (1996): 5–63.

In charting the emergence of ethnohistory, two essays are valuable: Calvin Martin, "Ethnohistory: A Better Way to Write Indian History," *Western Historical Quarterly* 9 (January 1978): 41–56, and Francis Jennings, "A Growing Partnership: Historians,

Anthropologists, and American Indian History," *History Teacher* 14 (November 1980): 87–104.

Several important works indicate the emergence of new ways of interpreting the history of the Five Tribes. See Michael Green, *The Politics of Indian Removal* (Lincoln: University of Nebraska Press, 1982); William McLoughlin, *Cherokee Renascence in the New Republic* (Princeton, N.J.: Princeton University Press, 1986); Patricia Galloway, *Choctaw Genesis, 1500–1700* (Lincoln: University of Nebraska Press, 1995); and Clara Sue Kidwell, *Choctaws and Missionaries in Mississippi, 1818–1918* (Norman: University of Oklahoma Press, 1995).

Modern Indian tribes seek self-determination. In that light, a valuable work that examines the nadir of Indian sovereignty is Carter Blue Clark's Lone Wolf *v.* Hitchcock: *Treaty Rights and Indian Law at the End of the Nineteenth Century* (Lincoln: University of Nebraska Press, 1994). See also Alvin M. Josephy, Jr., *Now That the Buffalo's Gone: A Study of Today's American Indians* (Norman: University of Oklahoma Press, published in cooperation with Knopf, 1984); and Sharon O'Brien, *American Indian Tribal Governments* (Norman: University of Oklahoma Press, 1989). For an overview on the legal status of Indians in the United States, consult Charles F. Wilkinson, *American Indians, Time, and the Law: Native Societies in a Modern Constitutional Democracy* (New Haven: Yale University Press, 1987).

An ongoing debate in Oklahoma is the site of the Battle of Round Mountain (or Round Mountains). See Angie Debo, "The Site of the Battle of Round Mountain, 1861," *Chronicles of Oklahoma* 27 (summer 1949): 187–206, and "The Location of the Battle of Round Mountains," *Chronicles of Oklahoma* 41 (spring 1963): 70–104. Charles Bahos largely agrees with Debo's analysis in "On Opothleyahola's Trail: Locating the Battle of Round Mountain," *Chronicles of Oklahoma* 63 (spring 1985): 58–89.

Index